The Capitalist Personality

Modern capitalism favors values that undermine our face-to-face bonds with friends and family members. Focusing on the post-communist world, and comparing it to more "developed" societies, this book reveals the mixed effects of capitalist culture on interpersonal relationships. While most observers blame the egoism and asocial behavior found in new free-market societies on their communist pasts, this work shows how relationships are also threatened by the profit orientations and personal ambition unleashed by economic development. Successful people in societies as diverse as China, Russia, and Eastern Germany adjust to the market economy at a social cost, relaxing their morals in order to obtain success and succumbing to increased material temptations to exploit relationships for their own financial and professional gain. The capitalist personality is internally troubled as a result of this "sellout," but these qualms subside as it devalues intimate qualitative bonds with others. This book also shows that post-communists are similarly individualized as people living in Western societies. Capitalism may indeed favor values of independence, creativity, and self-expressiveness, but it also rewards self-centeredness, consumerism, and the stripping down of morality. As is the case in the West, capitalist culture fosters an internally conflicted and self-centered personality in post-communist societies.

Christopher S. Swader is an assistant professor of sociology at the National Research University—Higher School of Economics in Moscow. He teaches social theory, focusing on individualization and modernization, critical theory (the Frankfurt School), the life course, and historical sociology.

Routledge Advances in Sociology

For a full list of titles in this series, please visit www.routledge.com.

54 **Twentieth Century Music and the Question of Modernity**
Eduardo De La Fuente

55 **The American Surfer**
Radical Culture and Capitalism
Kristin Lawler

56 **Religion and Social Problems**
Edited by Titus Hjelm

57 **Play, Creativity, and Social Movements**
If I Can't Dance, It's Not My Revolution
Benjamin Shepard

58 **Undocumented Workers' Transitions**
Legal Status, Migration, and Work in Europe
Sonia McKay, Eugenia Markova and Anna Paraskevopoulou

59 **The Marketing of War in the Age of Neo-Militarism**
Edited by Kostas Gouliamos and Christos Kassimeris

60 **Neoliberalism and the Global Restructuring of Knowledge and Education**
Steven C. Ward

61 **Social Theory in Contemporary Asia**
Ann Brooks

62 **Foundations of Critical Media and Information Studies**
Christian Fuchs

63 **A Companion to Life Course Studies**
The Social and Historical Context of the British Birth Cohort Studies
Michael Wadsworth and John Bynner

64 **Understanding Russianness**
Risto Alapuro, Arto Mustajoki and Pekka Pesonen

65 **Understanding Religious Ritual**
Theoretical Approaches and Innovations
John Hoffmann

66 **Online Gaming in Context**
The social and cultural significance of online games
Garry Crawford, Victoria K. Gosling and Ben Light

67 **Contested Citizenship in East Asia**
Developmental politics, national unity, and globalization
Kyung-Sup Chang and Bryan S. Turner

68 **Agency without Actors?**
New Approaches to Collective Action
Edited by Jan-Hendrik Passoth, Birgit Peuker and Michael Schillmeier

69 **The Neighborhood in the Internet**
Design Research Projects in Community Informatics
John M. Carroll

70 **Managing Overflow in Affluent Societies**
Edited by Barbara Czarniawska and Orvar Löfgren

71 **Refugee Women**
Beyond Gender versus Culture
Leah Bassel

72 **Socioeconomic Outcomes of the Global Financial Crisis**
Theoretical Discussion and Empirical Case Studies
Edited by Ulrike Schuerkens

73 **Migration in the 21st Century**
Political Economy and Ethnography
Edited by Pauline Gardiner Barber and Winnie Lem

74 **Ulrich Beck**
An Introduction to the Theory of Second Modernity and the Risk Society
Mads P. Sørensen and Allan Christiansen

75 **The International Recording Industries**
Edited by Lee Marshall

76 **Ethnographic Research in the Construction Industry**
Edited by Sarah Pink, Dylan Tutt and Andrew Dainty

77 **Routledge Companion to Contemporary Japanese Social Theory**
From Individualization to Globalization in Japan Today
Edited by Anthony Elliott, Masataka Katagiri and Atsushi Sawai

78 **Immigrant Adaptation in Multi-Ethnic Societies**
Canada, Taiwan, and the United States
Edited by Eric Fong, Lan-Hung Nora Chiang and Nancy Denton

79 **Cultural Capital, Identity, and Social Mobility**
The Life Course of Working-Class University Graduates
Mick Matthys

80 **Speaking for Animals**
Animal Autobiographical Writing
Edited by Margo DeMello

81 **Healthy Aging in Sociocultural Context**
Edited by Andrew E. Scharlach and Kazumi Hoshino

82 **Touring Poverty**
Bianca Freire-Medeiros

83 **Life Course Perspectives on Military Service**
Edited by Janet M. Wilmoth and Andrew S. London

84 **Innovation in Socio-Cultural Context**
Edited by Frane Adam and Hans Westlund

85 **Youth, Arts and Education**
Reassembling Subjectivity through Affect
Anna Hickey-Moody

86 **The Capitalist Personality**
Face-to-Face Sociality and Economic Change in the Post-Communist World
Christopher S. Swader

The Capitalist Personality

Face-to-Face Sociality and Economic Change in the Post-Communist World

Christopher S. Swader

Routledge
Taylor & Francis Group
NEW YORK LONDON

First published 2013
by Routledge
711 Third Avenue, New York, NY 10017

Simultaneously published in the UK
by Routledge
2 Park Square, Milton Park, Abingdon, Oxon OX14 4RN

Routledge is an imprint of the Taylor & Francis Group, an informa business

Library of Congress Cataloging-in-Publication Data

Swader, Christopher.
The capitalist personality : face-to-face sociality and economic change in the post-communist world / Christopher S. Swader.
p. cm. — (Routledge advances in sociology ; 86)
Includes bibliographical references and index.
1. Post-communism—Social aspects. 2. Social values—Former communist countries. 3. Capitalism—Social aspects—Former communist countries. 4. Former communist countries—Social conditions. 5. Former communist countries—Economic conditions. I. Title.
HN380.7.A8S93 2013
306—dc23
2012027697

ISBN13: 978-0-415-89221-6 (hbk)
ISBN13: 978-0-203-07271-4 (ebk)

Typeset in Sabon
by IBT Global.

Printed and bound in the United States of America on sustainably sourced paper by IBT Global.

But enough! enough! I can't take any more. Bad air! Bad air! This workshop where ideals are manufactured—it seems to me it stinks of so many lies.

—Friedrich Nietzsche, On the Genealogy of Morals (1967, 47)

Contents

List of Figures xi
List of Tables xiii
Permissions xv
Preface xvii

1 Introduction 1

2 Becoming Homo-Economicus 12

3 "The Wall in the Head": Mechanisms of De-socialization 45

4 The Chinese, Russian, and Eastern German Contexts: Social Values and Economic Change 77

5 Individualism, Ambition, and Work 96

6 "Get Rich First!": Materialism and Consumerism 113

7 Family Relationships and Friendship 133

8 Morality, Religion, and Politics 158

9 The Wild West? 172

10 Discussion: Ambivalent Individualization and Capitalist Culture 183

Appendix A: Methods 191
Appendix B: T-test Results 213
Appendix C: Results on Social Values and Gender 221
Notes 223
Bibliography 225
Index 235

Figures

3.1	Explaining enhanced latency of social values.	48
5.1	Value of independence by birth cohort in China, Russia, and Eastern Germany, WVS 1990–2005.	98
5.2	Non-materialistic job ambitiousness by birth cohort in China, Russia, and Eastern Germany, WVS 1990–2005.	100
5.3	Value of risk-taking by birth cohort in China, Russia, and Eastern Germany, WVS 1990–2005.	101
6.1	Value of thrift by birth cohort in China, Russia, and Eastern Germany, WVS 1990–2005.	116
6.2	Value of good pay by birth cohort in China, Russia, and Eastern Germany, WVS 1990–2005.	117
6.3	Value of being rich and having nice things by birth cohort in China, Russia, and Eastern Germany, WVS 2005.	118
7.1	Value of parental sacrifice for children by birth cohort in China, Russia, and Eastern Germany, wvs 1990–2005.	135
7.2	Relative importance of family compared to work, leisure, friends by birth cohort in China, Russia, and Eastern Germany, WVS 1990–2005.	136
7.3	Importance of friends by birth cohort in China, Russia, and Eastern Germany, WVS 1990–2005.	137
8.1	Importance of politics by birth cohort in China, Russia, and Eastern Germany, WVS 1990–2005.	159
8.2	Moral absolutism by birth cohort in China, Russia, and Eastern Germany, WVS 1990–2005.	160
8.3	Justifiability of lying by birth cohort in China, Russia, and Eastern Germany, WVS 1990–2005.	161
9.1	Value of independence by birth cohort in post-communist, OECD, and developing societies, WVS 1990–2005.	174
9.2	Value of risk-tasking by birth cohort in post-communist, OECD, and developing societies, WVS 1990–2005.	175

9.3 Value of thrift by birth cohort in post-communist, OECD, and developing societies, WVS 1990–2005. 176
9.4 Value of being rich and having nice things by birth cohort in post-communist, OECD, and developing societies, WVS 2005. 177
9.5 Value of parental sacrifice for children by birth cohort in post-communist, OECD, and developing societies, WVS 1990–2005. 178
9.6 Importance of friends by birth cohort in post-communist, OECD, and developing societies, WVS 1990–2005. 180
9.7 Moral absolutism by birth cohort in post-communist, OECD, and developing societies, WVS 1990–2005. 181
9.8 Justifiability of lying by birth cohort in post-communist, OECD, and developing societies, WVS 1990–2005. 182

Tables

A.1 Comparison of Country Cases 191
A.2 Basic Characteristics of 32 Informants (18 Businessmen, 13 Fathers, 1 Mother) 193
A.3 Description of WVS data used to compare China, Russia, and Eastern Germany 200
A.4 Description of Key WVS Variables, China, Pooled Waves 2 through 5 201
A.5 Description of Key WVS Variables, Russia, pooled Waves 2 through 5 202
A.6 Description of Key WVS Variables, Eastern Germany, pooled waves 2 through 5 203
A.7 OECD, Post-communist, and Developing Societies Included in Chapter 9 Analysis 204
A.8 Description of WVS Data Used to Compare OECD, Post-communist, and Developing Societies 205
A.9 English Interview Guide 206
A.10 Chinese Interview Guide 208
A.11 Russian Interview Guide 208
A.12 German Interview Guide 210
B.1 Two-tailed T-test Mean Comparisons of Key Variables Measuring Individualism, Ambition, and Work, WVS 1990, 1995, 2000, 2005 Waves 213
B.2 Two-tailed T-test Mean Comparisons of Key Variables Measuring Materialism and Consumerism, WVS 1990, 1995, 2000, 2005 Waves 214
B.3 Two-tailed T-test Mean Comparisons of Key Variables Measuring Family and Friendship Values, WVS 1990, 1995, 2000, 2005 Waves 216
B.4 Two-tailed T-test Mean Comparisons of Key Variables Measuring Morality, Religion, and Political Values, WVS 1990, 1995, 2000, 2005 Waves 217

B.5 Two-tailed T-test Mean Comparisons of Key Variables across Post-communist, OECD, and Developing Societies 218
C.1 Two-tailed T-test Mean Comparisons of Key Variables by Gender in China, Russia, Eastern Germany, 1990–2005 222

Permissions

Portions of the 'Homo-Sovieticus' section of Chapter 2 are reprinted with permission and courtesy of LIT Verlag, from: Swader, Christopher S. 2010. "Homo Sovieticus in Interpersonal Relationships Before and After the Collapse of Communism." In *Landmark 1989: Central and Eastern European Societies Twenty Years After the System Change*, edited by Heinrich Best and Agnieszka Wenninger, 62–79. Münster: LIT Verlag. Volume 32, 2010, 304 pages, 29.90 EUR, ISBN 978–3-643–10449–6; Series: Sociology: Research and Science.

Portions of this Chapter 4, specifically on the Russian transformation, are reprinted from CS Swader, "The Lost Years: Assessing Family Change in St. Petersburg, Russia, between 1983 and 2003." *Journal of Comparative Family Studies* 38(2): 317–336. Copyright © 2007 Journal of Comparative Family Studies. Reprinted by permission of the Journal of Comparative Family Studies.

Preface

Around the year 2002, the concept for this book grew out of the meeting of three ideas. First, I was aware that crime rates in many post-socialist societies had surged during the 1990's. Second, I had heard claims of family change, particularly family breakdown during this same period. Third, I had been studying social control theory and wondered if this could explain the first two observations. What if relationship breakdown had occurred in these societies because of economic transformation, and this constituted diminished informal social control, and thus social anarchy (See Liu et al. 2001)? Although I put the empirical investigation of crime to the side for then, and also in this volume, I began to investigate the social relationships and economic change question in detail.

From the beginning, I had approached this question in a way that was ambivalent to the leading approaches on value change and modernization. I found my approach compatible in some ways but critical in others. During my writing, I had also become immersed in the work of the Frankfurt School critical theorists. I found that their work resonated with and spurred some of my raw thinking and intentions. I was also lucky to be surrounded in Bremen by a variety of skilled life course sociologists, which was both theoretically and methodologically helpful for developing my project.

Briefly, I would like to offer a few road signs here in order to help the reader understand this book as I do. It is not about 'value change' as much as it is about 'values changing.' I want to look inside this ongoing process. Also, this is about more than post-communists. I claim that their condition mirrors some of the core features of a 'capitalist' condition. That said, this should not be interpreted as 'yet another' one-sided cultural-pessimist account of capitalism. Rather, I see the values-constellation of capitalism as ambivalent to the core, and I am highlighting a few of the aspects that are perhaps under-covered, in my view, in other recent accounts.

When I refer to 'family values' here, it is not from a conservative, politicized understanding. I am not supposing ideal families, but I am asking to which extent people pour time, mental energy, and intrinsic value into their closest ties, of whichever form they may take.

Every scientific work requires a leap of faith to cover the gap between the causal inferences made and the evidence provided to support them. I am acutely aware of this challenge also in this book. I have tried to narrow this gap and am still uncertain of how many will make the jump. My hope is that you will evaluate this work by first stepping inside of its arguments.

I would like to sincerely thank Ansgar Weymann, Steffen Mau, and Jeylan Mortimer for their advice on, and patient critiques of, the ideas of my dissertation, which eventually were transformed into this work.

Most of my time on this project was spent at the Bremen International Graduate School of Social Sciences (BIGSSS), where I enrolled as a PhD student and later worked for two years. This institution and its members provided me with time, space, and the financial and social support necessary for bringing this project to fruition. Especially Ansgar Weymann, Steffen Mau, Werner Dressel, Matthias Wingens, Walter Heinz, Johannes Huinink, Sibyl Kleiner, Vaida Obelene, Herwig Reiter, Benedikt Rogge, Reinhard Schunk, Volha Vysotskaya, Hao Yuan, and Chenjian Zhang have offered substantial input on my project.

The three-country fieldwork for this research could not have been completed without the help of three additional host institutions and many people. Shanghai University's Department of Sociology assisted me there during my stay. Yuzhao Liu, Guanbao Shen, Junhua Deng, Jiwen Feng, Jo Miao, Ning Shao, Larissa Weimer Swader, Ren Wang, Yawei Wang, and especially Chenjian Zhang deserve special mention for their support. In Moscow, I would like to thank members of the Sociology Department of the National Research University—Higher School of Economics. Thanks to Inna Deviatko for allowing me to present my research during my fieldwork stay. Especially, I am indebted to Olga Kuzina and Natalia Khalina for their tremendous assistance in conducting my fieldwork. Galina Kostova and Maksym Bilous also assisted me in preparing transcripts for analysis. In Leipzig, I was provided with office space and valuable leads by Georg Vobruba, and was assisted in my research by Heiko Beyer, Susan Henne, Konstanze Jacob, Greta Kahle, Elvira Möhring, Robert Zwarg, and especially Anne Grob.

I am also grateful to Jeylan Mortimer and the Life Course Center at the Sociology Department of the University of Minnesota. My stay there during the spring of 2006 was valuable for gathering feedback and for moving forward my analysis.

My past two years at the National Research University—Higher School of Economics (NRU-HSE) have provided me with the necessary support and intellectual stimulation to finish this manuscript. Verbal feedback from colleagues Leon Kosals, Eduard Ponarin, Ben Lind, and Rafael Mrowczynski on this topic has been particularly fruitful. In addition, my involvement with the NRU-HSE's Laboratory for Comparative Social Research has provided a continuation of the valuable opportunities I had earlier in Bremen to discuss modernization and values questions with esteemed scholars such as Ronald Inglehart and Christian Welzel.

A number of colleagues have been so kind as to read through portions of this manuscript at various stages. Thanks to Irene Broon for her work on the bibliography. For their critiques and suggestions on individual chapters, I am very grateful to Roberto Foa, Tatiana Karabchuk, Rafael Mrowczynski, and Priya Fielding-Singh. For her critical commentary and careful reading of wide portions of the book, I thank Larissa Weimer Swader.

1 Introduction

Recent transformations have affected the way that economically 'successful' people in China, Russia, and Eastern Germany care about their close interpersonal relationships. The shift in economic culture stirred the pot of values that motivates people in everyday life, and the resulting brew is rife with tension. This book addresses the question of 'how' values change in connection with the shift to capitalist culture. Contemporary economic culture favors values that conflict with the value of intimate social ties. 'success' is bought through sacrifice.

Psychological tensions burden modern life. Overwhelmed with information, responsibilities, and choices, we struggle to keep our lives, and our minds, in harmony. Conflicts over how to spend our time, our money, and our mental resources are so common that it is tempting to assume that they are universal. This is particularly the case with work–family conflicts. Yet this is what I would like to denaturalize. Tensions between work and family, or more broadly between economy and sociality, are an integral part of most of our lives. This is largely because most of us live in societies transforming themselves toward, or already within, capitalist models. The capitalist mode of economic organization spurs conflicts, particularly work–family conflicts, as a product of its operation. This book highlights how such tensions have grown more strident in post-communist societies as a result of their recent transformations toward market capitalism. More than twenty years after the fall of the Berlin Wall and the collapse of the Soviet Union, many sides of these transformations have been deeply investigated, but not yet this one.

Almost no scholars have earnestly attempted to answer the question of "what happened to the social psychologies of those who experienced the transformation from communism to capitalism?" (Kupferberg 1999, 24). Maybe it is because we take as self-evident the social-psychological 'nature' of communism, as described, for example, by the esteemed playwright, dissident, and later president of the Czech Republic, Václav Havel: "It is the worst in us which is being systematically activated and enlarged—egotism, hypocrisy, indifference, cowardice, fear, resignation, and the desire to escape every personal responsibility . . ." (The Economist 2011, 23). However true such accounts are, and they certainly meet many people's understandings about communism and social life, the inverse does not logically follow. The collapse of communism does not bring about a social resurgence by eliminating a source of human egotism and indifference. This is because capitalism also has an anti-social face.

There are two common ways to link the economic form and the mind. One involves the economy forging individual minds as a blacksmith hammers nails. This notion is top-down and structural, and the result of a mind that 'matches' the economy emerges from the economy creating the minds (and other products) that it needs in order to function. The second paradigm involves individuals choosing to become blacksmiths. This idea is bottom-up and agentic, and the match between minds and the needs of the economy is circumstantial to individual desires—apparently arbitrary—to become blacksmiths. The weaknesses of each of these stories are obvious. One neglects individual circumstances and action, whereas the other underplays environmental incentives and obstacles.

These views can be neatly meshed together. Instead of the economy 'forging' the mind or the mind merely 'choosing' to become an economic actor, both of these factors interact in individuals' 'becoming' economic actors in a cyclical process in which individual choices are both framed by and themselves frame economic culture. Continuing with the blacksmith metaphor, the choice to hammer nails and act as a blacksmith creates a tendency for an adaptive and reflexive person to increasingly 'be' a blacksmith in patterned ways that ensure success. These adaptations were not all consciously chosen themselves, but they are often side effects of the original decision to blacksmith. To blacksmith means to transform one's environment and oneself according to the imperatives of blacksmithing. Metal becomes something to be formed, melded according to the smith's will. Family members as well may be converted into supporters, apprentices, and servants. The smithy also learns to read his/her customers, to hammer just enough nails, horseshoes, and swords, and to convince the public of the high value of these products. On average, the person who achieves the greatest success *occupationally* as a blacksmith also becomes the most *personally* blacksmith-like, whatever those characteristics may be.

Of course, modern economies are not overpopulated with blacksmiths. Yet, just as for the medieval artisan, in order to be successful in the modern market economy—to become a successful manager, entrepreneur, or businessperson—an individual undergoes certain conscious and unconscious transformations toward behavioral 'best-practices.' What then are the tools of success for key occupations in a market economy? As I argue in detail in this book, they include calculative rationality, the commodification of time, the exploitation and instrumentalization of relationships, image cultivation and consumerism, personal ambition and independence, work focus, materialism, tolerance of failure, and moral flexibility. People who adopt these tend to reap benefits for themselves, and in having done so, they have adapted in ways which constitute the contemporary economic culture. However, to follow these rules of the game also results in important repercussions for life spheres beyond work.

Which side effects does this new mentality bring about in other life domains? In terms of politics, research has argued for strong links between capitalism and pro-democratic, self-expressive, and tolerant attitudes. The modern economy, through the economic growth it brings, appears to widen personal aspirations and self-expression and fosters liberation from tradition and material scarcity (Inglehart and Welzel 2005). Yet, aside from these repercussions with clearly political implications, which effects does this adaptation have within the realm of interpersonal relationships? If we look at the private sphere, at arguably the core aspect of human sociality, the face-to-face social bond, we see a very different picture. Capitalism produces tensions that challenge face-to-face sociality in everyday life. This book describes how capitalist culture tends toward the individualization of values in this sense, one that involves sacrifice, even for the economic 'winners.'

Such sacrifice comes about because those who adapt to these particular best-practices are likely to experience tensions with their social convictions, such as the high valuation of face-to-face ties. Two examples begin to illustrate this. "Time is money" is an adage adhered to by successful businesspeople. This means that every minute is potentially convertible into economic gain. Evenings and weekends are convertible as well. In fact, they count for even more if they are wasted by a competitor on the family but utilized by a smart entrepreneur for work. Time is, of course, valuable for other things besides work, such as leisure, and/or spending time with our families and friends, so its allocation to work can cause anxiety. In another example, personal relationships become 'useful' for business. A friend or a relative is also a potential client, investor, worker, or partner. Modern workers who successfully and cleverly instrumentalize their interpersonal relationships tend to be rewarded by the economic system. Yet many of those who are using or exploiting their interpersonal ties, or creating new ties for explicitly instrumental reasons, may feel uneasy a result, even aside from the effects of this form of behavior on their partners. The short examples above, the instrumentalization of time and of relationships, are two of the best practices talked about by successful post-communist businessmen. Not all people, of course, follow this perceived cultural code. However, those who do are likely to be rewarded. At the same time, people report that these adaptations cause them moral disquiet. I argue that this cognitive dissonance is itself a major force for adaptive change. The drive to resolve this dissonance is a prime factor leading to more individualized values, because people tend to relieve their mental conflicts by becoming *more* rather than less individualized and work-oriented. The capitalist personality is more at peace when it values face-to-face bonds less.

Yet why do I write of personality, and how is it linked to culture? The word 'personality' derives from the Latin 'persona,' which refers to the theatrical mask worn by Greek and Roman actors (Feist and Feist 2005, 3). There is much disagreement about definitions of personality, but a common one is that "personality is a pattern of relatively permanent traits and unique characteristics that give both consistency and individuality to a person's behavior" (Feist and Feist 2005, 4). Therefore, personality should help us to predict behavior (see also Ryckman 2008, 4–5). In this respect, personality overlaps with the concept of values. Often seen as less enduring than personality traits, values are the general cognitive constructs that allow individuals to prioritize their behavioral choices (Schwartz and Bilsky 1987). They are the meeting point between behavior and cognition. Personality can be viewed as a container for values.

This book argues strongly for a degree of malleability of personality features linked to patterned prioritization of behavioral choices, of values, in the face of radical social change. While it is often assumed that these traits are stable across time and between social contexts, this notion is contested. Particularly, in rapidly changing societies, such as in post-communist space, people do radically change some, although not all, of their key perceptions, priorities, and actions within the world, sometimes at the cost of dissonance and sacrifice (see also Kohn et al. 2002). Much of this book explains the reasons and directionality for a category of such changes: those concerned with people's valuations of intimate face-to-face communication and relationships. Furthermore, a key argument of mine is that personalities are patterned by a variety of cultural influences; economic culture is among them.

The 'capitalist personality' is the personality type favored by (in that it accrues rewards), and functional for, key entrepreneurial, business, and managerial roles within a capitalist economy. The most basic way that personalities are influenced by social constellations is not through imprinting upon them key and abstract functions, but rather through agents' own actions in response to the perceived environment. This model is not a deterministic one. Rather a capitalist economy embodies forces that tend to bring certain patterns of personality into effect through rewarding particular values.

Of course, we can think of many cultural influences that affect personality. We can imagine a communist personality (Wang 2002), an agricultural personality, the authoritarian personality (Adorno 1976), democratic personality (Lasswell 1951), a traditional personality, a middle class personality, an artistic personality, or a factory personality (Inkeles and Smith 1974). Each of these are, of course, in addition to national, ethnic, religious, and gendered patterns of personality, some of which social-psychologists differentiate and categorize, for instance into the individualist and collectivist dimension (Triandis 2001). These different spheres of cultural influence each contribute, in contending and combinational ways, to personality adaptation. An individual personality, such as you or I, is then the battling overlap of these contending spheres of cultural influence, intermeshed with genetic factors. Yet it is unsatisfying to simply say that we are formed from a variety of cultural raw-materials. It is rather important to identify how the main cultural spheres impact personality in specific ways. It is with this in mind that the capitalist personality is investigated. This particular personality has a secondary effect in that its favored values tend to result in the latency of values that allow intimate relationships to flourish.

This book draws evidence for these claims from societies that have recently undergone a transformation from a planned to a market economic system: economically post-communist societies, in particular China, Russia, and Eastern Germany. These three societies are chosen as the *most-dissimilar cases* among new free-market countries. Notably, China, Russia, and Eastern Germany vary radically in their cultures, languages, histories, ideologies, and centrally-planned and free-market economic conditions. However, the unifying factor is that they each experienced a near-total transformation to a market economy the past twenty years. Moreover, as I argue in this book, each has experienced shifts in social values during this same time period. Therefore, China, Russia, and Eastern Germany are chosen not only as a few of the world's most visible examples of new market economies, but more pointedly, because their starkly different ideologies, cultural and historical influences, and levels of transition-era economic prosperity demand that their similarity, the presence of social devaluation, be explained.

The post-communist condition in this sense is telling of capitalism at large. It depicts, through noting commonalities between different post-communist cases and elucidating the mechanisms directly linked to structural economic change, an aspect of the capitalism also very much alive elsewhere: an anti-social nature in terms of face-to-face sociality. What do I mean by 'anti-social?' The sociality dealt with here is one that is close at hand rather than abstract and far away. It deals with families and friends rather than institutions and strangers. It occurs through everyday conversation at the dinner table or over coffee rather than via memorandums or video-conferences. This face-to-face communication is a core means by which human norms are transmitted and reinforced, by which we receive much of our psychological well-being, and still where we spend large proportions of our time. It forms one of the most fundamental features of our social structure and social nature and is nonetheless highly sensitive to social change. Despite this, research on the close face-to-face bond is nowadays largely forsaken except for scattered ruminations about its demise, which form the 'dark side' of the coin of individualization referred to in contemporary sociological thought. In contrast to this relative silence, this problem was one of the prime interests among classical sociologists: how the development of the modern economy affects the social relationship.

Of course, capitalism is no homogenous monolith (nor behemoth) bridging all societies (See Hall and Soskice 2001). Rather, given our knowledge of the different forms of capitalism and the vast differences in specifics of the market-economic transformations in the post-communist world, the common cross-country observation of de-socialization despite these differences supports the idea of a capitalist *ethos*.

Breaking with practice, this book does not deeply investigate the underclasses who have been unable to stay afloat in capitalism's rising tide in Eastern Europe and Asia. Their stories are indeed filled with poverty, injustice, and private turmoil. Instead I write about those people who enjoy 'success' because so much has been made of their stories. They symbolize opportunity, and often, hope, as if only economic growth benefited people more equally, more would enjoy greater material, and therefore social, well-being, *like the newly rich.* We are told a similar story by social theories that highlight economic development as the first step to social and political evolution. Politics and society have moved "backwards" in Eastern Europe because of their lack of economic development, according to this view (Inglehart and Baker 2000).

There are some problems with assuming that value change stems only from economic conditions (thereby sidestepping the role of the 'economic culture'). First, China reports many of the same types of corruption and social anarchy—such as high rates of juvenile delinquency or property crimes—as Eastern Europe, despite its backbreaking and reliable economic growth. Second, many of the new rich in Eastern Europe achieved success in the 1990's through criminal activities (see Volkov 2002), are highly materialistic, and are hardly known for being pro-social. Third, as I will show in the following chapters, the social mentalities of post-communist states have not moved backwards, but in critical ways have become more 'Western,' with enhanced individualism, ambition, work orientation, and moral flexibility. Therefore, I have placed special emphasis on the new rich, the 'winners' of the transformation, as the flag bearers of the new economic system. To blame cultural problems solely on economic scarcity and inequality ignores the fact that the capitalist economic system, even in its ideal state, is also far from utopian. In other words, if the vanguards of new capitalism possess values that may be socially problematic, we can no longer write these problems off as due to inadequate economic growth or distribution. They are cultural and systemic rather than conditional, merely based on malfunction or harsh material conditions. These members of the new successful classes possess personality characteristics that are formed, not out of scarcity, but as a direct response to liberal economic culture. Comparative interviews with successful people and their own fathers illustrate this dynamic.

The central idea behind my interviews is to compare theoretically most-affected people with less-affected cases. With this in mind, two categories of informants were interviewed: the 'most-affected' young businessmen, entrepreneurs, and managers, and their own 'less-affected' fathers.

Men were interviewed, rather than women, as the 'most-affected gender.' Research indicates that women tend to be more compassionate, less competitive, and less materialistic than men (Beutel and Marini 1995; see also Appendix C). Therefore, interviews are conducted with men and their fathers as these interviews reveal the greatest contrasts and thus allow for an analysis of *how* capitalist value change occurs where it is found.

Shanghai, Moscow, and Leipzig were selected as the most culturally modern and economically developed cities of each society. Interviews were conducted in these 'most-affected' cities in order to maximize chances of finding the 'most-adapted' persons, in order to see how this adaptation works.

In his description, Becker (2006, 41) notes that "Shanghai is where modern China took its shape." Shanghai has always been the vanguard, foreshadowing China's future, for better or for worse. He also notes its Janus-face qualities as the pinnacle of Chinese modernity:

> Reviled in the 1920s and '30s as the "whore of the East" or admired as East Asia's greatest metropolis, China owes its first modern factories, banks, schools, universities, financial markets, newspapers, orchestras, and film stars to Shanghai. (Becker 2006, 41)

Historically situated as a center of early 20th-century Western economic power in China, its government has capitalized on Shanghai's economic history by forming it into the modern giant of China's post-Mao economic boom.

Non-Muscovite Russians are fond of noting "Moscow is not Russian." Only fifteen years ago, Moscow still felt like it had one foot in the Soviet past, while simultaneously being overrun by strip-clubs and casinos. Now, the city is packed with masses running on the heels of oligarchs, poor migrant workers from Central Asia, and streets lined with ritzy restaurants and cafes. Indeed, it hoards the majority of the country's wealth and vices and is sprawling with the new rich. In the city center, the famous grey of the Soviet past makes way for neon lights and sleek luxury automobiles. The reasons for resenting Moscow are obvious to most Russians; it represents the sharpened tip of the (admittedly quite long) spear of contemporary Russian economic and cultural development.

In Eastern Germany, Leipzig has been chosen for investigation. Berlin was not selected because of its unique East–West linkages. It would have been difficult to isolate former East Berlin social life as purely socialist in the same sense that it would now be impossible to designate it now as 'Eastern German.' Leipzig has an old commercial history, is host of the world's oldest trade fair, and its post-reunification business revival is marked by branches of big-name companies in its midst: Porsche, Siemens, and BMW. While certainly the major economic, technology, and business center outside of Berlin in the East, it is notably smaller and sleepier that Moscow or Shanghai. Nonetheless, it has a historical and contemporary business culture that makes it a center of economic development in the the new German federal states.

Because values are promoted and interpreted largely through family structures, this study used intergenerational qualitative interviews in order to gauge emergent tensions in social values. Interviews were conducted with new-rich businessmen (who have children) and with their surviving fathers. It can be assumed that the values of fathers and sons would roughly resemble each other, because fathers would be expected to socialize their sons with their own values. Differences then among the values of these generations thus represent the extent to which the father's values are no longer adequate and thereby indicate the potential direction of social change. Of course, younger generations may naturally try to distinguish their values from their fathers', as a form of rebellion, but the directionality of this shift would be highly affected by cultural influences, and within a stable cultural environment, we could still expect at least parallels between fathers' and sons' core values.

It is assumed that the businessman's father possesses the state of values closer to that which existed before the transition to the market economy. His values would have been much less affected by the economic changes than his son's because the father has been socialized long ago and now has minimal involvement in the economy and therefore less adaptive value modification. In contrast, economically successful businessmen, entrepreneurs, and managers are deemed to have adapted most to the new economic system and thus most-directly reflect the values of the new economy.

Based on representative quantitative samples from the World Values Survey, I also present results on how values are arrayed across the wider populations in China, Russia, and Eastern Germany. Specifically, I report on how key values differ between newer and older birth cohorts, between those in modern and other occupations, and between wealthy people and others. This allows the generalization of valuation gaps found in interviews between successful people and their fathers across the wider population.

The transformation from a centrally planned to a market economy spawned objective and subjective impacts in the lives of people in socialist countries. Much has been written of the objective effects, which have come primarily in the spheres of goods and work. However, in addition to these existential changes, individuals also came to face their new economic world with a new mentality functional within it, one that had profound consequences for face-to-face sociality. Ultimately the new value set tends toward an individualization also characterized by, in addition to some beneficial aspects, the diminished salience of face-to-face intimacy. As such, this book deals with the usually ignored subject of post-socialist everyday life.

This is not an account of a good society, either of a foreseeable or existing one. No utopia, or alternate utopia, will be constructed here. However, neither is this a dystopian work about sociality and economic modernity. This project is a critical-empirical account of one part of the underbelly of an aspect of modernization that many would interpret as 'good.' Ideology is like a blinding light focused on a few objects in the center of a large room. A 'critical' account should seek to balance the distribution of light. This both implies illuminating the dark corners where something important might be hidden and, at the same time, dimming the light shone on the objects in the center of the room, thus changing their appearance and revealing further textures and flaws. Furthermore, because this is an empirical account, I aim to provide you not with abstract theoretical claims but rather with arguments backed by evidence.

In the meanwhile, those who would hope that some solutions might be suggested for the problems I outline here may be disappointed. My task is one of analysis, deconstruction and reconstruction, not policy recommendation or condemnation. I am convinced, however, that facing the ambivalences and drawbacks of our economic and social reality is a prerequisite for constructing a better society.

REVIEW OF CHAPTERS

Chapter 2, "Becoming Homo-economicus" describes my main thesis in detail. I provide the reader with definitions and interrelations between the key concepts of capitalism, face-to-face sociality, individualization, and informal social control. In the meantime, I cover the scientific works most relevant to this theme. The following step critiques three aspects of neighboring scientific work: (1) the hostility toward critical thinking about capitalism among dominant 'grey area' economic-sociological approaches, (2) arbitrary assignment of blame for 'negative' post-socialist developments on 'homo-sovieticus' within transitology research, and (3) excessive focus on technocratic transformation questions while ignoring everyday life.

Chapter 3, "The Wall in the Head" outlines this project's principal finding and interpretive frame: the mechanisms of de-intimization. However, I will first introduce some basic information on my interviews and on the quantitative analysis. Thereafter, I describe how values change as a result of various factors. The most important of these concerns the cognitive dissonance that arises because of conflicting values. This dissonance is resolved in the direction of least resistance, which usually means in favor of the activation of economic values and the latency of social values. In addition, the roles of individual adaptation, intergenerational changeover, and ideological conflict and collapse are discussed as further mechanisms of value change.

Chapter 4 provides the "Chinese, Russian, and Eastern German Contexts" for this study. I provide the reader with a background on the topics of intimate relations before and during the transformation period as well as country-specific details related to the economic transformations of China, Russia, and Eastern Germany. Finally, I compare countries with one another across relevant features and highlight the logic of the most-dissimilar case design.

In Chapter 5, I detail tensions in "Individualism, Ambition, and Work" which appeared in these three societies. Results from an analysis of World Values Survey (WVS) data and from the qualitative interviews are presented. A key finding is the introduction of a temporal phasing of high familial valuation until retirement for ambitious persons. In other words, family time is a leisure activity to be engaged in once the 'work period' of life has passed. In addition, successful businessmen tend to see work as a matter of personal ambition, self-determination, and as a 'career,' and its priority is above other life domains. In contrast, the older generation views work as a duty performed for the benefit of the family and wider society.

Evidence for rising materialism and consumerism in China, Russia, and Eastern Germany is presented in Chapter 6, "Get Rich First!" This is based on WVS data and qualitative interviews. Important findings involve the centrality of profit-calculation, and its spillover into other life spheres, and the rising salience of consumer culture, whether instrumentally in order to demonstrate status or as an end-in-itself in the form of luxury temptation.

How have rising individualism, work-focus, and materialism affected interpersonal relationships? Chapter 7 presents results about gaps in "Family Relationships and Friendship" values. Various data sources are used to provide conclusions about how these key social values have been impacted by heightened valuations of work, the self, and materialism. A high valuation of competing values tends to push family values into latency. Furthermore, among younger generations, there is a noted emphasis toward individualized, naturalized values for children, toward diminished respect toward elders, and even toward the reduced importance of the notion that parents have a duty to sacrifice for their own children. In the meantime, friendship values expand in importance, but 'instrumental' friendships appear to be increasingly favored.

The increasing salience of rational individualist, work, and materialist values has also influenced the way that people value morality in general and the larger community. "Morality, Religion, and Politics" are covered in Chapter 8. Specifically, I report on how these spheres have experienced tension in the past twenty years, especially among the newly successful occupational classes. Adaptation is depicted here, to a large extent, as the 'selling out' of one's moral values. Indeed valuations of honesty or proclivities against exploitation are not seen as profitable for businessmen. As opposed to moral absolute standards in right and wrong, moral 'flexibility' is more relevant in the modern economy. Religion is also seen as opposed to these forms of moral flexibility, but its value tends to decline in younger generations. Also, I report on how younger cohorts are much less politically interested and community-involved than their elders.

How does individualization in post-socialist societies compare with other societies? Is it true that Western countries are even more individualized and morally flexible than the rest of the world? Chapter 9, "The Wild West?" addresses this question by comparing individuals from the OECD and developing countries directly with post-communists on a number of individualization indicators. My findings support the notion of a capitalist ethos, since highly individualized post-communist values are not a special case; in most respects, post-communist values mirror or are exceeded by the same values in the OECD.

The "Discussion," Chapter 10, provides a summary of results, further thinking about these in relation to individualization and social values in the Western world, a review of some of the monograph's shortcomings, and some commentary on praxis and policy.

2 Becoming Homo-Economicus

What does it mean to 'become homo-economicus'? This question can be best answered by the convergence of three concepts: capitalism, individualization, and values. This chapter moves forward in two steps. First, I will describe the research theme as I see it, at this convergence. Second, I will address it through related perspectives. This topic is located at the intersection of several 'camps': values studies, post-socialist studies, economic sociology, individualization, and criminology and social control. If I have failed to address a particular stream of thought, it is because this research area belongs to many scholarly territories, and I was forced to disperse my energy accordingly. Despite a limited history of other research that integrates these diverse strands, I hope that my effort helps the reader navigate this topic, while at the same time framing it within the neighboring terrain.

This chapter provides a set of definitions key for understanding my argument. To begin, how to define capitalism, and what is its relevance to face-to-face sociality? Capitalism will be described as a cultural system, one which contrasts to the planned economic system in socialist times. Thes values concept links culture and individual mentalities in patterned ways. I particularly describe the importance of 'social values.' Thereafter, presumed effects of capitalist culture on social values will be prescribed through the prism of individualization. These arguments provide the basis for the main hypothesis of this book: capitalist culture and the valuation of face-to-face social ties are in tension with one another. The connection of these issues to social control theory and social disorder will then be elaborated. Throughout my coverage of key concepts, I will be highlighting gaps in research into which I am stepping and my points of divergence.

The second half of the chapter examines my claims through other sociological lenses. I describe how three major trends in neighboring research allow it only to partially explain the phenomenon at hand. First, there is a hostility toward what is depicted as 'black and white' grand theoretical approaches and their empirical supports. The more recent trend is toward 'grey area' approaches to questions like mine. Although they dominate economic sociology and produce convincing empirical analyses, some of these approaches use the empirical complexity they find in order to delegitimize critical accounts of the ways that capitalism and sociality interact. The tendency of such research is away from conflict and critique and toward moral neutrality. Second, within another subset of research, 'transitology,' problems with both technocratic language and with 'homo-sovieticus' loom large. Often, changes that are deemed negative are blamed on the Soviet legacy, usually built-in as the homo-sovieticus mindset, while positive developments are credited to the present system. Also, much literature on the post-socialist transformations takes a technocratic approach, focusing heavily on economic institutions, elites, or networks, but ignoring questions of everyday life. The result of such research is that it tends to be useful to policy makers and economic practitioners, but it may less touch the "personal troubles" that matter to most people (Mills 2000).

CAPITALISM AND THE MARKET ECONOMY

Capitalism embodies three major components: market exchange, private property, and profit-orientations. It connects these together within a system where individuals work to extract the maximum surplus value, in the form of profit, for the goods and services they exchange in markets. This definition of capitalism, with its three components and contrasted to a planned economy, is close to that offered by Deirdre McCloskey, an economist with a very different view about capitalism's 'virtues' from my own: "I mean by 'capitalism' merely private property and free labor without central planning, regulated by the rule of law and by an ethical consensus" (2006, 14).

A common misperception arises from the terms capitalism and communism.[1] Both call us to envision the political poles characterized by the Cold War and the long struggle preceding it. As a result, we find it difficult to differentiate the different components of each system, the political, the cultural, and the economic. Except where noted, I use these terms in order to call up their economic significance, also encapsulated by the concepts advanced market economy or centrally planned economy. The argument here thus does not refer primarily to the political components associated with these terms but rather has to do with the advanced market and communist *economies* as contrasting economic structures. Therein, this project looks at the effects of these economic systems upon their subjects, the consumers and workers who function within them.

The first of the three components of capitalism, market exchange, implies a system where the forces of supply and demand are responsible for the setting of prices and the distribution of goods and labor. In ideal terms, the market economy is contrasted with the socialist planned economic system, whereby goods were centrally distributed by the state.

Without private property, a true market of exchange and the notion of profit are both nonsensical. Of course, it was common in socialist times to use social ties to secure a better apartment, some luxury goods, or to illegally trade products stolen from the factory where one worked. Certainly those in privileged positions were able to secure even more material advantage. Yet the degree of personal gain, especially in the form of liquid capital profit, which could be secured from such dealings, was greatly limited in comparison to a system where individually held property is legal and encouraged and culturally and legally protected. Where private property is publicly supported, the limits to informal personal accumulation are removed, and material accumulation is facilitated.

A third, but very important, component to capitalism as a system is the cultural and thereby personal incentive for and valuation of material accumulation: values beneficial for capitalism. As elegantly described within Max Weber's work (1984; 2003), it is far from 'given' that people will highly value profit calculation and material accumulation in a given place or a given time. Capitalism cannot function very well without at least some people who strive to, and know how to, maximize profit, alongside a variety of other market orientations.

Of course, there are many subtle hybrids between a market economy and a planned economy, with a plenitude of state control within market systems and shadow economies operating beyond the reach of planned economic systems. An excellent example of this type of argument has been forwarded by David Stark (1996), in his discussion on recombinant property. In a nutshell, Stark points out that market-like economies existed even during Soviet times, and therefore the collapse of communism did not leave a "vacuum." Rather, previous practices metamorphized, and new practices were built "with the ruins," not "on the ruins" of communism. In this case, "recombination" of multiple interwoven orders of reality, rather than replacement of one system by another, is the catchword. Yet, the Soviet second economies spoken of by Stark did not reach the masses with the same means as contemporary eastern European capitalism, through a mass consumer culture. These second economies were made real as human networks of informal exchange for scarce goods. This contrasts sharply with the faceless, and comparatively less-networked, effect of mass advertising, and the focus on luxury rather than scarce goods. Although it is clear that mixed, recombinant forms existed and still exist, individuals nonetheless *perceived and felt* the transformation years as a vacuum, a collapse, a transition from unitary communism to unitary capitalism. This had both subjective and objective dimensions.

Beyond the subjective, the complex recombination of market and planned economic orders with the collapse of communism had radical objective effects within the lives of real people. Historically, the freeing of prices, opening local currency to free exchange, and exposure of local businesses to international markets brought huge shifts in the lives of the citizens in these societies. These changes, brought about by the transition from the planned to the market economy, meant transformations in two main spheres: in work and in goods. Work became less secure, with greater potential variety, and there was a growth in service sector jobs, a greater income-gap between different jobs, and greater *potential* pay. In the meantime, goods arrived in much greater variety, in a greater price range as well; here the flood of the arrival of luxury goods is also important. A distinct, black and white, shift in the real lives of millions upon millions of people occurred as a result of the transformations to the market economic system. These changes, especially in goods and work, were *real* and necessitated reactions from those subjected to them. This fact both justifies the dichotomous distinction between the two economic systems and the goal to determine the effect of these transformations upon the values of their subjects. Interestingly, while this dichotomy between economic systems is often attacked where it appears within critiques of capitalism, it is rarely doubted in literature touting capitalism's benefits.

Therefore, it is necessary to distinguish between binary economic capitalism and communism as ideologically claimed, the really existing recombinant and hybrid forms of economy, and the meaningful (subjectively and objectively) patterning of such recombinations in the lives of real people.

VALUES

Social disintegration may occur through the advanced free-market economic structure's weakening of social norms through transforming traditional social values, causing them to increasingly reflect a market structure that is characterized by growing rationalization, individualization, and material aspirations. In other words, I argue that value change is the key mediator between economic structural transformation and declining normative power over the individual. Particularly, intimate social values are the foundation of the informal social control presumably uprooted by capitalist economic culture.

What are the 'values' referred to here? Hitlin and Piliavin (2004) provide a thorough review of the values concept and its potential for sociology. They answer several important questions about values. Some of their questions will be repeated in this section, albeit with slightly different answers.

What are values? A value is a theoretical construct representing the cognitive structure which makes possible a particular set of behavioral choices. In other words, values are where behavior and cognition meet. As a general definition of values, Schwartz and Bilsky's (1987, 551; cited by Hitlin and Piliavin 2004) is a useful one. They define values as "(a) concepts or beliefs, (b) about desirable end states or behaviors, (c) that transcend specific situations, (d) guide selection or evaluation of behavior and events, and (e) are ordered by relative importance." More simply stated, values should be seen as the individual's prioritized internalization of social norms used to guide his/her behavior. Values need not be consciously recognized as 'values;' they are presumed from their outcomes. Within this definition, the ambivalence in points (b) and (d) should be noted, in that values can concern "behavior *or* events" (emphasis added) and they may guide "selection *or* evaluation" (emphasis added). These ambiguities point to a critical point about values which should be made explicit: they contain a cognitive and a behavioral dimension. They are neither merely cognitions (attitudes) nor mere behaviors. This dual application of the concept of values to both cognitive settings and their outcomes requires a conceptual differentiation. For this purpose, the concepts of activity and latency will be used to describe the extent to which values are expressed in behavioral outcomes. An active value is more often expressed, while a latent value still resides in the mind but is less often revealed in behavioral outcomes.

Values are nested within individuals and should be contrasted with norms, which are at the group-level (Hitlin and Piliavin 2004, 361). Values can be seen as internalized norms. Furthermore, values are different from attitudes, which are rather positive or negative evaluations of specific social objects (Hitlin and Piliavin 2004, 360–361). Values are both higher in priority and greater in abstraction than are specific attitudes or opinions (Hitlin and Piliavin 2004, 361).

This book focuses the values concept upon *social values,* which are those values that emphasize and prioritize social relationships and face-to-face communication between individuals. These values are called 'social' not in a generalized or normative sense, but rather because they emphasize the most fundamental mode of sociality, face-to-face interaction, since it is this mode that underlies informal social control. Thus, this social values construct relies on the primary relationship as its central component, one that Carol Gilligan has called the "concrete other" in contrast to the abstract other (Ingram and Simon-Ingram 1992, xxxviii). In contrast, *non-social values* prioritize the self, materialism, or other non-social spheres or activities.

Furthermore, there are different modes of valuation, which give values different means of coming into being. Corresponding to a rational-calculative mode of valuation, we have both instrumental values, focused on the means of attaining a particular end, and terminal values, which focus on the ends themselves (Rokeach 1973). Indeed many individuals do not apply values according to this rational approach (Schwartz 1996, cited in Hitlin and Piliavin 2004, 365), and pragmatists tend also to reject this means-ends assertion as unrealistic (Hitlin and Piliavin 2004, 364). This problem can be overcome through an additional category of valuation. Many values are held intrinsically or innately; they are unquestioned, uncalculated valuations of particular ways of living without a premeditated reason to exist. They are seen as intuitively valuable.

Where do values come from? Hitlin and Piliavin (2004, 368–378) suggest many sources of values. They mention the possibility that biology and evolution may program us with sets of inborn values. In addition, race and ethnicity may provide values, for example, through particular "symbolic identities" (Waters 1990, cited in Hitlin and Piliavin 2004). Gender differences in values have also been illuminated; for example, Beutel and Marini (1995) have demonstrated that men are less compassionate and more materialistic than women. Hitlin and Piliavin also focus on a variety of socio-cultural characteristics and how they have been shown to affect values. Social class, occupation, and education are included in this category, as well as family characteristics, such as inter- and intra-generational influences. Immigration status, age cohort, and religion are also shown to be important sources of values (Hitlin and Piliavin 2004, 375). National and demographic roots of value change have been explored as well, and a variety of cross-national studies have been undertaken, but surprising is that, despite the variety of sources of values that has been cited, there is still a research gap.

Left out of values research is the effect that economic structures have in imprinting values. Certainly the economy itself, alongside its progeny, class and occupation, provides a certain pull in regard to the values found in its subjects. Inglehart (2000; Inglehart and Baker 2000) might be seen as approaching this problem through his embracing of the scarcity concept, but scarcity is less a question of economy itself than of economic conditions. In contrast, this work's focus on capitalism as a cultural system investigates economic structure.

Finally, Hitlin and Piliavin mention another key source of values, that they may be supplied by political ideologies (Maio et al. 2003, as cited by Hitlin and Piliavin 2004). Obvious applications of this notion for this topic are state and cultural supply of ideologies which emphasize or de-emphasize particular "value identities" (Hitlin and Piliavin 2004, 382). A key issue for this book is the extent to which capitalism and communism, as economic cultures, have produced their own conflicting 'value identities.'

How do such 'sources' of values relay their 'product' to individuals? This question has been left unanswered by most researchers. What Hitlin and Piliavin provide in terms of how values actually arise is the concept of adaptation to social and political circumstances (Schwartz and Bardi 1997, cited in Hitlin and Piliavin 2004, 379). The adaptation concept, while critical for understanding values change, is nonetheless blurry and insufficient. Adaptation must be better described and made more concrete. Additional mechanisms are needed which transfer values between the society and individual, with working components both at the macro- and cognitive levels. Such mechanisms will be elaborated upon within this book's Chapter 3, "The Wall in the Head."

Hitlin and Piliavin discuss some of the shortcomings of values research, and I have made efforts to overcome each of them in this study. One of the major weaknesses of most value research is the lack of empirical attention afforded to the *process* of valuation (Hitlin and Piliavin 2004). This book sheds some light on this issue, because its principal method of qualitative interviews offers clues as to how valuation occurs.

A further challenge of values research is that "values operate at the level of individuals, institutions and entire societies" at the same time (Hitlin and Piliavin 2004, 383). The approach of this book begins at the individual level, looking primarily at values within individual minds. Later, the production of values at the cultural and social levels will be addressed in terms of how these are then transmitted back down to the individual.

Hitlin and Piliavin make (2004) four suggestions for future values research. First, it should link social structural variables and individual values. I do this by explicating links between capitalism and values. Second, the authors question the mechanisms by which values are transmitted across generations, as well as how they remain stable. This book, making use of intergenerational interviews, explores some answers to this question. Third a temporal dimension is needed; this project incorporates temporality through focusing on social change, with a distinct emphasis on long- and short-term workings of individualization. Fourth, the authors suggest a focus on value variations within social groups. This study approaches this through elucidating a set of mechanisms of value change. Thereby, individuals' values differ according to their differentiated exposure to these mechanisms. While groups may tend to accumulate patterns of values according to their similar influence by the same factors, this does not prevent the emergence of heterogeneity. Nonetheless, while this project also has tools that enable it to explain within-group heterogeneity, it is the surprising emergence of partial value homogeneities *across groups* that are in other ways so different—in line with the most-dissimilar case approach—which is noteworthy.

Although much work (Inglehart 1990; Inglehart 1997; Inglehart 2000; Inglehart and Baker 2000; Rokeach 1973; Schwartz 1992; Schwartz 1994; Schwartz and Bilsky 1987) deals seriously with the research of *values*, a focus on the *de-intimization* of values has been rare.

The Inglehart discourse, which is based on the World Values Survey data, outlines broad trends of value shifts resulting from economic modernization, such as individualization and the growth of secular-rationalism (Inglehart and Baker 2000). However, this value shift is described as an exclusively positive event. This optimistic review of modernizing values is possible because Inglehart is concerned mainly with the political dimension of value shifts, specifically the connection between economic development, post-materialistic values, and democracy. Inglehart sees "materialist" values as a gateway to the post-materialist values that he views as critical for the development of democracy. In this approach, he does not engage in a full exploration of materialism and consumerism at the psychological level and the social consequences, such as normlessness, of shifting values. In contrast, Rokeach's (1973) values represent psychological ideals, terminal values such as 'a comfortable life,' 'wisdom,' 'courage,' 'freedom,' 'equality,' and instrumental ones such as 'broad-minded,' 'logical,' and 'intellectual' (Rokeach 1973). Rokeach's ideal psychological traits have less to do with the notions of sociality central to this book. In the meanwhile, Schwartz (1992; 1994; Schwartz and Bardi 1997; Schwartz and Bilsky 1987) deals with philosophical ideals such as egalitarianism and harmony, some of which are relevant to sociality questions. For example, he posits oppositions between self-oriented and other-oriented values. Yet Schwartz (1994) does not apply his tools to the communist-capitalist sociality question. He instead opts for an investigation of political value specificities in Eastern Europe during the early transformation years (Schwartz and Bardi 1997).

BECOMING HOMO-ECONOMICUS

The capitalist economic form can be connected to various value orientations. To begin with, there is a long discussion in the social sciences about the role of a so-called human 'nature' in relation to economic activity. Although older work poses human beings as *homo-economicus*—rational, self-serving, and calculating—much of current thought in sociology and in economics itself stresses the role of the irrational and the social elements of human behavior. As the story goes, classical economic thought is incorrect in its assumptions about human behavior, because human beings are, after all, *homo-sociologicus*, social and emotional, and thereby only boundedly rational by nature. Similar interpretations can be found in psychology, philosophy, and evolutionary anthropology. Human beings, we are told, are social and moral even as a result of our evolved brain physiology (Massey 2002; Dunbar 2003). What strikes me about these claims about our social nature is how they would mesh with discussions about economic performativity. Scholars point to the performativity of the field of economics, in that it *produces* in the world precisely the types of calculative, rational, behavior that its models predict, through its shaping of policies and expectations (Fourcade 2011, 41–45). Yet in the same way that economics as an academic discipline creates behavior and institutions that fulfill its expectations, the same can be said of the economy at large, of which, economics as a discipline forms a part (or shapes more profoundly). Individuals acting in such an economy, one that posits the unequaled value of profit maximization and individualism, come to act in ways that this economy prescribes and expects. In so doing, they simultaneously react to and perform 'economic culture.' Now I return to the social brain (Dunbar 2003) argumentation; in becoming more calculating, individualist, and rational, it is natural to ask how culturally 'becoming homo-economicus' affects members of the homo-sociologicus species. I attempt to answer this question through the idea of 'de-intimization,' which I nest within the paradigm of individualization.

The idea to connect de-intimization with capitalist economic culture emerged in connection to social control theory (Hirschi 2002). Researchers used this theory to attempt to explain why crime rates were rapidly expanding in many post-communist countries in the 1990's. The argument was that economic change uprooted traditional means of normative control over individuals, such as traditional family structures, and a result was more deviant behavior. Especially China-focused criminologists have tried to explain enhanced social anarchy through declining communal values (Liu and Messner 2001; Lu and Miethe 2001). For example, China's rising rates of juvenile delinquency (Feng 2001; Grant 1989; Rojek 1989) have been explained by the rise of materialist and individualist values and the decay of the traditional sphere. Such research spurred my thinking within this project in similar directions. The idea was that the post-communist economic transformation may have caused a rise in individualist and egoistic values, thereby undermining the informal social control that previously undercut deviance.

'Social control,' although rooted in Durkheimian social integration notions, was introduced within Travis Hirschi's (2002 [1969]) *The Causes of Delinquency.* The theory explains deviant behavior, and it does so by describing how social behavior is normally controlled by the society and its institutions. Hirschi breaks social control down into four forms: the direct, the indirect, the internal, and that of needs satisfaction. Needs satisfaction is not of relevance here, since it refers more to a motive for deviance than a mechanism through which deviance is regulated. Regarding regulation of deviance, which is Hirschi's principal contribution, it is helpful to see that his direct control represents *formal* means of behavioral regulation, and his indirect and internal control represent the *informal* variety.

This differentiation of social control into the formal and the informal is of key importance. Formal social control is exacted through abstract and distant institutions, such as the police and the law. Its means of correcting for norm violations and influencing pro-normative behavior tends to be external coercion and punishment. In contrast, informal social control (see Sampson and Laub 1993) is exacted through close and intimate institutions, such as family and friends, and critically, the source of its behavioral influence on the individual is internal, through an individual's very own emotions, feelings, and moral frameworks. It is widely accepted that informal social control is more effective in preventing deviant behavior. Informal social control works through intimate, face-to-face, connections with other human beings, through language, through eye contact, through visual cues, through our close and emotional bonds with the 'other.' Thus the concepts of intimacy and distance, even more so than 'informal' and 'formal,' represent the foundation of moral order.

When we socialize our children, it is our intimate connection to them, and their emotional bonds to us, which allows the facilitation of the normative structure at every turn. Our decisions to socialize our children would not be made if they had no value for us. Their decisions to listen to our messages would not be made if they did not value us. Even the automatic response of a baby to the mother's cues is actualized by the capacity for the emotional bond. The child's decision to actually follow a received message requires that it somehow values the message-provider. Importantly, the maintenance and punishment of violations of these norms also require intimate receptivity on the part of all parties. At every step, a high valuation of the process of intimate communication and the other is a prerequisite toward maintenance of moral structures.

The historical disappearance of Durkheim's classical mechanical solidarity (1933), as one might predict, is linked to historical developments in social control. Industrialization-era social disruptions brought to light the sudden inadequacy of traditional methods of maintaining order. The devaluation of social relationships as a result of urbanization, technology, capitalist development, and rationalization resulted in normlessness and deviance. The deterioration of traditional family life and mechanical solidarity during these times undermined traditional informal control, resulted in social disorder, and were responded to by the state through the establishment of formalized control through police and laws. It is no coincidence that the first modern police forces were established by Britain in 1829 as its industrial revolution was entering full swing. The establishment of the police could be seen as a formal response to rising deviance as a result of deteriorating informal social structures. Thereby, social control theory explains the historical conjuncture between social disorder and the onset of economic change in the form of rapid industrialization and economic development. It may also explain the social disorder experienced in post-communist societies as a result of their populations' adapting to a new model and becoming moreso *homo-economicus*.

ECONOMIC MODERNIZATION AND INDIVIDUALIZATION

A home for pro-sociality questions within sociology of late is within the study of 'individualization.' I will broadly use this notion in connection with economic development as a box into which relevant research can be categorized. In particular, there is a normative split within such literature between utopian, critical, and neutral approaches. The analysis conducted in this project is rooted as a response to the flaws of an optimistic individualization thinking that is in striking contrast to both classical and critical approaches. I support neither account exclusively, for it is through their synthesis that a fuller picture is obtained.

What is individualization? Despite the fact that individualization theory—embodied by the work of key thinkers such as Ulrich Beck (2002), Zygmunt Bauman (2001), and Anthony Giddens (1991) is rather diffuse and fractured, the core idea is that individuals become increasingly differentiated over historical time. Individualization scholars tend to agree that individuals today are more independent, self-driving, privately oriented, and less traditional than in the past (van der Loo and van Reijen 1992, 160). They increasingly shape their own lives and are less shaped by deterministic social forces completely beyond their control. As a result, Beck has argued that traditional sociological categories, such as class, lose their relevance and become 'zombie categories,' since they no longer substantially predict individual behavior (Beck 2002).

Depending on normative and thematic approaches, many 'individualizations' may be described. Within the spheres of work and creativity, for example, individualization is marked by increasing differentiation and expanded degrees of 'uniqueness' among individuals. If one rather looks at individualization in terms of locus of control, important may be the historical process of the development of a form of internal control, as per Norbert Elias (1979 [1939]), or of expanded responsibility of the individual in planning his/her own life, meaning both greater steering potential and risk, as per Beck and Beck-Gernsheim (2002). In addition, we may look at individualization as the development of enhanced forms of self-expression, which may have political repercussions as per their pro-democratic impacts (Inglehart and Welzel 2005). Yet a different arena, relationships and intimacy, is the focus here, one that refers to individualization as the adaptation of traditional forms of relatedness, to the extent that individuals come to value face-to-face communication with increasing latency as they come to interpret their interrelations in new, less bounded, ways. Therefore, I refine individualization into 'individualization as de-intimization' within this study.

Individualization is tightly embedded with modernization processes. Hareven (1990) notes that the "study of family has provided important linkages between individual lives and larger social and economic processes such as industrialization, technological change, urbanization, and business cycles" (215). Modernization, although not exclusively economic development or structural economic change, has been coupled with the individualization of society (See van der Loo and van Reijen 1992).

What scholars by-and-large agree upon is that modernization, especially economic modernization, is coupled with the growing salience of individual differentiation and self-focus. Where the debate becomes heated is not on whether or not individualization, broadly speaking, has occurred, but on how to characterize its effects in reference to human intimacy.

Optimists

Many scholars argue for an optimistic account of the various effects of individualization processes spurred by economic development. I do not agree with these solely optimistic accounts, so in presenting their views, I highlight aspects I see as problematic.

For instance, Adam Smith highlighted the ethical benefits of commerce, to include enhanced honesty, politeness, trustworthiness, and punctuality (Smith 1978, 538; cited by Fourcade and Healy 2007). According to Smith, these virtues are systemic outcomes of selfish individuals striving to maximize their own individual interests. Echoing this argument in recent years,

Deirdre McCloskey has served as one of the most outspoken proponents of the "bourgeois virtues." Virtue is, according to McCloskey (2006, 3), essentially the same as "smart business." Noting that Max Weber also argued that greed and capitalism are not synonymous (2006, 14), McCloskey claims that human beings are in a superior social state compared to years ago: "Modern economic growth has led to more, not less, refinement, for hundreds of millions who would otherwise have been poor and ignorant–as were, for example, most of your ancestors and mine" (2006, 25). McCloskey adapts the post-materialism and scarcity hypotheses, which I will discuss more in relation to Ronald Inglehart, in describing why the poor care more about money: "Richer and more urban people, contrary to what the magazines of opinion sometimes suggest, are less materialistic, less violent, less superficial than poor and rural people. Because people in capitalist countries already possess the material, they are less attached to their possessions than people in poor countries" (2006, 26). In short, richer, urban, bourgeois people, McCloskey argues "*are better humans*–because they in their billions have acquired the scope to become so and because market societies encourage art and science and religion to flourish and because anyway a life in careers and deal making and companies and marketplaces is not the worst life for a full human being" (2006, 28—29; emphasis added).

McCloskey is adamant that blaming capitalism for social ills is as pointless as "blaming everything on the weather." Yet when it comes to enriching the world, capitalism is responsible for everything from democracy, to longevity, to the full range of bourgeois virtues, and ultimately humanity. In this utopian account, capitalism has civilized a barbaric world, and "bourgeois virtues led us from terrified hunter bands and violent agricultural villages to peaceful suburbs and lively cities" (2006, 30). She argues strong ties are not to be sought after, noting their oppressive tendencies. Herein, she draws on Granovetter's (1985, 2005) notion of 'weak ties' as being more important in modern societies.

Other important advocates for optimistic individualization outcomes would be Alex Inkeles and David Smith and their seminal work, *Becoming Modern* (Inkeles and Smith 1974). It is based on an investigation, drawing on survey data, into the growth of the "modern personality" within six developing countries (Argentina, Chile, India, Israel, Nigeria, and Bangladesh). The authors identified a growth in personality traits that suit individuals well for work within the modern economy. They develop the idea of the factory "as a school" in forming personality. This clever idea is effective in explaining how factory-favored values become disseminated within individuals, and this concept is monumental in overcoming the Freudian assumption that values are mainly formed during the youth (Inkeles and Smith 1974, 9). However, a problem emerges with the values the authors call 'modern.' For them, these include the openness to new experiences and to change, likelihood to hold opinions about distant or abstract subject areas, awareness of the diversity of attitudes and opinions, orientation toward the present or future as opposed to the past, belief in the ability to dominate the environment, orientation toward planning and organization, the trusting of strangers, a belief in meritorious reward, an openness to education and learning new things, and, most revealingly, a greater respect toward the dignity of others (Inkeles 1983, 36–39). The problem is that each of these modern values is presented as positive and enlightened, naturally contrasting with an implicitly traditional and barbaric past.

An empirically and theoretically formidable argument for the 'virtues' of capitalism would be that of Ronald Inglehart's modernization approach. I argue that this approach alone is insufficient for investigating changing social values in post-socialist space. Inglehart empirically and theoretically links economic development to a range of outcomes, from gender equality to tolerance, self-expression, democracy, and pro-sociality. The World Values Survey, in collecting data in five-year intervals from dozens of countries, is far more ambitious than even the *Becoming Modern* data collection effort. In this regard, this survey, despite its size-related flaws, is certainly a monument within comparative data collection. Data aside, it is the political implications that are problematic. Inglehart supposes that individual values change through two parsimonious mechanisms: scarcity and socialization. The scarcity hypothesis proposes that individuals tend to value resources that are in short supply to them; prosperity tends to lead to post-materialist values emphasizing non-materialism, communicability, and tolerance, while poverty spurs the opposite. The socialization hypothesis implies that the implanting of values takes place primarily during the youth and these values change relatively little throughout adulthood. Furthermore, according to Inglehart, fundamental value change takes place primarily through cohort replacement. He predicts that, "after a long period of rising economic and physical security, one should find substantial differences between the value priorities of older and younger groups; they have been shaped by different experiences in their formative years" (Inglehart 2000, 221). In this way, Inglehart argues for a decline in traditional and survival orientations and the rise of secular and self-expressive orientations, the latter two of which he supposes to be good. Some problems with this model will be demonstrated, and alternatives will be suggested.

One flaw of this approach is its normative bias. This modernization of personality process is said to be driven primarily by economic development, which culminates in enlightened 'post-materialist' values, while economic stagnation and decline revert personality structures back toward the imagined anti-sociality of the past. Blame for "the bad" is reassigned away from the capitalist economy, while the good springs directly from its loins. An ambivalent approach that takes note of both positive and negative repercussions of the same individualization process is preferable.

Second, the socialization hypothesis is ill-suited for explaining the mechanism through which values may quickly change in times of rapid transition, such as for the former-communist countries, because it assumes values to remain somewhat static after socialization is complete and provides little means for their later modification within individuals. In contrast, I suggest that socialization is not the only mechanism of value change. The economic structure is also capable of modifying the values of individuals through their reflective adaptation to their perceptions of it and to the environment it creates.

Also, the scarcity hypothesis may not always be as salient as suggested. To begin with, China, Russia, and Eastern Germany have had varying, even opposite, levels of economic prosperity during the transition but apparently remarkably similar shifts in social disorder and social values. The transformation to capitalism may have affected people's social values in post-communist societies in a roughly uniform way, regardless of economic success or failure. Scarcity alone cannot explain the economic patterning of values. Economic cultures, 'structures' if you will, also shape the orientations of their practitioners.

Fourth, the Inglehart model does not explain social disorder in post-communist countries, perhaps because it assumes value changes associated with economic development to be positive. In contrast, if one focuses on basic social values, there are indications that these are deteriorating. This social devaluation may weaken mechanisms of social control that depend upon relationships to function, thus explaining rising deviance and other forms of social disorder.

My final critique here is that the Inglehart paradigm may overlook some of the negative consequences of economic development that are apparent even in the World Values Survey data. Ghana, for instance, is materially quite poor but has nonetheless one of the highest mean ratings of happiness in 2005 (World Values Survey Association 2009). This suggests that Ghana's definitions and interpretations of life satisfaction have little to do with material well-being, but are rather determined by something else, such as social (relational) well-being. Arguing in a similar manner, Ahuvia (2002) argues that economic development leads to subjective well-being by creating individualistic cultures where personal happiness is valued more than social obligations. Shanghai University sociologist Hao Yuan has suggested something akin in his dissertation about the reasoning for why Chinese well-being has not increased as much as material well-being would predict; a cultural shift may have offset the benefits of material well-being on subjective well-being (Yuan 2008; see also Brockmann et al. 2009).

Some of these suggestions may be difficult for the Inglehart model to pursue, since it assumes material well-being and strong social values to be linked from the outset. This may be a blind spot of a theory that, on other questions, offers formidable insight.

Optimistic accounts of individualization tend to explain the impact of the economy upon the individual through varying economic *conditions*. In other words, and as depicted in the 'family stress perspective' version, the thesis is that economic stress is a precursor to family stress, while prosperity alleviates such stress. One relevant formulation of this idea is found in a study on family stress during the post-communist Czech transformation (Pechacova et al. 2000). This study demonstrated how a family's perceived economic pressure caused increased marital instability. Families grew unstable as a direct reaction to economic crisis. On the other hand, *positive* economic conditions, such as success or wealth, are presumed to affect relationships in the opposite direction. In any case, economic conditions are the most often-assumed cause of value change in post-communist countries. This concern with economic conditions, while relevant, is not the whole story, and it tends to shift focus away from the economic culture.

With a focus on economic conditions, the economic system itself is invisible, and the only thing of concern is material poverty or wealth, since wealth is considered, within these paradigms, as the ultimate value. Moreso, the existence of 'wealth' provides a de facto legitimation for the capitalist system, since it, presumed as good, claims to provide an answer to its own effect, the spread of poverty. Therein, the supposed answer to the problems of capitalism is simply more capitalism, as economic growth cures all.

An example of a discussion on the economic conditions focus within literature on family and relationship change is Glen Elder's *Children of the Great Depression* (1974). Where Elder excels, in contrast to other 'economic conditions' literature, is his focus on the *process* connecting economic change to social and psychological effects, an often neglected aspect (Elder 1974, 8). Furthermore, Elder shows the "individuation" that arises—the non-historical differentiation of an individual from others through the development of a unique personality—due to economic deprivation (Elder 1974, 120). Yet Elder recognizes that "scarcity alone says far too little about the context in which it occurred" (Elder 1974, 274). In other words, what are the historical circumstances, the political conditions, and the economic culture within which scarcity is nested? These are equally important as economic conditions alone. What is called for here is a focus, in addition to conditions, on economic *structure*.

Even when excessive focus on economic conditions is overcome, structural accounts are often biased in favor of the dominant economic paradigm. Such a structural explanation for changing values is adopted by Xiaoying Wang (2002). She notes the rise of a broken "post-communist personality" in both Russia and China characterized by high levels of hedonism, egoism, and a lack of discipline. However, her analysis is perhaps led astray by her interpretation of Max Weber (2003), for she notes that the above personality is a far cry from the ascetic ideals which Weber links to the birth of capitalism. Yet, the asceticism which spurred the early formation of capitalism in Europe was contextually and historically nested; there is no expectation that capitalist systems always need or require asceticism to grow or survive. Furthermore, even in Europe, capitalism was catalyzed, according to Weber, by religious asceticism *only* in its initial phases by a value affinity, and he suggests that this non-economic core was in danger from the hardening of the iron cage of rational calculative values. Furthermore, the contemporary essence of capitalism has mutated in ways no longer reminiscent of its Weberian moral roots. Weber's thesis did not foresee the importance of the consumer class within late capitalism; it is consumerism that drives modern profits, and the consumer personality is thus produced as a necessity of the modern capitalist system. Of course, discipline is still required for certain specialized tasks: investment, strategic planning, calculation of profit, and the creation of new markets, for example, yet these tasks are today fragmented and differentiated as 'work' across many different persons, from the level of management to that of the CEO. Thus, even the successful capitalist today must be only *partially* disciplined and ascetic within limited spheres at work; in other realms, he or she may, and perhaps should, revert to a consumer mentality. Therefore, a modern reading of Weber may recognize that capitalism involves at least dual stages of development and dual class mentalities (capitalist and consumer). Yet Wang notices only the mismatch of the post-communist personality with the original Weberian ideal, and as a result, she blames this personality not on the capitalist present, but rather on the communist past. Corruption and negative personality traits, she argues, arise from the *incomplete* development of capitalism, one that, in China, is tainted due to the mixture of communist politics and capitalist economics. Thus, Wang is insightful in looking beyond the typical 'economic conditions' argumentation in relation to values, but her focus on economic structure places blame only on the communist past. In contrast, it is argued that her negative post-communist personality is largely a capitalist one; it also has roots within the capitalist economic culture.

Critics

Now I will introduce those critics who highlight the negative consequences of shifting values. While optimistic strands of individualization tend to focus on tolerance, equality between relationship partners, and choice, the critical strands turn this argumentation on its head. Thereby, individualization is ambivalent and involves a paradox whereby individuals acquire their own space and freedom at the cost of greater feelings of abstraction and anonymity (van der Loo and van Reijen 1992, 162). Therein, tolerance equates to indifference, greater equality within relations implies diminished social obligation, and the expansion of choice yields excessive narcissism, hedonism, and the growing preponderance of weak ties. Excessive choice culminates in relationship instability. I will state outright that I do not seek to replace a utopian view with a dystopian one. Rather, a much-needed critique of the dominant optimistic account leaves standing a fuller, more ambivalent picture.

Thinkers embodying a somewhat more critical individualization approach include Ulrich Beck and Zygmunt Bauman. Beck and Beck-Gernsheim's

(2002) ambivalent account overcomes more optimistic notions of individualization by highlighting the risks that individuals face in the world of choices, primarily alone. Nonetheless, they argue against a depiction of this condition as purely negative: "Any generalization that seeks to understand individualized society only in terms of one extreme or the other–autonomy or anomie–abbreviates and distorts the questions that confront us here" (Beck and Beck-Gernsheim 2002, 7). Yet the Becks make a crucial contribution in acknowledging, in rare form, the negative consequences of individualized society. Because of its focus on the more pessimistic implications of individualization, Bauman's (2001) work is valuable as a counter-force to opposing discourses. He highlights the modern individualized situation as a dilemma, symbolized by the Tantalus myth, whereby individuals in the modern world vainly yearn for a community that is lost. Thus, individualization is a personal predicament in which individuals long for an intimacy their societies can no longer provide. The approach in this book could be seen as closest to Bauman's because of his focus on individuals' elusive longing for sociality, but for me the sociality of interest is intimate and close, one centered on face-to-face interaction. In contrast, Bauman is interested in a more distant and abstract 'community.' Bauman's community is a grouping of persons de-centered from its individual members; attachment to community is therefore more diffuse than to a personal tie. Despite its affinity with the critical individualization approach of this book, Bauman's work, like that of the other prime individualization theorists, Giddens and Beck, incorporates little empirical evidence, and the theorizing has been seen as ambiguous enough to arouse only limited interest in this theme beyond social theorists.

Out of the possible critical foci of individualization, the one chosen here is the devaluation of intimate socialization, an historically enhanced self-centeredness corresponding to diminished value of communicability. There are many other scholars who have dealt with 'de-intimization' in relation to economic change in this wider sense.

Marx (1978) argued that through commodification, social relations are reduced to exchange relations, implying that social values may be weakened or destroyed when relationships and individuals imply quantifiable economic costs and worth. Therefore, from Marxism, we can take, first of all, a hypothesis placing the economy and human sociality in tension with one another. Of course, this can also be found in Durkheim's early distinction between mechanical and organic solidarity, within Tönnies' 'arbitrary will' underlying *Gesellschaft*, in Simmel's (1995) pondering on the leveling effects of money, and within a host of Marx-influenced thinkers, such as Polanyi and members of the Frankfurt School of sociology. The core idea here is that human sociality, within the advanced capitalist economy, becomes commodified and subservient to economic exchange (Marx and Engels 1978). Marxism also paints for us a *character* for capitalism. Whether or not it was true or false, this is the same symbolic language that was known by post-communist citizens, thus framing their transformation experiences. The communist system handed these symbols to its citizens. They were digested, rejected, and interpreted in various ways, and it is worthwhile to see how people adapted to the capitalism for which they had already constructed a symbolic meaning. From Marx we also have the notion that individuals may have great incentives to exploit their relationships for the sake of economic gain (e.g. Repetti 2002). The existence of private property allows a struggle over the means of production and accumulation of wealth, allowing a ruling class to exploit the others for gain. The possible extent of this exploitation would have been less in previous times because of lesser potential rewards (because of the limited accumulation potentials of individuals within socialist economies) and aspirations. As a result, because of these limited incentives and rewards, social relationships during the communist era could not have been purely instrumental or exploitative, despite their usefulness in accumulating scarce goods.

Written later than Marx, Tönnies' (1988 [1887]) idea about a shift from *Gemeinschaft* to *Gesellschaft* refers to a historical transformation in social structures. He notes that different motives of action on the part of individuals characterize these two phases. In *Gemeinschaft*, individuals are motivated by an essential will to contribute to society, while in *Gesellschaft*, they view society instrumentally, through an arbitrary will. On this point, Durkheim's (1933) take is similar, as he notices the dissolution of a mechanical solidarity based on likeness, collective knowledge, functional simplicity, and the intimate interdependence within traditional social groups, such as the family. He predicts this solidarity's replacement by organic solidarity, one based on the division of labor, and ultimately, corporate social integration. However, if solidarity is defined, as done here, from a perspective that emphasizes normative control as linkages and interdependence between human beings at the face-to-face level, Durkheim's organic model, characterized by the division of labor and abstracted interdependence, clearly fails to crystallize into real face-to-face solidarity. Tönnies' focus upon actors' orientations toward society allows for a more pessimistic outlook than Durkheim, since it is exactly those orientations which undergo transformation. Instead, Durkheim's focus is a functional one, on solidarity, and since a functional equivalent can always be imagined (in this case, organic solidarity), his prognosis is more optimistic. This book situates itself more closely with Tönnies, both in its assignment of interpersonal motives as a fundamental feature of social organization, and in its darker prognosis when these motives turn sour.

Perhaps the most relevant of the 'critical' approaches to capitalism and individualization could be seen as critical theory itself. Stemming from a flavorful mix of Freud, Nietzsche, Hegel, and Marx, the Frankfurt School of Critical Theory is known for its pessimistic account of capitalism and modernity. Within the *Dialectic of Enlightenment*, Horkheimer and Adorno (2002) suggest, in a manner relating to Weber (2003), that rationality itself may be a root of domination and injustice. The capitalist economic system uses this rationality in order to subvert everything according to its whims, using such mechanisms as the manipulations of the culture industry, which serves, in a gloomy turn from Marx, to limit the possibilities of the working classes from ever realizing their true position and interests. In terms of personality, the capitalist economic system is associated with authoritarianism and subservience: a herd-mentality. A hallmark of this approach is to criticize the status quo in ways that are fundamentally in opposition to the ideal strands of contemporary modernization theory. Where modernization sees progress, classical critical theory sees regress.

Also in the Marxian tradition, Karl Polanyi, in his book *The Great Transformation*, has covered the relationship between capitalism and human sociality extensively. To Polanyi (2001 [1944]), gain and profit are alien and unnatural to human relations and played no part in governing markets before the 19th century. Polanyi describes the land-enclosure process within English history as an example of the forceful uprooting of the peasantry as part of the development of capitalism. In this way, human beings are converted into a 'fictitious commodity,' labor, only through stripping them of their previously existing social relationships. Thereby, social relations become 'embedded' within the economy. In contrast, market exchange in early societies was governed by social relations, rather than by profit (Sahlins 1971). In support, the economic historian Moses Finley (1973) demonstrates how many of the modern principles of "economy," such as labor, production, capital, investment, income, circulation, demand, the entrepreneur, and utility, were non-existent in ancient times, even within ancient Greece and Rome, and such concepts were actually untranslatable from English into Greek and Latin as late as 1890. He asserts that there were no "enormous conglomeration of interdependent markets," "extreme division of labour," nor "absence of household self-sufficiency" in ancient times; in contrast, ancient markets were characterized only by a "few isolated patterns" (Finley 1973, 34). Some scholars, such as R. Firth or Smelser, reject Polanyi and Finley's assumptions as historically inaccurate (Humphreys 1969). Despite the debate, there is an important contribution within Polanyi's ideas. Polanyi shows us the historical direction in which our economic systems have moved along a spectrum of social- to economic embeddedness. Within this model, capitalism, in its shift away from socially-based toward profit-based economic structures, represents the epitome of de-intimization. This point is similar to making a Braudelian (1977) distinction between capitalism and a market economy. Braudel shows that market exchanges have always existed, but capitalism as the epitome of market exploitation arrived only later in history, and its initial growth was gradual.

Max Weber, of course, is also a prime figure in relation to the question of affinities between economic and non-economic values. Misunderstandings of Weber's *Protestant Ethic and the Spirit of Capitalism (PE)* (Weber

2003) twist him into being an apologist for the 'humanity' of capitalism, despite his sober prophesy about the iron cage of rationalization. The iron cage prophesy should not be viewed as an odd moment of misgivings at the climax of a piece dedicated to demonstrating the religious roots of the values underlying economic power. Rather, it is the dialectical result of the said analysis: if modern capitalist values were solidified partially through religious beliefs, how is it that they have come to entrench themselves secularly within such a short period so that they begin to function as a cage? In other words, Weber is providing us with an interpretation of one aspect of the birth of capitalist values, the fact that they were originally intertwined with religiosity, *in order to* ask us a serious follow-up question: why have these values become so inhuman despite these roots? He then recommends a follow-up study, in which capitalism itself is seen as an independent variable, in order to examine its effects on spiritual and other human values.

Following in the Weberian tradition, and also relevant to my analysis of contemporary capitalist values, there are arguments that the modern economic environment increases the frequency of rationalized cost-benefit analyses within everyday life. This means that rational calculation is promoted over more social and intuitive forms of decision-making. For example, the effects of calculating the costs of marriage and birth can be seen in plummeting birth and marriage rates in new free-market societies. Similar rationalization argumentation may be inferred from Simmel's (1995) *Philosophy of Money*. Simmel elaborates on how money depersonalizes relationships and inserts rational exchange values and profit-calculation into the social sphere. According to Simmel:

> [T]his fear of contact seems to me to stem largely from the steadily deeper penetration of a money economy, which more and more destroys the natural economic relationships of earlier times (though this work of destruction has not been fully completed). Money is placed between man and man, between man and product, as a mediator, as a general denominator into which every other value must be translated, so that it can be further translated into other values. (1968 [1896], 79)

In fairness, Simmel's account of the effects of money is not merely negative, as it assigns to it enormous potential of liberation as well. Yet this freedom comes at a price, because although our time possesses "more freedom than any other before," we seem "to find such little joy in that freedom." (1993, 68). Weber (1984) has also demonstrated this rationalization trend in his analysis of peasants in East Elbian Germany during the early industrial revolution. He indicates that the act of profit calculation was slow to dominate the peasants' thinking, thereby illustrating a differentiation between pre-industrial and industrial rationalities. This rationalization focus parallels other arguments as well, such as Habermas' later (1989) "colonization of the lifeworld," Marx's (1978) "commodification of workers," or the related "commodification of relationships" (Gold 1985).

Psychologists have also identified this effect, one that they label as the "bleed over" of materialist values into interpersonal relationships (Kasser et al. 2003, 20). Specifically, people with "materialistic value orientations" are more likely to use their friends, to possess Machiavellian personality traits, and be more likely to compete (Kasser et al. 2003, 20–21). In other words, materialistic values are not conducive to warm relationships. The common theme is that the insertion of rational calculation within the new economic environment challenges intrinsic social valuations. Yet there is disagreement about the long-term endurance of this opposition between rationality and sociality. While for Marx, it may be overcome through the abolition of the exploitative economic structure by an energized proletariat, Weber, Horkheimer, and Adorno suggest something more sinister, that rationality (and thereby modernity) is dominating by nature, and as a result, capitalism is more likely to become more entrenched than collapse or evolve due to its internal contradictions. It is a system of domination, and while it certainly causes forms of resistance, it also has means of co-opting its subjects, veiling its intents, and 'digging in.'

Habermas (1989a) provides us with helpful language, wherein rationalization and bureaucratization affect social relations by "colonizing" them with alien forms of logic. Abstract and legalistic bureaucratic frameworks can negatively affect social life through replacing the logic of the lifeworld with their own (Habermas 1989a). An example of this from Hareven (1990, 240) is that, in America since the 1920s, institutional and legislative changes have contributed to the fragmentation of the family's functioning as a collective work unit through the implementation of anti-child labor and mandatory school attendance laws. The result of this is that family functions were passed on to other institutions. This loss of the family's collective control over its members' work implies colonial replacement by bureaucracy of the family's social influence over its members. Habermas' lifeworld concept is a valuable one in that it establishes a sphere of action that is governed by intimate sociality and communication alone, one that can be damaged by outside "colonial" logics. Habermas argues that social relationships are also colonized through the insertion of profit motives and cost-benefit analyses into the intimate sphere, a process he calls "monetization" (Habermas 1989, 356–373).

One catalyst for materialist value change is that advertising, the media, and other cultural messages conspicuously try to influence people to adopt more materialistic lifestyles (Kasser and Kanner 2003, 3), which leads to a neglect of competing social spheres, such as the family and communication. This process leads to an "internalization" of culture from media and advertising (Kasser et al. 2003, 16) and bears relevance to Horkheimer and Adorno's (2002) discussion of the "culture industry" wherein culture reinforces individuals' objectified locations within the economic system and removes any hope of their revolt.

When culture successfully transmits materialist values to individuals, research has come to critically assess these impacts on social relationships. For instance, heightened material aspirations may lead to a higher valuation of work and a corresponding devaluation of non-work activities, such as socialization within the family. Such aspirations may increase the value of entrepreneurialism, materialism, and competitive consumerism at the expense of less-materialistic and more cooperative modes of living. Psychologists have correlated the role of such "materialist value orientations" with poor relationship quality, such as through relatively shorter and more conflicted friendships and love relationships (Kasser et al. 2003, 19). Other researchers, using the paradigm of Shalom Schwartz, have noted the tendency of conflict between material and collectivist values (Burroughs and Rindfleisch 2002). In addition, there is the Durkheimian danger of anomie resulting from hedonism and aspirations that may spin out of control (Kupferberg 1999, 179).

A formative work concerning modernization and social psychology is Norbert Elias' *The Civilizing Process* (Elias 1979 [1939]). Elias eloquently argues how, since the middle ages in Europe, there has been fostered a growing emphasis on internal emotional control that replaced more external constraints, exemplified through the state's seizure of the monopoly over physical force. This process amounts to a 'civilizing' effect, in which an inborn barbarism is alleviated by internal control, shame. At first glance, Elias' findings might appear to challenge this study's claims, since I equate modernization with growing latency of sociality, but Elias links modernization with enhanced social refinement. However, there are several grounds on which to reject such an interpretation. First, there are many civilizations, and each of them implies different types of restraints or shame, but these civilization-specific restraints vary, as do fashions. In other words, they are largely arbitrary, and many are without moral content; as such, they say little about intimate sociality. On the other hand, there are some restraints that are not arbitrary, as they embody a communicative meaning, and in most of these cases, the communicative content of Elias' manners develops in a direction toward greater repression of communication and greater silence. For example, he documents increasing control over topics of conversation, gesticulations during conversation, proper modes of addressing persons of a different class; each of these amounts to a restriction of communication. Even some of his, at first glance, 'neutral' manner developments, such as the transition from eating from communal dishes to that of each person eating from his/her own dish, can be seen as a an individualization of social relations.

Furthermore, it is hard to imagine that Elias' central thesis is valid, that shame and internal control are fresh inventions of civilization. In order to back this claim, he forwards a Hobbesian view of nature whereby the past was dominated by the use and threat of physical force alone. An objection to this is that, within the historical record, the use of physical violent force has hardly decreased over time. This has led Bauman (1999, 12–18, as cited by Outhwaite and Ray 2005, 176) to name the 'civilizing process' a myth, as he argues that "violence, genocide, and the Holocaust were made possible by the formal bureaucratic procedures of modern societies." Such an argument is in line with a critical theoretical standpoint, which shows civilization as a system of *increasing* external and internal totalitarian domination, stemming from rationality itself and its spawn within social structures (Horkheimer and Adorno 2002). Apart from this objection, however, one can also challenge the Elias thesis by continuing to trace the existence of informal controls indefinitely back in time. All groups develop cultural criteria for proper behavior, and more importantly, this culture is at least partially internally held and regulated by the individual through self-control. Elias' assumption of a Hobbesian state of nature would have us believe that, 10,000 years ago, there was no patterned behavior at all, except for the habitual use of, and threat of, force. This myth is displaced by referencing what we know of the complex cultural content of hunter-gatherer societies.

Another well-known book often equated with the critical individualization genre is David Riesman's (Riesman, Glazer and Denney 2001) *The Lonely Crowd*. Therein, the authors described the historical shift in American society from the dominance of the traditional personality to the inner-directed, and eventually to the other-directed personality in America. The key problem with the book lies in its conceptualization of three types. Essentially, it relies on an inner versus other-directed dichotomy of personality types, with an archaic tradition-oriented type proceeding it, but this "traditional" type presumably inherits its values and rules from thin air, as it is neither inner- nor other-directed. Subsequent thinking, for example on the individualist-collectivist dimension, identifies traditional societies as more other-directed, with people in advanced societies being more self-directed. Therefore, a more useful distinction is rather between *other and self* than between *outer/other and inner*. The book's under-conceptualization of the traditional and of inner and other-directedness make its main claim, the decline of inner-direction and rise of other-direction, opaque. It lamented the decline of inner-directedness caused by the growth of mass culture and associated this with a decay in American society's individualism. In this light, the study should be contextualized within American history as a worry over the decline of the frontier type, the rugged yet moral individualist. Yet the main point, especially when applying the Riesman study elsewhere, is that this moral individualist is a facet of the American myth, one perpetuated as a celebration of the free market spirit. The American pioneer spirit still lives today in the businessman, we are told. It is claimed as the mythical source of both profit and morality. This tacit level of ethnocentrism spills over in the following passage:

> Inner-directed men were able, for a relatively brief historical period, to act as if the Chinese, Indians, Malaysians, Africans they encountered were radically different from themselves (and from each other); they could act this way because they were obviously so much superior in power and hence, in many encounters, *in poise as well.* If they were missionaries they might ask of the others, even in the heart of darkness, that they learn to act like white men; and—astonishingly, as it now seems to us—millions sought to do so and were converted, *impressed by the rectitude* as well as the power of their captors and models. It has now become difficult for *thoughtful Western men*, not encapsulated by prejudice and ignorance, to take their own cultures and practices as absolutes; they cannot, by merely willing it, take them with deadly seriousness—in fact, the current wave of talk about the American Way of Life is a propagandist's vain defensiveness against this very discovery. (Riesman, Glazer, and Denney 2001, xlix—l; emphasis added)

Stated differently, sensitivity about the historical domination of Western culture might, as a side effect, be derailing us from discussion of the 'discovery' of the core of our Western culture, which is claimed to be actually superior to alternatives. The 'poise' and 'rectitude' of 'thoughtful Western men' is bound inextricably to Riesman's idealized inner-directed frontier type. It is less an analytical category than an ideological one.

Not so surprisingly, Riesman's types become inverted when removed from the American bias of frontier morality in which they are found. Riesman's inner-directed type, characterized by moral direction and guilt, should be better labeled as other-centered, since he/she inherits those moral regulations from his/her intimate relationships. In contrast, Riesman's 'other-directed' type, characterized as amoral, anxious, self-gratifying, and instrumental in relations, is actually the self-centered type more commonly referred to within individualist-collectivist literature and within this project. Most alarming, however, is the *Lonely Crowd*'s inability to explain how these types emerged. The authors comment, for example, that "historical and cross-cultural investigation would be necessary before one could better understand how inner-direction came about—and why it may now be disappearing" (Riesman, Glazer, and Denney 2001, xlviii).

Precisely on this point is where this book inserts itself. I want to explain how specific sociality orientations become distributed within particular populations during a particular type of social change.

In a relevant recent account, Melvin Kohn (Kohn et al. 2002) looks at personality change during the very period in question, the post-socialist transformations. Perhaps motivated by Durkheimian concerns, he wishes to determine whether or not personalities are *stable* during the transformation years. In other words, he wishes to determine to which extent the change in social structure equates to instability in personality. Kohn's research, while intriguing, does not speak to the core of my problem because it mostly bypasses the question of the directionality of the personality change at hand. Are they becoming more egocentric or altruistic? Are they becoming more materialistic or post-materialistic? Kohn's work does not appear to yet answer these questions although it provides much insight into the overall stability, and lack-thereof, of personality during economic change. In addition, it is a rare example of concentrated comparative work on personality and the post-socialist transformation, a work less affected by excessive optimism in relation to modernization.

Other scholars as of late have produced intriguing critiques of the modern economy in relation to individualization. Richard Sennett's *Corrosion of Character* (1998; See also Bellah et al. 1985; Putnam 2000), for example, links the modern American capitalist economy to forms of impersonality, heartlessness, and immorality because of the conflict between the conflicting demands between work and family. In addition, Daniel Bell's (1976) work is relevant in revealing *The Cultural Contradictions of Capitalism.* He claims that the guiding principles of the polity, economy, and culture—respectively equality, efficiency, and hedonism—are at odds with one another. His worry is that the hedonistic contemporary culture attacks the core efficiency required by capitalism to function. I suggest, in contrast, that capitalism spurs hedonism, indeed builds it into one of its core modes of operation: a split between the rational worker and the irrational consumer within individual minds. More to the point, after work and the self have had their fill, intrinsically valued relationships are left fighting for the leftovers.

Denial of Individualization: "Nothing has changed"

In contrast to the optimists and critics, some argue that individualization in society is empirically unsupported. Graham Crow (2002, 2–7), for example, disagrees with the claim of declining solidarity in modern society, noting that many versions of the "loss of community" perspective have rested on shaky ground, such as the "dubious" claim that the "historical record supports a pessimistic interpretation of social change in which social relations in the past are treated as having been somehow better than they are now." He thereby supports reviving the Durkheimian connection between individualization and solidarity in the form of organic solidarity, thereby critiquing "romanticized notions of informal relationships." In a similar vein, within her informative review of sociological work on families and intimate relationships, Val Gillies (2003, 16) also criticizes this "breakdown" or "demoralization" perspective, a criticism that she equally applies to the optimistic "democratization" hypotheses, arguing overall that "the concept of *social change* in personal relationships is profoundly overstated" (emphasis added). Her critique hinges on the "theoretically tinted lens" and "politically grounded versions of the truth" that inform each of these social change narratives. In contrast, she argues that "personal values and practices of trust and caring have remained *relatively stable over the years,* reflecting ingrained identities and power relationships" (Gillies 2003, 16; emphasis added).

On the one hand, Crow and Gillies' objections are understandable, given that both utopian and apocalyptic discourses make steady use of individualization argumentation to make normative inferences. On the other hand, although acknowledgment of the political content of these approaches may ring true, this does not negate the real material- and empirical content being addressed. Regardless of the variety of political consequences of these findings, the way that we live with our social relationships may indeed, empirically, be changing. More fundamentally, Gillies' assertion about the stability of personal relationships "over the years" becomes more untenable as any sort of reasonable historical time-frame is inserted; at the extreme, to claim that ancient hunter-gatherer societies and our techno-urban virtual modernities espouse basically the same social relations demonstrates the limits of this 'everything is the same' approach. Finally, a 'continuity' approach serves to only strengthen the status quo by failing to recognize it as patterned and by therefore denying the need to seek possible structural alternatives. Critique is thereby located superficially within the existing structure of society, thereby undermining attempts to reach beyond it. 'Nothing has changed' helps to ensure that nothing will change.

ECONOMIC SOCIOLOGY AND TRANSITOLOGY APPROACHES

I have just completed an overview of ideas that are central to my approach. I argued my case for connecting values, social control, and capitalism concepts through a particular 'critical' type of individualization approach, one that focuses on de-intimization. Now I will address some neighboring scholarly terrain in economic sociology and transitology that nonetheless tends to verge from this book's core interest and, in my view, is less suitable for grappling with it.

'Becoming homo-economicus' is about capitalism spurring individualization through the culture it promotes. These mechanisms will be described in detail in the following chapter. Yet why is it that this notion has not been a point of concern or focus within relevant studies on the post-socialist transformations? I focus on problems within two bodies of literature. First, within contemporary economic sociology focused on intimacy and embeddedness, hostility toward "hostile worlds" approaches breeds moral neutrality toward 'economy and sociality' questions. Second, transitology approaches tend to have two flaws. First, this literature has focused on political and economic policies, actors, and elites. As a result, everyday life has been neglected. In addition, this literature comes with a pre-packaged ideological scapegoat, homo-sovieticus, a bogeyman for attempting to explain changes that are less than ideal.

New Embeddedness Within Economic Sociology

Contemporary economic sociology is less than infatuated with studying the effects of macro-level social change upon individuals. In my view, this is an unnecessary side-effect of the empirical richness of two dominant approaches. The research paradigms of Viviana Zelizer and Mark Granovetter share a common strength and a resulting weakness. This dilemma, and its solution, can be framed within the language of two types of embeddedness: the embeddness of Karl Polanyi (old embeddedness) and that of Mark Granovetter (new embeddedness). New embeddedness tends to reject old embeddedness in whole because new embeddedness claims the old interprets socio-economic activity through a black and white lens which is not matched by empirical reality.

Polanyi's embeddedness refers to the hierarchical ordering of the social system and economic system in terms of which principally influences the other. He argued that economic life became, within the modern industrial capitalist economic form, disembedded from the social relations that enabled it. Instead, social relations became an appendage to economic life. An illustration of this is his depiction of labor as a fictitious commodity, and crucially, that in order to make human beings commodity-like, their previously existing social relations must be uprooted and reshaped. Key to this type of embeddedness is the classical sociological portrayal of economic structure and social relations as in tension.

Granovetter's embeddedness, in contrast, focuses on the empirical inseparability of economic structure and social relationships. They are intimately intertwined in an "intermixing" of economic and non-economic activity (2005). Economic life is actualized through ongoing social relationships, through really existing human beings and their social ties. Viviana Zelizer's (2005) approach is similar, in that she notes that the "hostile worlds" of sociality and economy, as depicted by classical theories, are not in tension at all, for it is actually subjective individual actors who assign complex meanings to their economic activities. Again, it is only through social practices and subjective meanings that 'economic' activity exists at all.

Therefore, Zelizer and Granovetter point to the actually existing thick web of relationships and meanings that make up socio-economic life in order to argue that classical theorists positing economy and sociality tensions are, at best, missing the point. As a result, scholars that follow 'new embeddedness' tend to be skeptical of research that might begin with a critical-classical view of the economy-sociality mix.

There are two major problems with a view that would replace old embeddedness with new embeddedness. First, such research tends toward ignoring morality. Fourcade and Healy summarize this problem well:

> The dominant paradigm of embeddedness implies that culture and institutions mediate, and often trump, the moral implications (good or bad)

> of capitalist markets. In this view, markets do not have a moral nature outside the particular social and cognitive arrangements from which they emerge and that sustain them. (Fourcade and Healy 2007, 286)

Some might interpret the moral disinterestedness mentioned above as a good thing, but on which basis can the paradigm of new embeddedness critique slave relations, child labor, or any other exploitative practices? Slaves and child laborers are also thickly 'embedded' within their economic activities, and we can describe the relevant and fascinating layers of human relational networks and subjective meaning with which their slavery functions. Yet, if we remain hostile to 'hostile worlds' approaches, we can no longer explain particular macro-economic structures or their exploitative potentials. As a result of the grey-approach's moral void, it is easily hijacked by utopian accounts, such as McCloskey's, where the weak-ties/strong-ties argument is simplified into a binary system, whereby strong ties are oppressive and weak-ties, linked to capitalism, make the world turn (2006).

A second problem is that new embeddedness approaches do not help us to understand or explain macro-level social change. This is important because economic forms differ in their effects on human social organization, result in varying arrangements of personal networks and subjective meanings, and these forms change over historical time. Granovetter writes about his focus away from 'big-picture' questions:

> I have had little to say about what broad historical or macrostructural circumstances have led systems to display the social-structural characteristics they have, so I make no claims for this analysis to answer large-scale questions about the nature of modern society or the sources of economic and political change. But the focus on proximate causes is intentional, for these broader questions cannot be satisfactorily addressed without more detailed understanding of the mechanisms by which sweeping change has its effects. My claim is that one of the most important and least analyzed of such mechanisms is the impact of such change on the social relations in which economic life is embedded. If this is so, no adequate link between macro- and micro-level theories can be established without a much fuller understanding of these relations. (1985, 506–507)

Neither does Zelizer deal with the question of how micro-level conflicts and tensions can be linked to more "large-scale shifts in categories of worth" (Fourcade and Healy 2007, 301). Even if we understand how economic networks and economic meanings are used by individuals, we still cannot explain the differences without a system of understanding how economic forms differ with one another or change over historical time. This is what 'old embeddedness' provides.

I try to provide some reasons for why 'new embeddedness' approaches are not always sympathetic toward 'old embeddedness' projects, but the divide is not large. The two forms of embeddedness are not in logical opposition. Polanyi never argued for really existing 'hostile worlds,' black and white distinctions between social or anti-social economic practices at the individual level. Rather he argued for the increasing salience of tensions in really existing social relationships and practices as a result of patterned, macro-level economic change. These tensions are displayed clearly within Zelizer's work; she just assigns a different framing to them. Granovetter as well points to normative labels as proofs that relations have not been reduced to a cash-nexus. Old embeddedness does not claim that modern capitalist economic practices are not taking place through human beings; it points out that the manner in which these practices takes place is often highly conflict-ridden and problematic for the people involved. Such evidence has been demonstrated by new embeddedness accounts, but they often reject the old embeddedness sense-making frame capable of fully analyzing it. There is no reason to leave the rich emprical details of micro-level new embeddness findings unconnected to macro-level old embeddedness concerns. This book strives to interpret micro-level thick complexities in social values through a macro-level explanation, the transformation to capitalist culture.

Technocratic Transitology

A different body of literature, the transitology paradigm, provides an example of the normative and utopian elements of modernization harnessed in scientific form. This work focusing on the post-socialist transformations can be broken into two major spheres. On the one hand is the transitology that serves as a technocratic 'how-to' manual for implementing transition, which is contrasted with a "pure" academic interest in transition (Tökes 2000). This first type can be readily dismissed as "hubris" because of the unstated, yet profoundly manipulative qualities of the ideology it promotes (Tökes 2000). Others have more pleasantly labeled this hubris as "the neoliberal discourse of radical reform" (Bönker, Müller, and Pickel 2002, 5). An example of such research is the monograph aptly entitled *Successful Transformations?* which nicely explains the aims of this genre:

> With the collapse of communist power in central and eastern Europe in 1989, the great question for economic policy became the best means to ensure a 'successful' transformation of the various countries of the area into 'modern' market economies. A 'successful' transformation would be one that enabled the country to create a new economic system, to ensure rapid and sustainable economic growth so as to reduce, and ultimately to overcome the gap with the advanced countries of western Europe and, above all and most conclusively, one that led to acceptance as a developed

> market economy by the world's financial institutions, by governments and by intergovernmental organizations. (Myant et al. 1996, 1)

Many books, however, even have a less abashed celebration of the Western economic model, employing, alongside "success," lingo such as 'being ahead' or "catching up" with the transformation:

> Although most transition strategies are based on a three-pronged approach—liberalization, institution building, and macroeconomic stabilization—countries have, in practice, adopted distinctive reform agendas and achieved varying degrees of success. Whereas some countries have moved decisively ahead with their transformation, others are making a steady effort to catch up . . . (Blejer and Skreb 2001, 3; emphasis added)

To continue on transitology as 'hubris,' Grancelli (2002, 97) has cited Stephen Cohen's (1999, 42) apt recognition of the Orwellian knowledge produced by transitology, including:

> the worst industrial depression of the twentieth century has been called reform; a decreed market, featuring contract killings as the supreme form of litigation, has been called a free market; the decimation of the highly educated and potentially entrepreneurial Soviet middle classes has been called the creation of a middle class; and, finally, the disguised form of Russian authoritarianism that has presided over all this is called political reform. Grancelli (2002, 97)

Transition literature only very rarely focuses on real people. Kupferberg (1999, 10), one of the few exceptions to the rule, describes the point well: "Whereas most theories of transformation assume that what is transformed are structures or institutions, I argue that transformation is fundamentally about people, that is, individuals." This social psychological dimension of the transformation process has been conspicuously underemphasized in transformation literature as a whole and nearly ignored by transitology.

Aside from the openly normative transitology, the other 'pure' academic category focuses mostly on the institutions and gears of political and economic transition, on questions of efficiency. The social sphere is woefully neglected. The primary drive of most, even Tökes' 'purely' academic transitology literature, is to attempt to learn the proper sequences and factors required for 'successful' transition toward capitalism and democracy. The focus is on the mechanisms and efficiency of transitions, often from an institutional perspective. One example, indeed a progressive one, of this literature may be the edited volume by Burawoy and Verdery (1999), entitled *Uncertain Transition*. The editors spend much energy critiquing those who interpret the collapse of communism as "the final victory of modernity's great achievements," but the volume's focus on institutions, political actors, economic policy, and the meso-level workings of the economic transformation neglects both the intimate sphere and the macro-levels, and thus serves, despite the authors' intentions, as a how-to manual for analyzing the operative contours of the political and economic machines. For example, they pursue the following questions:

> "Why does the Russian economy continue to decline year in, year out, while the Chinese economy continues to grow? Why has the Polish economy done better in some respects than the much acclaimed Hungarian and Czech models (Burawoy and Verdery 1999, 15)?"

Within this ethnographic-technocratic mix, the effects of the economic transformation on real everyday people—not persons as abstract actors, classes, or elites—are cloudy, as are the cultural characteristics of the systems in transition. In many such works, we are left with what feels like a fatalistic and mechanical process, with institutions and elites reified in a realm separate from both personal and from generalized overarching meaning. Transitology does not touch the field of personal values because it rather dissects transformations through a technocratic language, one divorced from both people and subjective meaning, so that, in the end, it remains 'useful' to modernization.

This all misses the question of how real people dealt with socialism and the transformation in the 1990s. How did the transformation impact them, not merely as elites, decision-makers, or functionaries, but also as full human beings, with families, ideals, dreams, and friendships? In other words, how did the collapse of socialism impact everyday life? Unfortunately, "no one has bothered to study the phenomenon in question:" the fate of the intimate and private sphere in a post-communist setting" (Kupferberg 1999, 24). Fourcade describes well the need to focus on everyday valuation processes: "sociology's critique of economics must shift away from a focus on economic markets, in which the value problem remains confined to things that are effectively traded, to *a focus on economic valuation processes, where the value problem is much more general and encompasses everything that people care about* (or are believed and made to care about)" (Fourcade 2011, 46; emphasis in original).

Homo-Sovieticus: Transitology's Bogeyman

Contrasting with transitology's sterile technocratic edge is its opposite face, one clothed in an emotional rejection of everything communist, especially the people. The following passage captures one author's frustration at this fact:

> It's high time you realized that these people want to promote a false picture of Soviet man because it keeps them in business. And truth doesn't provide anyone with a good job. (Zinoviev, 1986, 118)

Transitology tends, at its best, toward scientifically framed technocratic hubris that is useful for implementing ideological agendas. We can see it at its worst when the technocratic language melts away, revealing its true nature. Much of transitology is engaged in a witch hunt for "homo-sovieticus," a person whose socialist socialization has rendered him/her a human being "completely deprived of its social roots" (Malysheva 1992). Damnation of homo-sovieticus has become more frantic with the fall of the Soviet Union. An explanation lies in the meaning of 'victory' within a charged Cold War environment. Particularly, there arises a dissonance between the West's Cold War victory and the obvious struggles of Western ideals of democracy and capitalism on the ground in post-socialist Central and Eastern Europe. However, the red-tinted glasses still exist which allow scientists from both East and West to assign blame: the Soviet culture still existing within former Soviet individuals in the form of residual institutions and personality traits (see also Yurchak 2006). For example, Tarasulo (1994) warns that "the old ideology remains in Russia like *an unexploded bomb* covered over with a new layer of wind-blown soil" (emphasis added), as the Russians test "the shortest road from darkness and backwardness" (Tarasulo, 1994). Kupferberg's description of the communist sickness is also quite colorful:

> Sociologists would therefore profit by studying the origins of this moral erosion, how it *grew like a cancer*, and gradually forced society to its knees. When you travel around in Eastern Europe today, this is precisely the impression you get: it is a society that has barely survived. It has been *through a long bout of illness* and is only now recovering. (Kupferberg, 1999, 30; emphasis added)

This particular case of "binary socialism" (Yurchak 2006, 5) was written in 1999 and is typical in its linking of moral rot exclusively to the communist past with no reference to the existing cultural formations of the present, variations of capitalism and democracy. There is no causal reference to capitalism or democracy because these, in transitology research, tend to be sacred cows made sick by multiple highly contagious diseases carried by homo-sovieticus. Anything but capitalism is a disease eating away at present possibilities of success. Yet, like all good doctors, transitologists are reminded to maintain at least a small degree of sympathy for their 'patients:' "one should not turn a blind eye to what is often subjectively felt as deprivation by at least some of the participants" (Kupferberg 1999, 175).

In another example indicative of the negative influence of homo-sovieticus, Morawska (1999) points to the negative impact of Central and Eastern European transnational migrant entrepreneurs within their home countries. She writes of the match between homo-Sovieticus and new global variants of inferior "booty capitalism." Homo-sovieticus' "beat the system/bend the rules" mentality, reliance on crony patronage and connections, and need for immediate gratification and consumption make him/her perfectly suited for inferior modes of capitalism which ultimately stymie economic growth. Morawska's prognosis for Central and Eastern European transformation is bleak, since the former communist regimes have replaced with their own "distortions" the basic infrastructure which could have eventually influenced citizens' worldviews in a direction more conducive to successful transformation.

A comparable well-known formulation by Piotr Sztompka (1993) explains the failures of post-socialist societies to adapt to modern civilization as due to their "civilizational incompetence." In the realm of interpersonal relations, which are depicted as more enhanced in the West than in the East, he declares, in stark contrast to Cold-War era scientific depictions, that "shortages and poverty *preempted any concern with everyday virtues of civility*," (Sztompka 1993, 89; emphasis added). In addition to its other incompetences, now homo-sovieticus was seen as anti-social. This incompetence was caused via the same evils already laid out in the 1950's: direct indoctrination, totalitarian control, and the defensive mechanisms developed by persons against these. Sztompka also reports on the problem of anomie in interpersonal relations during the transition years, indicated by loneliness, amorality, and hostility, as helping to preserve the communist-legacy.

The dominant paradigms in economic sociology and in transitology research have not yet fully researched the effects of capitalist cultural transformation on intimate relationships in post-socialist societies. They tend to focus on other problems. In the instances where questions close to this book's are dealt with, there is a normative polarization in scientific accounts. Either the moral implications of economic transformation are not taken seriously or they are presumed as uniformly positive, contrasted with a sick homo-sovieticus. In contrast, this volume explores de-intimization related to recent economic changes while keeping emergent moral tensions and value conflicts in central focus. The core mechanisms of this individualization process are described in the following chapter.

3 "The Wall in the Head"
Mechanisms of De-socialization

> You feel kind of like in a running wheel. You constantly move but never really reach the finish line, because, then you are doing neither one nor the other right. Then you are not really at home, and if you are, you are somewhere else in your thoughts, and the other way around.
>
> —Leipzig businessman, L1

I am less dealing with the question of 'if' values changed than indicating 'how' social values become more latent. This chapter does this through describing the mechanisms through which the values of the post-communist persons in my study have individualized. These mechanisms, my most succinct story of 'what happened,' provide the interpretive frame to be applied to the following chapters of this book. The "wall in the head" of post-communist people (this term is used by Hessel et al. 1997, cited by Flockton, Kolinsky and Pritchard 2000, 17), representing both psychological conflict and ideological tensions, is one of the main ways that individualization is driven forward. In describing this and the other mechanisms, I make use of my informants' own interview accounts. However, let me first briefly provide some additional information on the design of my research.

RESEARCH NOTE

As I have already discussed in the introduction, I employ a mixed-method research design, using both qualitative and quantitative data. Within the qualitative portion, I make use of a most-dissimilar country design and look at the most-affected cities and at the most-affected gender, men. Besides this, I compare interviews with successful businesspersons, entrepreneurs, and managers with their own fathers. In total, the qualitative data being analyzed here consist of interviews with 32 informants that include 18 younger generation businessmen and 14 from the older generation. Information about these interviewees can be found in Appendix A (Table A.2). Throughout this book, I will refer to these persons mainly by their anonymous numbers, which will allow us more easily to keep track of where they are from and to which generation they belong. Herein, the "L" interview numbers represent Leipzig interviews and "S" and "M" represent, respectively Shanghai and Moscow. Furthermore, each odd-numbered interview represents someone from the businessman cohort, while the subsequent even number is their own father. For example, M1 is the son of Moscow informant M2.

The younger businessmen range in age from 32 to 49, while their fathers were between 60 and 80 years old at the time of the interviews (2005–2006). Each of the informants was male, with the exception of M12, the Moscow mother of M11, since there was no surviving father. With two exceptions (S11, L7), each of the younger cohorts were either married or divorced, and only one of these two (S11) is childless, whereas all other informants have children. In terms of occupation, each of the younger cohort members is a manager, businessman, owner, or an entrepreneur. They vary considerably in terms of wealth. At the low end, M9 could be described as middle to upper middle class, while the wealthiest informant is M5, a marketing tycoon.

Semi-structured interviews were conducted by native-speakers. On average, these lasted approximately 90 minutes and covered, in an open-ended manner, the informants' values now, values 15 years ago, value changes, and value conflicts (See Appendix A, Tables A.9 through A.12 for interview guidelines in English, Chinese, Russian, and German). In addition, 'typical' time diaries were collected for work and vacation days now and, retrospectively, 15 years ago.

Appendix A describes, in addition to further qualitative details, my usage of quantitative data from the World Values Survey. I have used four waves of data beginning with 1990 and as recent as 2005. In addition to samples from China, Russia, and Eastern Germany used in Chapters 3, 5, 6, 7, and 8, I use samples from additional post-communist, developing, and OECD countries in Chapter 9.

THE MECHANISMS OF DE-SOCIALIZATION

How do values tend toward weakened face-to-face sociality? Four processes work together as the mechanisms of this shift: conscious adaptation, ideological conflict, cognitive dissonance, and intergenerational changeover. These keys for understanding the growing latency in social values function in the following way. For individuals in post-socialist societies, the capitalist transformation embodied objective changes in goods and work. At the individual level, *conscious adaptation* to these new structures and conditions, the economic culture, is the general process describing how individuals cope with and adapt to the new social system in order to ensure success. This and the other mechanisms will be described in more depth later. Yet this individual adaptation is also embedded within a macro-level cultural frame characterized by rapid ideological change and *ideological conflict*. This frame affects how individuals interpret events and subjectively react to them. Capitalism was perceived by individuals in post-communist countries somewhat crudely, because it was already pre-formed, filled up with valuations and counter-valuations because of the claimed ideological opposition to socialism. Thus, people partially adapted their values in order to match their perception of the new order, one not only formed by objective shifts in goods and work, but one that is also shaped through the antagonistic ideological lens of the previous system. For many who adapted, there occurred a clash between the values of the new society and existing normative structures, and individuals felt *cognitive dissonance* as a result. Interestingly, people often mitigated this dissonance by further enhancing their individualized values. Finally, *intergenerational changeover* dynamics also result in individualized values in a number of ways: through fresh contact (Mannheim 1952), the lack of appropriate role models, the influence of peer groups, and the breakdown of socialization of the younger generation. Such intergenerational changeover effects occur within any social change, and this particular one was no exception and has resulted in a younger generation better adapted to the new system than its elders.

Through these four mechanisms, this chapter explains enhanced latency of social values in our three post-communist countries. These explanations are grounded within empirical data, some of which is presented in this chapter, but the bulk will be found in the remaining book chapters. The overall model of explanation is illustrated by Figure 3.1. This dynamic model shows both catalyzing and buffering effects of the main process of individualization, which occurs at the core through individuals adapting and being socialized to the key 'tools of success' within the capitalist economy. The diagram is not intended to imply an immediate deterministic notion of individualization but rather indicates the tendency toward the individualization outcome for reasons to be explained here. People are hardly unthinking drones dominated by impersonal systems, but neither is their behavior unpatterned (see de Certeau 1985). Rather, agentic action by successful persons in the modern capitalist economy produces individualization both through individually intended and unintended means.

On the left of Figure 3.1 is the independent variable, the capitalist market economy, whereas on the right, we have the main outcome noted in the following chapters: an individualized value set whereby intimate sociality becomes latent. The principal mechanisms taking us from the left to the right are the joint processes of socialization and adaptation. Socialization refers mainly to the naturalized 'top-down' value-schooling enacted by social-structural agents such as parents, schools, and workplaces. More neglected in paradigms that assume individuals have mostly static personalities once formed is the notion of conscious adaptation. This is the more agentic form of value modification whereby individuals consciously enact behavioral adjustments according to their own desires and preferences, attempting to achieve a match with the needs of the ruling economic culture. To the right of this socialization/adaptation box in the diagram are 'tools of success.' These correspond to the societal rules of the game by which individuals are rewarded for adapting their behavior in certain ways in order to be successful within the capitalist economy. These particular tools involve concepts to be discussed in this chapter, such as profit-oriented calculative rationality, skills of interpersonal exploitation and instrumentalization, the commodification of time, image cultivation and consumerist display of luxuries, a high degree of personal ambition and independent self-sufficiency, a strong focus on work, a materialist mindset, and moral flexibility. Each of these generates its own unique individualizing effect. Overall, those who acquire these tools, which are matched to the needs of the economic culture, are thereby more likely to achieve success than those who do not. Yet those who adopt these tools are less likely to be able to devote their time and mental focus to the intimate social sphere.

Numerous processes catalyze and slow ('buffer') this transmission of individualized market-economic values. Among the catalysts are intergenerational changeover effects. Specifically, Mannheim's (1952) notion of 'fresh contact' is used to demonstrate how younger generations always tend toward a more radical adoption of new cultural forms than their parents. In addition, the older generation's lack of knowledge about the new economic system exacerbates the younger's reliance upon peers as a source of knowledge and as role models, thus enhancing the fresh contact effect. Finally, the breakdown and modification of the socialization of values into children also result in a value set which is less intimately social.

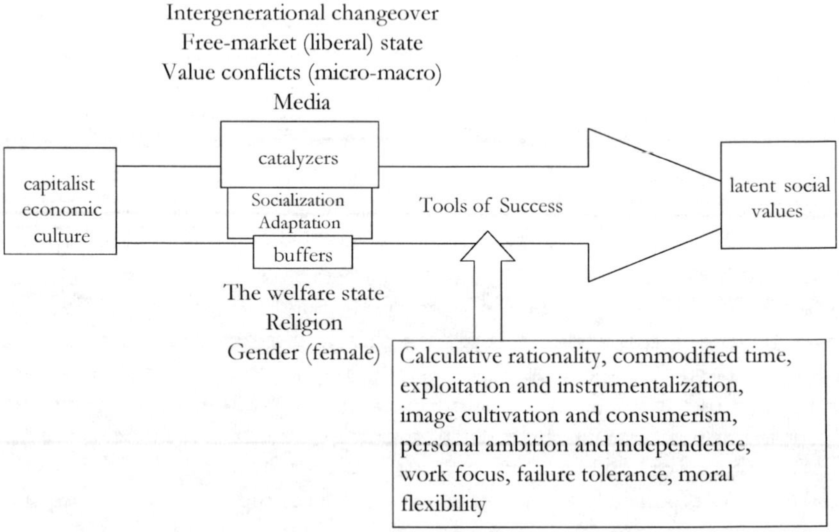

Figure 3.1 Explaining enhanced latency of social values.

In addition, the liberal free-market state, epitomized by the American or British model, catalyzes the individualization process through promoting individualist ideals. The American 'frontier mentality,' 'pulling oneself up by the bootstraps,' the 'do it yourself' mindset, the demonization of welfare and of receiving social help, plus the glorification of business, creativity, and the entrepreneurial spirit; these all characterize how the capitalist economic culture is supported ideologically by a particular form of state, one that mostly ensures the transmission of values functional to the economic machine. The Chinese and Russian states have both adopted this model of 'values policy.' The Russian state, upon the Soviet collapse, adopted a laissez-faire approach regarding values, one resulting de-facto in the furthered interests of values conducive to economic health. In the last decade, however, this was reversed, as Russia has started to promote a form of nationalist familism within pro-family advertisements in order to promote fertility. Meanwhile, the Chinese Communist Party actively encouraged consumerist and capitalist values through propaganda. In the past decade, it has subsequently reversed its course a bit, through reintroducing Confucianism into school curricula, but this will be written of later, in Chapter 4. Therefore, state policies may contribute to slowing down or speeding up the individualization of values.

Value conflict and the resolution of this conflict is also a major source of value change. At the micro level, considerable energy will be spent in this chapter elucidating the role of cognitive dissonance within value change. When conflicts occur, as my data show, between work and family, and between money and morality, these are most often resolved in the direction of least resistance, which is the direction of the economic impulse. enhancing work at the expense of family and intimate relations. Furthermore, the parallel of individual-level cognitive dissonance at the macro, cultural level is ideological conflict, by which individuals interpreted capitalism through a communist ideological lens, and thus adapted to capitalism in its 'ideal' communist presentation: as a wholly individualized, immoral, and anti-social entity.

Finally, the role of media and advertisements in furthering individualization is also established. The goal of advertisements, in locking persons into consumerist lifestyles conscious of image and sensitive toward material success markers, is one at odds with the individual goal of shielding oneself from spending more time shopping and working than necessary. Modern movies and music may also sell ideals which are aligned with the dominant cultural motif, one of economic success. Among our informants, there is evidence of the media's role. While many informants deny the manipulative effects of media upon their own values, others nonetheless show that they are influenced by what they see. L3, for instance, admits that he has no television, as he claims that it "dumbs people down" and "prevents them from thinking."

Yet media have been successful in transferring certain images of success to businessmen. In China, for example, where media is state-controlled, there are television programs that glorify the lives of great entrepreneurs, attempting to firmly establish them as role models. S13, for example, wants to learn all he can about famous entrepreneurs from several well-known television programs. S15 is also influenced by advertisements that tap into this "entrepreneurial image":

(S15)

Q: When you see the advertisements which encourage people to spend more money or buy certain goods to show their success, how do you feel?

A: Personally, I agree with that. There are many high-level advertisements which affect me a lot. What I care about is the enterprise culture the advertisements have embodied. I don't care which star helps to promote the products. What attracts me most is the persuasive culture the ads have embodied. If the enterprise culture is embodied to full extent, I think the products would be also very good. So the quality of the products lies on the level of its enterprise culture. By the way, I will buy whatever products Tony Leung (a Hong Kong actor) helps to promote because I think he is very masculine.

Nonetheless the majority of informants claim they are uninterested in and unaffected by media. On this note, M11 equates contemporary Russian skepticism with advertisements with the former Soviet-era skepticism toward propaganda. Yet, this informant notes in another portion of the interview that he *believed in communist ideals*. It is likely that this propaganda had a long-term effect despite the resistance that it generated at the immediate level; in this way, it was effective at a level below consciousness. The same 'creeping' effectiveness could be claimed for advertisements. It is scant to believe that billions of dollars in advertising attempting to influence individuals to consume have no influence. Yet, individuals are unlikely to admit that they are unconsciously affected by a stimulus.

Several factors have been identified as buffers working against the transformation toward individualist values. One of these appears to be the welfare state. Eastern German informants, when faced with moral and social conflicts over their work, were quite ready to admit or pursue the *possibility* of shifting jobs because of the existence of a social safety-net. In addition, pro-family laws and work-family harmony ideology may have also played roles in allowing the Eastern German informants to at least feel the acceptability of a balanced work-family routine. This is in stark contrast to the non-welfare states that promote work, self-realization, and profit ideologies. In addition, religion appears to be a powerful bastion of pro-social values. Each of the informants that espoused religiosity also displays a high degree of respect for sociality and work-family balance. This is likely due to religion's espousal of ultimate values in conflict with those of the ruling economic system (i.e. god versus profit). Finally, gender is also a strong indicator of pro-social values, based on outside research and the quantitative findings of this study (See Appendix C), as women are more likely to hold onto pro-social, religious, and anti-materialist values.

Now that these mechanisms have been briefly introduced, I will describe the roles of conscious adaptation, ideological conflict, cognitive dissonance, and intergenerational changeover in greater detail.

CONSCIOUS ADAPTATION

There are two ways in which adaptation is understood. First, it is a generic process that describes how individuals come to match their environments, whether they do so through intentional learning, less intentional processes such as ideological manipulation or acculturation, or through traditional notions of socialization. This concept is a key one in explaining how, within the capitalist economic structure, former communist citizens may come "to be socialized in a way which makes disorder, uncertainty and risk-taking an element of everyday life" (Kupferberg 1999, 11). Yet there are many ways through which such adaptation or socialization may occur; the notion is a black box within which many varieties of behavioral modification may fit.

With this in mind, the way in which adaptation is used in this book is more specific. The adaptation analyzed here occurs in a mostly conscious form. Conscious adaptation implies actors learning the rules of the game and the means to success within a particular system. Thereby, conscious adaptation should be seen as the reflective adaptation of individuals to their environments. Yet this 'conscious' adaptation is only one of several mechanisms of value change provided here. The unconscious dimensions of value change in post-Communist societies will be described in later sections on ideological conflict and cognitive dissonance.

A prerequisite of conscious adaptation is recognition by the individual of the structure or 'sense' of society. This sense was referred to within the interviews. Our informant, L3, points out that this recognition is one of a concrete economic structure, even a "natural one," according to which one must adapt in order to be successful in work. When speaking of money and material things, this informant used as a subject the German impersonal pronoun '*man*,' meaning 'a person,' as in, 'a person should do this or that . . .' In contrast, when speaking of his own values and ideals, he used "*Ich*," or "I." This may show that he depersonalizes the demands of the economic structure into impersonal rules and pressures that he must obey, while he sets these in contrast with his own innate interests. In contrast, his father,

L4, notes that "since I am not working anymore, one is a little shielded by the problems of the working world." L6, as well, found it unnecessary to adapt to the new society due to his age and lack of economic integration. Similarly, M12 notes how her lack of economic involvement meant that she did not need to adapt, which is in contrast to her son:

> *Q:* Did these changes somehow affect your values, your points of view or not at all?
>
> *A:* They happened. I saw what happened. But I can't say that they have affected me too much. I haven't participated in all these happenings, so my point of view could be subjective, it's not objective at all.

In contrast to the non-workers, L7, as a businessman, describes how his reflective adaptation implies value change. He notes that, over the transformation years, he has "grown into the business" as a result of his focus over time upon career, personal progress, leading the business, and being successful. Thereby those working are 'playing the game' and therefore must adapt to the 'rules.' Yet there are specific conditions that motivate them to adapt: material conditions and, more importantly, personal ambition.

Certainly, one of the prime motivators of adaptation during the transformation years was economic scarcity and material survival, or at least the threat of economic insecurity (Kasser et al. 2003, 13). In this view, scarcity is a factor motivating value change (Inglehart and Welzel 2005), but not the only or principal factor. During the transformation years, individuals were motivated by the threat of poverty to secure a material foundation for themselves and their families. Indeed the economic conditions in Eastern Europe were miserable. Some observers note that the economic depression resulting from the transformation was comparable or worse than was the Great Depression for developed countries (World Bank 2002, 5; as cited by Outhwaite and Ray, 51). The shock of adjusting oneself under such conditions of material insecurity proved especially poignant, for example, in Eastern Germany, where upon transformation individuals entering the Western labor market had to learn to "prove themselves" constantly (Offe 1994, cited by Kupferberg 1999, 179).

There are many observations within the interviews of the relevance of material insecurity. The father-son pair M7-M8 is an example. During the transformation years, the father, M8, was still working and thus had a frantic rush in order to successfully commercialize his business for the sake of material well-being. This sacrifice resulted in the situation that the family became important only "by default" for him. In contrast, the son M7, is more family-oriented, because his transition occurred more smoothly and less suddenly since it was experienced concomitant with his youthful socialization and without the same material burdens shouldered by his father. It was a 'natural' part of growing up, part of the known social environment being adapted to by him and his peers. As a result, the son is more family-oriented than the father. For these cases, shock because of material insecurity stimulated a radical transformation in the direction of heightened valuation of work, to the detriment of active valuation of the family.

Yet material insecurity was only one of many motivators among people who experienced the transformation. Also important was the enhancement of personal ambition and aspirations, whereby the accumulation of money and material subsidence for many are only side-effects of striving for personal achievement. This individualistic personal achievement cult is part and parcel of the "western ethos of winners and losers" (Pollack 1992; as cited by Kupferberg 1999, 26).

A rise in the value of individual achievement is strongly documented within the interviews. Typically the young informants have a sturdy achievement-orientation. As an illustration of this trend, S13's focus on self-realization is quite strong:

> *Q:* What is the most important thing in your life?
>
> *A:* Self-realization. I won't be suppressed by anyone. I am not a presumptuous man, but I have such a nature that if I find that someone wants to prevent me from developing on purpose, I will resist.

Similarly, S9 notes "The first value is to devote myself to the cause I love and make some achievements." These high-achievement oriented people typically channel these drives toward their careers. In contrast, the older generation notes that a strong personal drive toward individual success was not necessary and may have been frowned upon in the past. For example, S14, the father of the 'insuppressible' S13, recalls, "Planned economy means whatever assignments the leaders gave to you, you should strictly take their orders. Nobody would refuse to finish the assignment and nobody would say 'I'm sure to succeed'." S7 points as well to the tendency of the younger generations to "overestimate themselves."

This focus of members of the younger generation on personal ambition and personal achievement is clearly one of enhanced self-focus, differing greatly from the more group-oriented work orientations of their fathers' generation. A high degree of self-confidence and ambition should be seen as both a motivator and as a tool of success within the new system.

Tools of Success

Individuals' recognition of the nature of the objective economic conditions—within work and consumption—in which they live also implies that they learn something about how to achieve success within these systems. In addition to the personal ambition and independence already outlined above, several tools of success are outlined here: enhanced work focus, tolerance of failure, cost-benefit analyses, image cultivation, interpersonal exploitation and instrumentalization, and commodified time.

An important finding is the inflated value of work among successful businessmen. This work focus, work as an end in itself and for 'the self.' has major repercussions on social relationships and catalyzes the need for adapting each of the other work-related tools of success. This self-oriented notion of 'work as career' contrasts greatly with the 'work as duty' orientation of the older generation.

The seeking of and taking on of more risk by individuals, due to their high drives toward personal achievement, also implies the suffering of more failures (Beck 1992). Therefore, the younger generations must also adapt a 'thick skin.' Since plans do not always work out as they should, one must have an enhanced tolerance toward enduring failure. S9, for example, notes that he will attempt to transmit such a value to his son: "If he can endure many problems, he will be sound in mind. And that's a requirement for me as well." S13 similarly values endurance of failure:

> *Q:* What do you think is the most important quality for a successful entrepreneur?
>
> *A:* The ability to endure failure and difficulty.

The ability to endure failure enhances the individualism inherent in the high self-achievement mentality noted above. It allows the individual to become continually more self-confident, risky, and self-directed. The enhancement of these traits improves the likelihood of both economic success and excessive self-centeredness.

Businessmen need to learn cost-benefit analysis, specifically profit-calculation, in order to survive. This economic thinking is attached to particular roles; L12 points out that a businessman knows cost-benefit thinking "from the cradle." This is also noted in a comparison of the L5-L6 pair, whereby the younger definitely notices a change in his cost-benefit thinking during transition years, while his father did not change in this regard. The following remark is typical in demonstrating the importance of profit calculation as a tool of success of the businessman:

> *(S17)*
>
> In life, we think we can afford to spend money when there is need to do so. However, as an enterprise, I will consider the inputs and profits. If the profits are not so good, I won't do so.

There is a widespread recognition of the importance of profit calculation. L7 also describes this newfound frugality:

> Professionally of course, [there developed] a much bigger conscience about the costs. It's not that one saves money endlessly, but yet one considers what one needs. I think today it's certainly more important to get high quality things cheaply.

L7 also remarks that, in comparison to his father, he personally tends to "scrutinize" more closely in business matters, compared to his father, who tends to deal with commercial things "calmly" and intuitively. However, L7's frugality notion is applied to work *and* home, implying a partial 'colonization' of the lifeworld (Habermas 1989) by this rational form of calculation. Other informants, such as L1, also perceive the threat of rational calculation in their private lives. They attempt to resist it by refusing to focus too much on costs and benefits when it comes to activities within the family.

L4 describes how further rationalization occurs within informants because of the new requirements that they learn to "manage" the state and its new requirements by themselves. L4 describes this change:

> New is that with the state, with the fiscal office or with the health insurance, or as regards the pensions, with many things you have to act on your own. You either have to get informed and one has to take care of things more actively, and it wasn't like that in the GDR—which had formed us. Everything was done for you, it was just like that. But one couldn't change anything either. Today one has to be careful.

Therefore, several aspects of rational cost-benefit analyses described here relate to the individualization in question. First, the rational thinker is also more independent, separated by his/her calculative logic from the world, which then must be 'managed.' Therein is the second danger, that calculative logic itself will objectify everything and *everyone* into objects of analysis, thereby raising dangers of estrangement, instrumentalization, and exploitation. Finally, these both imply that calculative logic may "colonize" other more innately communicative spheres of life (Habermas 1989).

Examples will be noted in Chapter 6 of the role of image cultivation and its importance for the entrepreneurs, businessmen, and managers who were interviewed. Image cultivation is given as a justification for conspicuous consumption, whereby individuals consciously choose to buy a nice suit or a nice car in order to be perceived as successful by their peers and customers. Thereby, however, a habitus of consumption develops which later may liberate itself from its original pragmatic intent or justification. This liberated consumerism may become an end in itself, potentially blinding its victims to other forms of ultimate valuation, such as the family, or communication for its own sake.

The following chapters also describe the enhanced roles of exploitation and instrumentalization within post-communist relationships. The word exploitation is more often used as a critique of the behavior of others, while informants rarely admit they are exploitative themselves. Nonetheless, certain informants admit to "using" others in an instrumental style, one that is "normal" within capitalism; they thereby reject the negative valences of "exploitation" as communist rhetoric, while incorporating its essence as normal.

L1, for example, feels more used by others nowadays because money plays a greater role since there are more goods on the marketplace. He remembers how money was worth less back in those days, but now, the possibilities are greater, which "makes people do things they shouldn't do." Thereby, he indicates the expansion of the field of exploitation through explaining the growing incentives of exploitative behavior. This exploitative and instrumental style of relating to others explains the prevalence of larger and thinner friendship networks in the post-communist setting as well as the older generation's reaction against this style of communication, one that views relationships as instrumental objects rather than as inherently valuable.

The previously-described conscious adaptive processes each embody their own forms of individualization. However, there is a powerful multiplier in exacerbating their joint individualizing effects. Time itself has become more scarce, as it has become commodified and inflated in value (Neidhart 2003). Whereas socialist work embodied somewhat stable working hours and limits upon productive capacities, partially supplied by the lower psychological incentives for working harder, the capitalist system in contrast transforms time into money. Thereby, the enhanced focus on work found within post-communist businessmen and entrepreneurs is one that demands every minute of available free time. A system that commodifies time, converting it into money and 'success,' also commodifies the relationships which rely upon this same precious resource. Informants often complain about the time conflicts between work and family. These conflicts are usually resolved in favor of work, with the 'family phase' of life, as emphasized in Chapter 7, being postponed until retirement. In other words, the resource of time is granted to the family and primary relationships only when the informants' true loves—work and the self—have had their fill. The inflated and commodified value of time causes individuals to change their rhythms of time (see Outhwaite and Ray 2005, 181) so that life sequencing itself is altered.

The interviews provide many examples of the inflated value of time and of work-family time conflicts. Many informants, especially the East Germans, complain that time is too short to simultaneous manage work and family. The indication is that, at the beginning of the transformation, money was short and time was replete, whereas now the opposite is true. L9, for example, complains that he has the money to go on vacation but has no time.

The pace of modern time, aside from taking time away from intimate relationships, may also lead to uprooting. L3 describes:

> But time is so fast and ephemeral, that one . . . that one asks oneself whether one personally even has such a big influence in those matters. One is able to determine a certain set of values for oneself and his own life indeed and this set of values is going to be valid in 5, 10 or for me even in 20 years from now, but one doesn't have the ability to, I simply say it that way, predict the progression of one's environment any longer. Time became too fast-moving for that.

The pace of life makes stability difficult to ensure.

This perpetually scarce time, which the interviewees complain about, is commodified not directly by the economic system but rather through the informants themselves, as made clear by the prevalence of this problem especially among the self-employed. One Eastern German claims that self-employment is a form of slavery. Another, L2, remembers how, 15 years ago, the amount of time that he spent at home and at work was about the same as today, except that today he unfortunately brings more work home, since he is a freelancer.

> But if you are in a position where you have responsibility, as entrepreneur for example, then this conflict is given, because if you decided to do something like this then you have to do it like this in order to get it working. Certainly you could organize things differently, I mean everyone does things as he thinks it is right and that is why I invested a lot of time that I didn't have at my disposal for other things.

Important here is that he notes, "certainly you could organize things differently," but he chooses not to.

IDEOLOGICAL CONFLICT

Aside from the conscious adaptation discussed above, I will now introduce the second mechanism for de-socialization: ideological conflict. The previous section on adaptation focused primarily on conscious and willed responses to the new economy which resulted in a de-intimization of values. In contrast, I now begin to frame some of the unconscious responses to change. In order to adequately do so, we must consider how the post-communist transformation was perceived, based on the ideological context within which individuals faced the 'objective' economic structure. This ideological step lays the ground to introduce one of the most surprising of individualization mechanisms: cognitive dissonance.

Individuals adapting within post-communist societies were certainly faced with *real* changes in the realms of work, such as greater instability, and consumption, such as the range of available products and luxuries. Certainly many responses to these changes would be somewhat automatic and 'natural,' but nonetheless the way that post-communist citizens came to *evaluate* these changes would be unique because of the ideological baggage they inherited from the communist past. In other words, the capitalism inherited by post-communist citizens was one viewed through the glasses of a cultural bias, the communist ideological lens (compare to Yurchak 2006, "Chapter 5: The imaginary west"). Of course, each culture produces a 'biased' view of the world. Just as many Westerners triumphantly greeted the communist collapse as a victory against totalitarianism and oppression, many individuals in those countries met it as the victory of what had until that point been known as an immoral, hedonistic, and materialistic capitalist economic power. Communism and capitalism presented one another in pure forms, and such stubborn presentations are difficult to eradicate for individuals within either system.

This is not to suggest that either communist or capitalist populations naively swallow the ideology they are handed in whole or unquestioningly. As will be reported in Chapter 4, there was indeed widespread disillusionment in socialist societies prior to the economic transformation, exemplified through widespread mistrust of all official information in Soviet Russia and East Germany. Nonetheless, these ideologies *do form* one part of the cognitive environment of individuals in transition since this 'information environment' functions at levels of unconsciousness as well as on the more apparent level of ostensible resistance. Despite convictions to the contrary held by many in Western Europe or the United States, communism did have a "grip on the hearts and minds" of its citizens (Kupferberg 1999, 1; Yurchak 2006, 8–9). In Eastern Germany, for example, even after the regime lost its appeal, many citizens still saw the communist experience as an "'error' growing out of good intentions" (Offe 1997, 170).

This is not mentioned in order to underplay the internal resistance to Communist regimes, the poor material conditions they provided, or the real oppression they inflicted. However, individuals experiencing the economic transformation also experienced an ideological one. As Kupferberg (1999, 31) notes, although the communist regimes were a "system of lies," they had to nonetheless "persuade" the great majority of citizens to join them. This is why "information policy" and information control was a key aspect of the former communist regimes (Kupferberg 1999, 40).

This notion of opposing ideological systems implies culture shock for those transitioning from one to the other. One either adapts the new ideology, neo-liberalism, alongside its condemnation of the communist past *in pure form* or clings to the past, issuing a strict condemnation of the capitalist present. Among those who adapt, taking on the new ideology, this creates a hardened mindset in which, to quote one of the elder Moscow informants (M10), "everything except economics is crap." Those who adapt can be quite candid of the meaning of this personal shift in values, as our Moscow informant 11, a successful businessman, noted, "In my case, all the communist ideals I cherished collapsed." In other cases, people refused to adapt. Many East Germans still support the previous regime ideologically, specifically the moral superiority of socialism (Kupferberg 1999, 145). Especially for older people, this transformation came as a shock. For the younger, the transformation in values was equally tangible, but held more of an air of excitement, at least at the onset.

For many post-communist citizens, socialist collapse brought a profound sense of disillusionment. This is demoralization in the first, standard sense. Many individuals experienced culture shock when confronted with commodity civilization (Kupferberg 1999, 135). This created an "anomic effect" in the sense that previous norms ceased to hold value. With rapid social change, previous "meaning-constructions" were made irrelevant, which threatened individual self-worth and sense of reality, creating a demoralization to be coped with (Kupferberg 1999, 55–56).

Beyond a general form of demoralization, implying the loss of 'morale,' it should be stressed that *morality* also ceased to hold value. This is demoralization in a second sense. Communism defined itself in opposition to a capitalism that was morally abhorrent, with heightened rates of crime and prostitution, rampant exploitation, egoism, and hedonism. Communism, in contrast, *claimed* to be the 'city on the hill,' a system that put community over self, morality over exploitation, gender equality over patriarchy, responsibility over hedonism. Therefore, the collapse of communism and socialist society, and even more, its apparent exposure as a massive Potemkin village (Kohak 1992, 202; as cited by Kupferberg 1999, 32) also undermined its claim to moral authority. Castells (1998, 64) has also referred to this "mockery that the Communist state made of the values of human solidarity" (as cited by Crow 2002, 2). Yet when solidarity and morality are exposed publicly as propagandistic frauds and myths, as happened within the post-communist setting, especially in Russia, they may be thrown out with the bathwater. For those who fully adapted to the new economy, there was a tendency for morality itself to be dismissed as a thing of the past, one of the lies exposed by the victory of capitalism. In turn, there was a tendency for the capitalism of their perception to be adopted in its ideal (from the communist perspective) form: egoism, 'profits first,' hedonism, and immorality. Therefore, the widespread recognition of "demoralization" noted within the early transformation years (Malysheva 1992; Shlapentokh 1991) was more than just a feeling of loss and collapse; it was real in a second sense: an abandonment of morality itself as a vestige of the failed and naive communist past. This second demoralization has made value adaptations, and thus dissonance, more extreme.

Part of the adaptation to new values is the fading of old values, one of which, because of its poor match to the needs of the capitalist economy, is robust moral reasoning. At the same time, those who did not adapt to capitalism, such as many of the elderly, claim that many blatant Marxist-Leninist accusations became realized: "capitalists are greedy and capitalism as a system is immoral because it allows people to be thrown out into the street without either job or roof;" this particular perception is, of course, irrespective of the "real' greed or victimization of this system (Kupferberg 1999, 138).

When even well-adapted, successful persons do not value morality, this can not be explained by economic scarcity. Kukolev (1999), in describing one of the new elite classes, the "free artists," notes how their lack of moral scruples aided them during the transformation years:

> In Soviet times, they were engaged in small-sized speculation with imported goods, audio records, and so forth. Those who did not find work went to the bottom of the social scale and often developed problems with alcohol and drugs. During the perestroika years, many of these people rushed into the business world. Being very aggressive, cunning, and unprincipled, they were often quite successful. They ascended the management of large financial empires. Their knowledge and experience of life permitted them to balance legal and illegal activity through good relations and connections to the highest levels of the establishment as well as with criminal structures. (292)

In other words, Soviet era criminals were perfectly suited to build empires within the new economic environment (see also Volkov 2002).

As individuals come to perceive high-level economic activity and adaptation as 'natural' for themselves, they also come to perceive immoral behavior as a key to economic success. This becomes clear among the businessmen interviewed for this project, who noted the benefits of dishonesty and exploitation within work. Those who put profit first will achieve the most profit. Morality is not needed in the times of the capitalist "Wild West" (M10).

Across large portions of post-communist populations, political cynicism became widespread. It was a reaction both to the demoralizations described above and to the failures of the initial hopes of the transformation (Trotsky 1969; Sztompka 1991; as cited by Kupferberg 1999, 131). Cynicism regarding political institutions has been "linked to a legacy of corruption and a moral vacuum in which social solidarity was weak and crime rates were soaring" (Outhwaite and Ray 2005, 17). This cynicism could be seen as an advanced stage of demoralization, in which individuals no longer hold 'naive' thoughts about the nature of the new economic system and are rather coming to terms with its corruption:

> People are growing impatient and believe that change is being blocked or delayed. The result is a high degree of alienation and anomie among the people. The lack of ultimate values and ends reduces all social action to an instrumental level, especially action in the political system by elites. It is not surprising that crime, corruption, suicide rates, and lack of adherence to governmental regulation are the accompaniments

> of the collapse of communist regimes. (Shlapentokh, Vanderpool, and Doktorov 1999, 10)

This process involves the overcoming of old communist values since the possibility of a classless society is erased:

> For a citizenry raised in the belief of a Marxian utopian vision of a classless society and rudely suffering under the yoke of the selfish greed of the communist party elite and its dominant bureaucracy, the hope of a humane society that cares for its people is shattered. (Shlapentokh, Vanderpool, and Doktorov 1999, 7)

The impossibility of classlessness in modern Russia is exacerbated by the corruption of its elite structure, driven by oligarchs, ex-KGB, and corrupt politicians, leading one scholar to note that "Russian society is in a suspended state, its institutions in disarray, its idols broken" (Keller 1999, 355).

Within my interviews, political cynicism seems tied to growing self-centeredness (M11, for example). Informants turned inwards, toward their goals of personal achievement and strong foci on work in lieu of their previous goals. M7 describes this notion of cynicism and its relation to the destruction of old values:

> *A:* The attitudes of a lot of people are cynical because they realize that the country does not serve the people's interests but its own.
>
> *Q:* Was your attitude more positive in the beginning of the '90s?
>
> *A:* Of course, there was the hope that the new government will take care of its people and that freedom of choice, enterprise will be present.
>
> *Q:* Do you think that this does not exist anymore?
>
> *A:* To a big extent this period was devoted to the annihilation of all these values.

COGNITIVE DISSONANCE

Individuals therefore consciously adapt to the more objective elements of economic culture such as changing work and consumption possibilities, but their evaluation of the culture itself occurs through the lens of ideology and is impacted by ideological conflict. In order to move further, the idea of merely conscious adaptation will be put aside in order to look at the unforeseen and unconscious cognitive consequences of cultural-level ideological conflict. Therein, the tools of success previously mentioned, as individuals adopt them, come into conflict with other deeply held values. These conflicts, and particularly, how they are resolved, constitute the third mechanism for de-socialization: cognitive dissonance.

With years of ideological struggle between opposing forces of 'capitalism' and 'communism,' it should not be surprising to find that the collapse of communism triggered value conflicts among the citizens experiencing it. There are at least several reasons why such conflicts are of greater scientific interest. First, it is quite useful that they can be explained in ways consistent with cognitive dissonance theory, thereby allowing a thorough exploration into the rise of, forms of, and resolution of dissonance among this population. In this way, the at-first vague notion of 'value conflicts' becomes transformed into the more exploitable concept of cognitive dissonance. Second, because of the central place of the concept of dissonance resolution within the theory, we come to an important finding from analyzing these data: cognitive dissonance among these post-communist informants is consistently resolved in a way that is relevant for a broader trend of social change, one representing a devaluation of sociality. Successful post-communist informants tend to resolve their dissonance through enhanced valuation of the economic sphere at the expense of their valuation of intimate sociality. Third, it is apparent that the source of dissonance among these post-communist people is closely linked to their work within the new capitalist economic system.

Cognitive dissonance (as per Festinger 1957) is the negative feeling that arises from simultaneously possessing two opposing cognitive states. That feeling spurs a drive to dispel it by eliminating the conflict. There are two primary preconditions for dissonance to arise. First, conflicts stem from the competitive environment within which cognitions are seated because of limited time in which to distribute behavior; this is the environment within which dissonant cognitions are forced into a zero-sum game. Furthermore, in order for dissonance to arise, the cognitive elements in question should tend toward opposition. Our post-communist informants and their conflicting values display both of these: time conflicts and cognitive oppositions.

Limited Time

Festinger's focus on decision-making, forced compliance, and involuntary exposure to dissonant information signifies the importance of a cognitive environmental quality which allows cognitive oppositions to emerge. There is no reason to expect that opposing mental states, such as the valuation of different objects or conflicting means in one's mind should necessarily result in opposing mental states *a priori*. The conceptual transition from difference to opposition requires the addition of a competitive environment. Indeed, most people have a wide array of values that, on the surface, appear to coexist harmoniously although they might imply competing ends or means. The majority of persons, to some degree, value their relationships, money, work, achievement, comfort, and political freedom, but it is a mistake to believe that this coexistence of values implies harmony. To do this would involve an incomplete notion of values, that of values merely as cognitive entities. However, values are not only relevant as they sit in the mind. It is also relevant how they crystallize into behavior. This is why scholars cite the importance of the prioritization of values (Nye 1967, 241–242; Schwartz and Bilsky 1987). Values are important to us, as social scientists, because they are our construct for how the will selects its behavior, and it is in this act of behavioral selection that valuation as prioritization occurs and conflict becomes visible.

The pressure of behavioral selection becomes most apparent in reference to limited time. Limited time is an oft-cited cause of dissonance, specifically of work-family conflicts (Frone, Russell and Cooper 1992; Voydanoff 1988). Such examples of time pressures are abundant among those who are conflicted within the post-communist sample. For example interviewee L2 and his son both note a conflict between their family and work time. His son, L1, describes it in this way:

> Yes, well, that sometimes is a problem. I do have to work a lot, first because I am a freelancer and second because lawyers have a very time-consuming work in general. Unfortunately, that is the way it is and it is certainly not that easy if you have a family and also two little kids because my wife does a lot, meaning she does the most but also would like to do something else once in a while.

L3 also relates his own work-family conflict to his limited time:

> If I look for example at the time I am spending on work here and add the work-time in the region, which in fact means all of Germany—well if I get more specific: we are having projects in Dortmund and Frankfurt at the moment—then there certainly is this distance between me and the family. It isn't very good for the family . . . or it isn't necessarily beneficial for the family.

In nearly every case of conflicting values, the informant refers to limited time as a main cause of his dissonance. Here are some examples from the other two cities, Moscow and Shanghai:

> (*M7*)
>
> The conflict now is that I work for a company where I have to stay at work longer. I leave early and come back late. This contradicts my family values because I cannot see my children enough.
>
> (*S15*)
>
> Take my family values for example. I think family values are very important while my family members and friends don't think that I

> regard them as important. Nowadays I don't spend much time with my family members for I have little time to do so . . . In fact, I regard family as very important from the depth of my heart. I don't think I have spent as much time with my family members as my friends have.

Likely these informants would not experience dissonance from time pressure alone if they were choosing between a set of inherently compatible options, but in fact their limited time makes it possible for inherent cognitive oppositions to become manifest because they have to choose how to act.

Cognitive Opposition

The second prerequisite to cognitive dissonance, aside from limited time, is cognitive opposition. This notion of an inherent opposition separable from the problem of time constraints is often overlooked in work-family conflict literature (See Frone, Russell, and Cooper 1992), although it may be found implicitly through the notion of inherently conflicting behaviors (Greenhaus and Beutell 1985, 77). Festinger (1957, 13) describes such cognitive opposition in detail: "two cognitive elements are in a dissonant relation if, considering these two alone, the obverse of one element follows from the other." Festinger (1957, 14) gives, as examples, several different types of opposition: logical, cultural, violation of past experience, and a specific case opposing a general rule.

The informants of this study, when they are conflicted, consistently display conflicts between their family and work values, or more generally, between morality and money, thereby suggesting an opposition between these spheres. This opposition, it will be shown, is both a logical and a cultural one.

Leipzig interviewee number one (L1) describes how his mind is caught between the two spheres of work and family:

> *(L1)*
>
> *Q:* How do you feel when those kinds of conflicts arise?
>
> *A:* Well . . . torn back and forth, well, you feel kind of like in a running wheel . . . you constantly move . . . but you never really reach the finish line, because, then you are doing neither one nor the other right. Then you are not really at home, and if you are at home you are somewhere else in your thoughts, and the other way around.

Notice this informant's report that he is "somewhere else in his thoughts" while at home and his complaint that he can "neither do one thing nor the other right," meaning neither work nor family. This implies an opposition between these cognitive elements for him. Combined with his limited time and the negative feeling he has associated from this opposition, he is experiencing a classic case of cognitive dissonance. Describing his family as important, he depicts managing his work-family balance as "a highwire act." He is typical of a class of informants feeling torn between family and work. Another informant, M7, when speaking of work and professional values laments "Of course, they contradict each other, but you cannot do anything." L8 summarizes the conflict in vivid words:

> I mean, during times when we built something [in the business] in order to give something to others the family had to suffer from it. Maybe the children of entrepreneurs can buy bigger ice cream cones but have to pay for it with their 'worse' family situation.

In other interviews, it becomes clear that some informants feel they have to sacrifice their social morality in general in order to be successful in the modern economic environment. Leipzig 5, for example, a technology advisor, has to sacrifice his honesty, a value about which he speaks repeatedly during the interview, mostly in the form of nostalgia for the honesty he formerly possessed. He complains that he has to set this value aside while at work in order to convince his clients to purchase services they do not need or at a price that is too high, thus causing considerable dissonance:

> Well, of course mostly I am in conflict with the value honesty. That depends on the situation. That's clear. . . Well, with business partners or with customers, the honesty thing is unfortunately not always the guiding value. That's how it is. . . . I can't generalize how I handle it. That is, I have lots of difficulties to. . .to give up this value but I decide in the situation what is more important for me and sometimes it's not the honesty.

Other informants feel that they have to exploit and pressure their employees while at work in order to maximize efficiency, thus generating another form of dissonance. In the words of L2:

> I'd say if you are an entrepreneur you have to see to it that your work generates a certain profit, if not, it doesn't work. To do so, you have to put your employees under pressure and maybe you also have to or you can't pay them the wages you think they are worth . . . sure enough you are in a conflict then.

M10 faces a similar conflict between workplace efficiency and treating people well. He notes that at work "I have to force people to do some things, I see that they cannot do them but I cannot fire them as well. This is a conflict which should find its solution." M11 also sees a conflict between dignity and humanism "on the one side, and the desire to earn money and establish a successful business from another." Toward the end of the interview, he comments:

> For example, I want to run a business and earn money and therefore I have to fire this worker because his work is bad. I feel sorry for him. Well, here you have a conflict. I have to constantly change when I talk to my mother. It often happens that you do not say what you mean at work. I do not like this at all.

This situation is reminiscent of L1, who reported that he felt as if running in a wheel, trapped between work and home modes of thinking. M11 also feels this way, as if the modes of thinking in work and at home are contradictory. Workplace efficiency has no place at home when speaking with his mother (who lives in his house supported by him and his wife), and home's humanism has no place at work when it comes to firing an employee or negotiating a contract. This cognitive opposition is also expressed by one of the other informants:

> *(L7)*
>
> *Q:* In what way do you think do some of your values conflict with others?
>
> *A:* Yes, considerably . . . there is for example the value of family versus the value of business and making progress vs. the value of social thinking, that is for example the work at the Red Cross.

Notable here is that the specific modes of thinking pertaining to home and work form not merely a logical cognitive opposition, but there appears to be a broader cultural dissonance between business, economic thinking, and money on the one hand and social contribution, non-instrumental communication, and morality on the other. This points not to a generalized work-family conflict as the source of dissonance, but rather to a *specific form* of work, that which is necessary for success within the modern capitalist economy.

Money versus Mensch

Before moving on to the resolution of cognitive dissonance among the informants, it is helpful to theoretically frame the above dissonance. The particular form of cognitive opposition found within these examples of dissonance in post-communist individuals is well-theorized in classical sociology and touched upon in value-change research, but it has been inadequately applied to the post-communist case, especially in the explicit language of cognitive dissonance. These opposing logical and cultural elements may be broadly labeled as 'money versus Mensch,'[1] in order to highlight this tension between economy and sociality. Admittedly, it would be folly to argue that these two spheres are really existing "hostile worlds" (Zelizer 2005), but at the same time it would be brash to suggest that they are harmonious in light of evidence of dissonance. Therefore, talk here of the spheres of sociality and modern capitalist materialism and work values being in conflict should be read to understand there is a tendency toward conflict and an inherent tension, but not quite an open hostility. There is, of course, a wide body of classical sociological work that suggests that materialist and social concerns may conflict with one another, which has already been discussed within Chapter 2. Within this body of theory, cognitive opposition is usually seen as based on the fact that the economic and social spheres entail different *modes* of valuation. In the economy, the rational-calculative mode and its means- and ends-focused forms of quantitative valuation are themselves tools of success. In contrast, social relations are ideally governed by an intuitive valuation which qualitatively values others and relationships as intrinsically valuable.

Relevant research on the topic concerns work-family conflicts, a specific variety of cognitive dissonance, where it has been noted that "work and family roles still have distinct norms and requirements that may be incompatible with one another" (Greenhaus and Beutell 1985, 77; Voydanoff 1988). More specifically, the "managerial stereotype" emphasizing self-reliance, emotional stability, aggressiveness, and objectivity may experience role conflict with his family members, who expect him to be "warm, nurturant, and emotional" (Bartolome 1972; Schein 1973; as cited by Greenhaus and Beutell 1985). More broadly, Burroughs and Rindfleisch (2002), through their analysis of survey data and an experimental study, find considerable support for the position that materialistic values conflict with more collective values, such as those values dealing with the family or religious belief. These researchers base their claims on the work of Shalom Schwartz (1994), which supposes that self-oriented values are inherently in opposition to other-oriented values. Schwartz posits, for example, an opposition between hedonism and achievement on the one hand—which use self-centered satisfaction as a motivation—and benevolence, conformity, and tradition on the other (Hitlin and Piliavin 2004, 363). For Burroughs and Rindfleisch, materialist values are self-oriented and are therefore posed in opposition to other-oriented values. On this point, they rely upon theoretical roots partially in cognitive dissonance theory. This position, compared to classical approaches to this particular cognitive opposition, focuses more on differing *objects* of valuation, since cognitive opposition arises due to the economy and society valuing incompatible objects of value, the self and material wealth on the one side versus 'the other' on the opposing side.

The two approaches to the 'money versus Mensch' incompatibility, based on differing *modes* and on differing *objects* of valuation, are reconcilable. A desire to maximize material acquisition or self-gain is best pursued by using rational calculation with a clear end, *terminal valuation*, and a selection of appropriate means, *instrumental valuation*, toward that end. In contrast, the pursuit of meaningful social interaction tends to forsake a calculative approach in lieu of valuing interaction and 'the other' according to an *intrinsic valuation*, in which "life itself is a cornerpiece" (Nye 1967).

This point is best illustrated through a thought experiment. In order to solidify the three valuation categories introduced above—terminal, instrumental, and intrinsic—and more importantly, to test their value against plausible and relevant scenarios, a series of ideal types representing the tools used for success within important roles can be introduced and classified according to the scheme. The purpose of this is to demonstrate how the differences between the modes of material valuation and social valuation, with these representing logical and cultural oppositions, open the way for cognitive dissonance.

Within individuals' actions in different everyday roles, such as father, worker, husband, friend, and investor, different modes of valuation are implied by the tools best used to fulfill these roles. Aside from the intent of performing a particular role, the tools required to accomplish that role will be illustrated through ideal types in order to show how the tools of success within different roles may conflict with one another. This focus on tools is chosen because of an issue mentioned earlier: an analysis of cognitive values does not reveal conflict until those values are transformed into behavior. The tools used to fulfill roles are likely to conflict with other competing tools because of behavioral time constraints.

To start with, ideal types representing the tools crucial for fulfilling successful roles in work are examined. For an individual involved in competitive capitalist business, *profit calculation* is a rational-instrumental value toward the terminal goal of profit. In addition, someone in a *supervisory role* over other people is expected to rationally calculate his/her employees' efficiencies as a means toward the higher goal of group efficiency or effectiveness. Similarly, a person in the role of *customer service* must instrumentally treat the customer well as a means to earning future business; again, this is a rational calculation. The successful worker must focus on *production*, and whether on a farm or in a factory, must also value his/her output of high quality materials or knowledge as the end of his/her efforts, an end toward which all means must be rationally aligned. Of course, by using the word "must," I am not implying that reality matches these prescriptions. Rather, I am indicating the prescriptions for certain types of behavior within certain roles, and how sometimes these prescriptions may conflict with one another.

In contrast, roles that are not directly work-related often must use a very different variety of tools. As a tool of parenthood, *motherly love* is an intuitive, uncalculated, intrinsic concern from the mother directed unconditionally toward her child/children. Similarly, *best friends* are those friends who employ a longstanding respect and emotional bond with one another; in contrast, the tool of *networking* rationally links the pursuer to the pursued, either through calculated assumptions of reciprocity or through direct usage. In another example, *religious belief* also employs intrinsic valuations; those who believe in god tend to value god or their spirituality based on intuitive expressions of faith.

When individuals act within work-related roles, success requires tools that use rational and means-ends valuations. When acting in non-work-related spheres, such as the family, within friendships, or as a person of faith, success requires tools that employ intuitive and intrinsic valuations.

The reader might recall the Burroughs and Rindfleisch hypothesis that materialistic and collectivist values ultimately conflict because they value different *objects*: the self versus the other. Surely self-oriented and/or materialist values do conflict with other-oriented values, but this conflict may be rather due to different valuation *modes* (intrinsic, instrumental, terminal) used within the materialist/ego-centric and social spheres. Work- and materially-oriented roles demand rational valuations, while social roles demand principally emotional and intuitive valuations. This is one fault-line, which when confronted with pressures such as limited time, may erupt into cognitive dissonance. As one of our Moscow informants noted, he has to "think differently" when at home and at work.

Of course, one might soundly object, noting that a degree of sociality is required in work, and a mode of rationality is often used in relationships; in reality, emotion and rationality are mixed. However, it is likely that, as our society understands it, the greatest success within the role of the mother is probably achieved through emotion, not rationality, and the greatest success as the CEO of a large firm is achieved more through calculation than through intimate relations; it is a matter of propensity. Furthermore, the cultural, subjective perception of these tools as prescriptions is already enough to create dissonance, whether or not these tools objectively lead to better outcomes. The mother's ideal tool is love, and the CEO's is to keep an eye on profits, or at least dividends, for the shareholders. This is not to say that the CEO, or a mother, do not possess other tools; it is rather that some of these are understood as primary compared to others.

Dissonance Resolution

Now that the nature of this dissonance between spheres has been discussed, it is time to return to those who experience it. When such dissonance between work and family, and work and morality indeed occurred with the economic transition among this study's informants, and continuously increased in intensity, how was it resolved?

Within the interviews, a devaluation of family in comparison to work appears to be the favored resolution of cognitive dissonance, one influenced by the domination of the new capitalist work culture in post-communist societies. Informants report feeling no choice but to adapt to the economic culture if they wish to become successful in the modern economy. L3, for example, sees material survival and looking after material conditions as a "natural" structure to which one must adapt. Similarly, L7 notes that struggling within the business implies a form of personality modification, causing one to become "grown into the business." L2 describes this process of adaptation:

> If you are in a position where you have responsibility, as an entrepreneur for example, then this conflict is given, because if you decided to do something like this, then you have to do it like this in order to get it working. Certainly you could organize things differently or so, I mean everyone does things as he thinks it is right and that is why I invested a lot of time that I didn't have at my disposal for other things.

This necessity of adapting to the economic culture, and the family-work conflicts that come with it, leads to a sense of fatalism in some of the informants. They learn to accept such conflicts as a natural part of life, as evidenced by the following passage:

> *(L3)*
>
> I just have mentioned that both my wife and I are conscious of the fact that there is potential for conflicts there. In any case there are things which are restricting the family life but we are both also very aware of the fact that it doesn't work in a different way.
>
> *(L2)*
>
> *Q:* How do you feel if conflicts like this occur?
>
> *A:* Well, that is not nice . . . that's for sure. But I also have to say that after the years you put up with it. You know it is not good, but it's like that and you think about it less than if you are confronted with it again now.

As evidenced in the above passage from L2, this sense of fatalism quickly leads to a blasé escapism, as he learns to "think about it less." Escapism is also quite evident among other informants. M11, for example, feels bad that he does not spend enough time with his child. How does he handle it? He answers, "The best way to deal with it is with the help of adrenaline. You sit behind the wheel at 200 km/h." After digging deeper, he reveals progression from fatalism to escapism to activity to frustration:

> I do not like the fact that the world is wrong, that I cannot shape it the way I want to. And I try to form it. . . . I can be depressed but this will not be for a long time and usually afterwards I start being very active.

Thereafter, his cycle loops back to the beginning, a sense of fatalism and demoralized acceptance that "absolute truth does not exist." Ultimately, his conflict is covered up by the motto of "continue swimming." He remains active in the economy, pursuing his career ambitions and economic success, de facto accepting fewer behavioral choices that benefit his family. Perhaps he (M11) will eventually opt toward the direction of M9, who from his similar position of escapism approaches nihilism as a solution to his dissonance. He declares that the solution is "very simple. Stop worrying and start to live."

While some, like M11, tell themselves that the conflict cannot be resolved, many rationalize their behavior as benefiting the family economically. Furthermore, many informants highlight that time can be spent with the family "later." For example, L9, who, as most of the young informants, has children, sees a strong focus on work *today* as a solution to his dissonance and plans to spend time with the family *later.* As goals for the future, when he has obtained his material security, he imagines his focus will be "family and *also, in general,* spare time. [emphasis added]" Family time becomes another free-time activity which he will pursue upon his early retirement if it materializes. Hopefully, it does not occupy the same mythical place as his youthful (as he recalls from 15 years ago) dream to move to his "own island" by age 40.

In the midst of these processes of resignation, fatalism, escapism, and postponement of the family in regard to work-family conflicts, work gradually becomes an end in itself. L7, for example, expresses a degree of dissonance between his work and family values. His solution to this, however, involves a further entrenchment of work, in his words, more work "rigor," with the intent that this would free more time for him at home:

Q: How can these conflicts be resolved?

A: (He laughs) . . . I don't know if Einstein can come with something. . .well, through further improvement, essentially of the main part of work, that is, the cycle of things here at work, and thereby getting more spare time for the family, for the club, for other activities .

Q: How could this improvement look in your opinion?

A: Rigor . . . that is really, but that can be brutal, also on colleagues. . . Documenting norms of effort in written way, checking the clock and stuff like that, well, checking the clock itself doesn't help much but there are systems of time recording and eventually also changing the personnel. I'd say, it is a functioning business. Yes, that's it basically . . . better self-organization, even higher discipline . . .

His solution is ironic. The same rational calculation which causes dissonance with his intrinsic social forms of valuation, is then posed as a solution to the dilemma. He has a faith that more rigorous, calculating, and efficient work may both solve his time-crunch with his family and liberate him from work-family dissonance, both of which were caused in the first place by rigorous, calculating, and efficient work.

Similarly, M10, a scientist, notes that he 'resolved' conflicts with this daughter by escaping into his work. He notes that "work saves" in an allusion to Weber's (2003) *Protestant Ethic*, but the meaning is inverted. It is as if Weber's fear has come true, that the disciplined and rational calculation of capitalism has liberated itself from its religious and moral roots and become an end in itself.

Nonetheless, this new work ethic *does* tend to free the informants from their dissonance. M1, for example, a workaholic yet carefree architect, also refers to "the protestant ethic" and the idea that "the job saves." He believes that if he works well now, the future will be "happy and joyful." Notice that the spiritual salvation motivating the classical protestant work ethic becomes replaced with a secular aim, a comfortable early retirement with lots of wealth, free time, hobbies, and the family. In the meantime, although he only takes, on average, three days off from work *per month*—he works most weekends—he experiences no qualms or dissonance related to his time away from the family:

Q: It happens sometimes that people, for example, have the value of family and from the other side is the value of work which takes all available time . . .

A: I say, I don't know it exactly as there's not any conflict here. We spend so much time together so it looks like it is enough. And it looks like we work also so long, so it is enough as well. Probably one should work less because I suspect that there could be a conflict and one should spend more time together. I don't know, I'm not sure. My daughter doesn't need it for sure that I stay home for the whole day. And I think, my wife doesn't need it either. Most probably we have very balanced situation.

By reducing his expectations and valuation of family time, he frees himself from the specter of cognitive dissonance.

Many of the other informants do not display cognitive dissonance. These fall into two categories. On the one hand, there are retired persons, who, since they do not work, have not had to adopt modern work values at odds with their own social values. For example, L4 notes, "since I am not working anymore, one is a little shielded from the problems of the working world." Many of these older informants note that they too would probably have adapted in the same way as the younger generation, even after negatively evaluating such behavior, if they would have been involved in the economy:

(L6)

Q: What do you think of people who behave 'capitalistically' (this is the informant's terminology) and use others?

A: I am refusing this, but I can understand them. Everybody has to see to making ends meet. That's how I see it as outsider, you know. If I was 20 years younger, or 25 or of your age, I would see things like they do. But I don't have to see it like them. I do understand them, but I refuse it. . . .But I think this probably has to do with my age, I'm standing outside. If not, I would possibly see things differently. I suppose my sons see it differently than I do. I don't know, but I assume it.

Another informant, M12, the only mother in the sample, also notes that her lack of involvement in society explains her lack of adaptation, in contrast to her son, the man who earlier mentioned he must "talk differently" with his mother.

On the other hand, the second group that experiences no dissonance consists of the young businessmen who have already devalued the family. Those for whom work is highly-valued, such as L11, may declare that "what is good for the business is good for the family," even though social concerns are irrelevant in work, because "work is for making money." In this case, the family becomes subjugated as an appendage to work, a mechanism for supporting the worker. In some cases, work is explicitly valued more highly than the family, as in this example from S13:

Q: You have to show your responsibility for your work, your family and your friends. There may exist conflicts among them and if you think more of one aspect, you may think less of the other. How do you handle it?

A: I will think more for the enterprise and less of the family. My wife supports my work very much. For example, she will understand me if I can't go home to have supper with them. I think if you have a sense of responsibility, some conflicts can be resolved successfully.

A pattern emerges. Those with no dissonance are either not working (the older generation) or not highly valuing the family if they are working (the younger businessmen). The two members of the older generation who *were* still working at the time of the interview, who founded new businesses within the new capitalist environment, were as dissonant as the younger generation members. When arranging the young informants, since the older informants exhibit very little dissonance, according to the amount of psychological discomfort shown when they speak of family and work in the interviews, the Leipzig informants show the most dissonance, followed by the Muscovites, and then by the Shanghai informants. Interestingly, this appears to be directly proportional to the informants' family valuations, their amount of focus on child socialization, and their respect of the older generation. The most-family oriented individuals tended to be the most psychologically conflicted as well.

What does this suggest in light of cognitive dissonance theory's means to resolve dissonance? If two cognitive elements (A and B) are in conflict, the most direct way to resolve this dissonance, aside from inventing a "cognitive overlap" between the elements—as already noted by those who adopt the 'work for the family' or two-stage 'work then family' strategies—is simply to either reduce the value of A or the value of B (Festinger 1957, 44–45). It is likely that the least conflicted informants are so because they have *already* devalued the family in comparison to work. The conflicted Leipzigers, in contrast, remain conflicted because they, more family-oriented, have *not yet* devalued the family as a response to overwhelming new cultural pressures to enhance the value of work. Congruent with this hypothesis is that the Leipzigers also still hold members of the older generation as role models and take an active role in socializing the next generation, two family-value support mechanisms which are comparably lacking among our less-conflicted, more work-centered informants. Furthermore, the most-conflicted Leipzig informants tend to be religious, another factor that would strengthen their family orientations. Finally, it is possible that the German welfare-state, the equivalent of which doesn't exist in Russia or China, has somewhat shielded the Leipzigers from the insecurities of the market culture which otherwise might have enhanced their work valuations at the expense of family; some conflicted Leipzig informants are willing to take the risk of quitting their elite jobs in order to find something new in order to relieve their dissonance, thanks to German unemployment insurance as a safety net.

In summary, it is striking that 'modern' values of materialism and individualism emerge partially as a result of patterned individual resolutions of dissonance. This pattern emerges in the favor of modern economic values and at the expense of traditional sociality because the economy presents itself as a "reality" to be adapted to, and one that is perceived as difficult to change, two factors demonstrating the firmness, or resistance to change of pro-economic value sets (Wicklund and Brehm 1976, 3). Along these lines, some scholars have noted that family boundaries are more "permeable" than work boundaries, meaning that work more often interferes with family life than vice versa (Frone, Russell, and Cooper 1992). This is likely because of the strong negative sanctions associated with violation of work role demands (Greenhaus and Beutell 1985, 77) in comparison to family roles, which is especially the case within the contemporary capitalist economy, where non-adaptation may threaten material survival.

INTERGENERATIONAL CHANGEOVER

The last of four value change mechanisms I review is intergenerational changeover. It contributes to individualization in four ways: through "fresh contact," the lack of role models in the older generation, the role of peers in the younger generation, and the breakdown of socialization values among those in the working generation.

"Fresh contact" is a term used by Karl Mannheim (1952) to indicate how the new generations interface with the society as they mature. Since a young generation encounters the new society without baggage from a prior socialization, its initial socialization occurs simultaneously with social change, and as a result its adaptation will be more full and direct than that of older generations. In contrast, older generations come into contact with social change through the lens of their own experienced pasts. Therefore, the unique social location of the youth tends to result in a value bias toward the more modern value set, in comparison to older generations. Important here is that this "fresh contact" effect is universal to all social changes, since the specific nature of a social change is irrelevant to it.

Another result of intergenerational changeover during a period of rapid social change is that the older generation ceases to provide adequate role models for the youth. This has been noted many times within these interview data.

To select a few examples, L9 does not mention his father as a role model, but rather selects his role models from the world of business. This trend of informants choosing famous role models and bypassing their mal-adapted parents is notable. Among one of the more bold informants, M11 mentions Julius Caesar as his role model and admires him because of his ability to manage and plan complex situations. This is a role model that the informant developed only later, because during the time of the early transformation, he said there was no one who served as a moral authority. This is common; most of the businessmen had no role models at all during the transformation years or chose them from popular culture or from their peers. It is very rare that they mention their own parents in this regard. This lack of role models of the younger generation exacerbates the fresh contact effect noted above, as it forces individuals to adapt either alone or with their peer groups, with thereby less reference to the previous cultural value stock and a bias toward the new system.

As a mirror image to the lack of parental role-models, those who experienced the transformation in their younger years had to look into themselves and to their peers in order to see proper and effective modes of adaptation, thereby ensuring the 'freshness' of their adaptive response. S11 describes this how this worked for him:

> I become sophisticated gradually, which has a loose connection with my parents. Other qualities of how to behave were learned from my colleagues and friends after stepping into society.

His process of 'sophistication' and 'self-improvement' is one that simultaneously involves estrangement from his parents and their values. If anyone, he looks to his peers for guidance, who have also severed their roots to the past.

Emphasized very strongly within the interviews, especially those within China and Russia, is the devaluation of socialization itself among the businessman-parents. In other words, despite their structural roles as parents, many opt for 'natural' or 'independent' socialization of their children by the society at large, while others are either confused about their roles as socializers or unable to implement the values that they envision as important because of completing claims within their lives of work and leisure. This withdrawal of parents from socialization ensures that the children will be affected by, at best, random and arbitrary socialization forces, or at worst, will become ideal pawns of economic, political, and cultural propaganda.

Many post-communist individuals do not realize their parental roles because they see the role of socialization as one that primarily belongs to the state, for example to the schools. During communist times, those families who exercised less than ideal parenting practices were nonetheless helped by the thick role that the state, for obvious reasons, played in the socialization of the youth. Uhlendorff (2000, 208) has noted this trend in Eastern Germany. After the collapse of the socialist schooling system, which involved state involvement in moral upbringing, many East German parents now are insecure about their socialization responsibilities. Nowadays even the more progressive families may have their values influenced in the direction of greater apathy toward socialization. As a result of each of these processes, individualization is enhanced as children learn to fend for themselves, and are socialized 'naturally and independently' according to the consumerist whims and designs of mass society.

In the previous chapter and in this one, I have outlined my research question, theoretical framing, and described the central mechanisms by which I have found the value change process to operate. Specifically, individual social values become latent because of concerted impacts of conscious adaptation, ideological conflict, cognitive dissonance, and intergenerational changeover. The next chapter, Chapter 4, will outline important contextual information specific to Chinese, Russian, and Eastern German economic and social transformations in recent years. I will highlight those profound differences in order to make their similar value tensions, outlined in Chapters 5 through 8, more striking.

4 The Chinese, Russian, and Eastern German Contexts

Social Values and Economic Change

Values do not frivolously shift only according to current whims or without influence from cultural, political, and economic histories. Path-dependency is an enduring aspect of cultural change (Inglehart and Baker, 2000). Especially important for unraveling the economy-sociality interface under investigation are the paths of the economic and social spheres in each country. Therefore, a history of family and intimate relations during recent socialism will be summarized for each country, followed by a short economic history of the transition period.[1] Thereafter, a collection of findings on intimate relations during the transformation period is provided. Intimate relationships typically receive short shrift compared to other transformation topics, such as economic and political institutions and elites. As a result, research on the valuation of intimacy in these three countries is rather scant. However, through various sources, we can begin to get a picture of what intimate relations were like before the transformation and how they might be changing. Throughout these country reports, I will also remark on other relevant factors—whether political, religious, or other—that may have obvious influences that affect social values in each society. After these individual reports, I will also compare countries across dimensions and demonstrate the value of the most-different case design.

CHINA

Family and Intimate Relations in Post-Mao 'Planned-Economic' China

Communist rule failed to completely dislodge the core of traditional Chinese values. This is despite the widespread social disruptions brought about by the Cultural Revolution, 1966–1976. One ethnographer notes, based on his 1986–87 fieldwork in a northern Chinese village in Hebei province, that, "it soon became clear to me that under Communist rule family life had hardly undergone total transformation" from traditional structures based on late imperial family organization (Cohen 2005, 77, 79). Of course, impacts on families could still be seen alongside these continuities, such as through major restrictions on family size as a result of the one-child policy (Cohen 2005, 80). This unique aspect of Chinese families should be highlighted, as the one-child policy means that each Chinese child receives the undivided attention of two parents and four grandparents; as a result, Chinese speak of growing egoism among the youth, as they develop into "little emperors."

Furthermore, while by 1986–87, property relations within families had maintained much of their traditional flavor (Cohen 2005, 81–84), marriage customs had changed, such as through the growing frequency of "love" marriages as opposed to arranged marriages (Cohen 2005, 86–87). Customs in family living arrangements had also changed, with brothers increasingly opting for obtaining their own homes rather than living together, and household sizes tending toward simplification and conjugalism. In addition, there is evidence of weakening inter-familial solidarity, parental authority, and de-hierarchization of the wife and mother-in-law relationship (Cohen 2005, 118, 145, 148–149). Cohen (2005, 148) also reports how this breakdown of traditional familial ties is exacerbated by "growing consumption-oriented individualism and the popular culture nourishing it." This later observation hints that the driving force behind these developments is not so much communist political rule as it is the rapid pro-capitalist changes that have come to light as a result of the open-door policy since 1978.

The Post-1978 Economic Transformation of China

Following the passing of the Mao era, Xiaoping Deng is credited with the major economic reforms that have taken place since 1978. Especially over the past 20 years, the scope of Chinese economic development has lifted hundreds of millions of people out of poverty, and thus, the Chinese economic 'success' contrasts sharply with Russia's 1990s collapse and Eastern Germany's stagnation during its transformation.

Xiaoping Deng and his supporters intended to utilize the economic powers of the market to further the material means for further socialist ends (Meisner 1999, 452). As a result of Deng's "open door" policies, China's foreign trade nearly doubled between 1978 and 1988, and it quadrupled again over the following six years (Meisner 1999, 457). Importantly, the transformation was also instituted at the level of the individual through slogans such as "getting rich is glorious," which were intended to blatantly twist socialist values in a new direction (Suliman 1998a, xv). All in all, China's economic transition is set apart from others by its caution and gradualism, symbolized by Xiaoping Deng's notion of "crossing the river by feeling for stones" (Suliman 1998b, 24). This caution is in stark contrast to Russia's "shock" transition and Eastern-Germany's colonial transition.

During the first economic transition phase, involving the de-collectivization of agriculture from 1979 to 1984, China decided to begin linking farmers' payments to their output, thereby canceling the system of the 'people's commune.' In addition, large amounts of grain were imported in order to lift the burden on farmers in regions with poor agricultural output. At the same time, however, the prices of agricultural products were increased in order to raise individual motivations to produce more. The maximum-allowed size of private plots was also increased in order to spur private farming (Meisner 1999, 454). As a result, agricultural output increased enough to nearly satisfy the domestic demand for food and clothing, while also raising rural incomes and consumption (Meisner 1999, 454; Shi 1998, 4).

The second stage of China's economic reforms, lasting from 1984 to 1992, involved a new focus on urban areas. The government aimed to reinvigorate medium and large-sized state-owned enterprises, both through increasing managerial responsibility over enterprise output and limiting direct government intervention, and later by the introduction of mechanisms to encourage competition between enterprises (Shi 1998, 6–7). Key to success was the promotion of enterprise profitability and the state's attempt to "smash the iron rice bowl," which promised lifetime job security, and to establish a flexible capitalist labor market through expanding contractual labor (Meisner 1999, 472; Werz 2007). An improvement of the market system was also implemented, with a partial reduction of the planning and pricing of goods and services. In addition, this second stage of reforms also included a reduction of state monopolies for purchasing commodities, the reform of tax systems so that state-owned enterprises paid taxes rather than delivering all their profits to their government, and a reform of the banking system (Shi 1998, 6–7). The urban reform program and the rural marketization reforms together brought in "spectacular industrial growth and intense social disruption" (Meisner 1999, 473).

The third and final stage of Chinese economic market reforms was initiated in 1992, as Chinese authorities embarked on accelerating the growth of their contradictory "socialist market economic system," embodied by Deng's famous remark, "It doesn't matter if a cat is black or white, so long as it catches mice." From this point on, the intent was to make the market economy the fundamental means of distributing resources. By 1994, market-determined pricing systems had been established, and commodity markets, financial markets, labor markets, real-estate markets, and technology and information markets had been developed (Shi 1998, 6–8; Werz 2007). In 1998, China continued with its long economic reforms by deepening its privatization efforts (Werz 2007).

The inclusion of China as a 'capitalist' case in this book can be justified by the character and extent of its economic reforms. Although it has a government that still calls itself communist, I consider its consumer sector to be more capitalist than Germany's, whose domestic economy is heavily taxed and regulated. Indeed the consumer sector is most relevant to me, as it strongly affects the everyday lives of most Chinese. Although its banking and construction sectors are still heavily state-influenced, the everyday urban

Chinese citizen works, shops, and lives in a world driven by market principles. Doubters are encouraged to take a trip to Nanjing Street in Shanghai or to Wangfujing in Beijing, where, if the bustle of economic life fails to convince them otherwise, efforts on paper would certainly fail as well.

China's economic rise has been steady and remarkable. In 2011, it overtook Japan in GDP, becoming the world's second largest economy. Projections in the same year predicted that it would overtake the United States in 2016. Such extreme growth has not been without social consequences. There is massive migration from rural to urban areas, wealth disparities, overinvestment in banking and construction sectors, powerful middle-classes, and increasingly vocal Netizens that cause many observers to question this trend's sustainability.

Post-Transformation Social Values in China

Recent studies have found that family values are under stress in modern China. Chu and Ju (1993a) found that by the early nineties, Chinese parents had become less authoritarian in their child-rearing practices and less controlling over negative behaviors, such as drinking and smoking. These authors also found indications of the fading of the traditional Chinese value of filial piety, especially among young parents (see also Yan 2003). A recent ethnographic study has explored the disappearance of traditional dinner table customs among young persons in Beijing. These have previously functioned according to filial piety and hierarchical principles (Jura 2004). However, in an opposing view, older research in 1997 suggested that, at least at that time in Baoding, a mid-sized city near Beijing, such a finding on the decay of family obligations was premature (Whyte 1997).

There is evidence of enhanced work values in modern China. Froese (2007), for example, in a comparative survey of elite university students in Shanghai, Tokyo, and Seoul, found that the Shanghai students were even more career- and occupation-oriented than their peers in Japan and South Korea. Froese (2007) also notes that an overall rise in work values has been observed over time in China.

In addition to an enhanced value of work, other scholars (Chu and Ju 1993b) report the expansion of material aspirations, even in the early years of the transition, and they point out the link between these untenable aspirations and the rising frequency of family disputes about money. These scholars allege that money plays a greater role in undermining social relationships which used to be based on shared traditional values and are now governed increasingly by instrumental concerns. Other scholars confirm the alleged shifts toward both individualistic and materialist values today in China (Lu and Miethe 2001, 109; Rojek 2001) as a result of the recent market transitions.

Related to the growing material aspirations, Smith (1991, 47) has also found that "the instrumentality of the *guanxi* system"[2] has become more important than ever in the time of the post-Mao reforms. This finding of heightened instrumentalization is also linked to other research citing the rising importance of friendship. For example, Chu and Ju (1993a, 102) find that urbanites in the early transition period in China were already developing more relations outside of the kinship structure. They state that this growth of social networks outside of traditional kinship has led to the erosion of the quality of social relations, putting these in "a state of ambiguity" (Chu and Ju 1993b). Indeed the decay of traditional authority and growth of friendship networks appear to be linked:

> Those heavily exposed to Western cultural influence not only tend to rely on friends rather than relatives for financial help, they are more inclined to argue with elders when they disagree. This behavioral pattern would not be tolerated under the kinship system. Interestingly, those individuals are far more likely to be consulted by others in the role as "opinion leaders," as if what they have learned from Western cultural programs in the mass media has some instrumental value in the new changing social and economic environment. (Chu and Ju 1993a, 102)

Each of these changes outlined above is in line with Xiaoying Wang's (2002) "post-communist personality," characterized by a lack of discipline, nihilism, expanded hedonism, and materialism among China's younger generations (See also Ci 1994, as cited by Wang). However, other scholars may doubt these findings, noting there was already evidence of many of these personality traits on the rise before the recent transformation, even since 1949, including declining dependency, conformity, modesty, self-suppression, parent-centeredness, and self-constraint, together with rising values of autonomy, individual achievement, and hedonism (Smith 1991, 41). Furthermore, Tsai has pointed out that, despite their high degree of political connectedness, media consumption, and economic involvement, China's entrepreneurs still trust their family members and friends most (Tsai 2007, 89).

Yet most recent indications claim the rise of individualization in China, even since the 1970s, as a result of the "untying" of peasants from the bounds of the planned-economic system and the simultaneous expansion of consumer culture (Yan 2009; Hansen and Svarverud 2010). Some have pointed to this cultural shift as responsible for undermining the subjective well-being of Chinese citizens (Brockmann et al. 2009).

Traditional Chinese values can be broadly depicted as Confucian: in short—respect oriented, familial, partriarchical (Swader and Yuan 2010). During its transformation, however, the Chinese state aggressively promoted materialist values through propaganda. In the meanwhile, observations of contemporary Chinese cities and rates of deviance point to the success of their campaign, as traditional values apparently hold somewhat less sway. Even the government points to their dissolution as one of the causes of juvenile delinquency (see Wong 2004), and has, as of late, reinstituted the teaching of Confucianism within public schools (Carr 2006; Fan 2010). It has even moved to protect and promote Confucian shrines in an effort to 'return' to this traditional core.

RUSSIA

Family and Intimate Relations in Late Soviet Russia[3]

How could one characterize Soviet Russian families? On one hand, the Soviet state was highly anti-social and espoused policies that were destructive for families. Shlapentokh (1991) describes how the Russian family in Stalinist times lived under three immense pressures. First, state ideology, not the family, was the chief determinant of social values, and these values both emphasized public life over private life and work over family. Second, the Soviet state before and through Stalin's reign existed in conditions of stark material poverty. According to Shlapentokh (1991), this poverty exacerbated the low-priority of family life because the poor living conditions within Soviet homes and communal apartments of that era provided little incentive to spend time with the family within them. The third and most direct pressure exacted by the Soviet state against the stability of families was that it pitted family members against one another in its mechanisms of repression. Stalinist intelligence services set children against parents, wives against husbands, and neighbors against each other by encouraging them to spy on one another. This sort of treachery, woven into every-day life by the state made family life tense (Shlapentokh 1991). These pressures on the family were apparently great because people reportedly "devoted little time and energy to their families" (Shlapentokh 1991, 267). Another researcher, Malysheva (1992), has dubbed the Soviet person of this era a human being "completely deprived of its social roots."

On the other hand, the Soviet family became a sanctuary from the state, a place where state ideology could not intrude. Under the strain of the above pressures, family members relied more upon one another. As Shlapentokh (1991, 267) puts it, "when faced with the Stalinist leviathan, the Soviet people turned to their families for protection against the horrors of everyday life." Similarly, Malysheva (1992) called family "the only place of expression and resistance in a spiritual vacuum." Yet the pressures that affected Russian families especially in Stalin's time weakened considerably at the latter end of Soviet rule, to the benefit of the family. The ideological collapse entailing the failure of communist ideals and the declining authority of the state, the improvement in living conditions, and the decline of repression allowed family life to "re-emerge" (Shlapentokh 1991, 269). Kupferberg (1999), in speaking of this "overdeveloped private sphere" across the socialist world remarks that:

> People stuck together, they helped each other. They had to, there was no one else to lean on. Not only for purely materialistic reasons, I believe, although this of course also played some role, but for emotional reasons as well (in real life these two motives were hopelessly intertwined). Psychologically it is impossible to live in a society where no one trusts anybody. (22–23)

This strengthened private sphere is typically seen as a direct response to a lack of trust between public institutions and their citizens. Typical of a Western skepticism—stemming from individualized culture—of intimate relations, yet also revealing something of the lost private sphere of Soviet times, is Kupferberg's (1999) warning:

> Now such clinging to personal relations should not be romanticized. The need for human warmth and mutual trust was real enough, but the overdevelopment of the private sphere as the haven of this feeling was an **abnormal** phenomenon. We know of similar tendencies in the Southern part of Europe which are more 'familistic' in their institutionalized value structure than further north, but the overdevelopment of the private sphere in the communist countries was something unique, something **unheard of**. (23; emphasis added)

The private sphere, according to the above scholar (Kupferberg 1999, 23), who spent time in the Soviet Union starting in 1978, "meant much more for the Eastern Europeans than for any Western European nation, including the Italians." Kupferberg reveals much about the private sphere in the Soviet Union, where primary relations "became a value in themselves, the highest value. The tendency was to make a cult of the private sphere, to live for it and in it and forget about the rest" (Kupferberg 1999, 23–24).

This post-Stalin re-emergence of the importance of Soviet family life was apparently short-lived, for signs of family decay and of a greater Russian social deterioration were obvious by the late 1980s. Descriptions of Russian families in the eighties and in the years afterwards often use the mantra of "demoralization" (Malysheva 1992; Shlapentokh 1991). This demoralization did not reach a critical mass until it was catalyzed by the total loss of popular trust in socialist reality and ideology with glasnost and perestroika in the 1980s. By the moment of the collapse of the USSR, the decline of the family was fully visible. For example, in 1991, Shlapentokh (1991) called the demoralization of Soviet society and the erosion of social bonds the main threat to the Russian family. He notes that many Soviet writers of this period decried the "loss of prestige of family in society," "the devaluation of the family," and "the collapse of the family" (Shlapentokh 1991, 272). Malysheva (1992) also argued during this period that the demoralization of society was causing the demoralization of the family and would lead to a subsequent rise in crime, alcohol consumption, drug use, prostitution, runaways, and divorce rates.

The Post-1990 Economic Transformation of Russia

Russia's initial transformation from a centrally planned to a market economy entailed at least five significant aspects. Ironically, the architects of this transformation called it 'shock therapy.' These reforms initially caused a fall in living standards of nearly all parts of the population (Komozin 1993).

First, in January 1992, prices were freed from their artificial fixed levels, causing massive inflation. Second, the government had to balance its budget. It instituted an austerity plan which made large cuts to almost all public welfare programs, such as health, education, pensions, and social services (Malysheva 1992). Third, the Ruble was opened up to international trade, and its drop in value made it even harder for Russians to deal with rising prices. Fourth, privatization was implemented. What was supposed to be a transfer of property to workers and managers instead became a sale of state property to government cronies at well-below market prices (Koliandre 2001). This "sale of the century" (Freeland 2000) created a new class of Russian oligarchs who became rich by stripping state enterprises of their assets, resulting in a loss of enterprise efficiency (Stiglitz 2002, 144). Fifth, the inefficient Soviet industrial economy was subjected to market forces with paralyzing consequences. Eighty percent of the Soviet economy fell somewhere within the military industrial complex. The subjection of these industries to market pressures caused a partial industrial collapse. In 1992, the country's GDP decreased by 14.5 percent from the previous year. In 1993, the decrease was 8.7 percent, and in 1994, 12.7 percent. The decline of the rate of industrial production was even greater: 18 percent in 1992, 14 percent in 1993, and 21 percent in 1994 (Polozhevets 2001). The human result of these GDP downturns was, of course, unemployment.

To make matters worse, in addition to the shock therapy characterizing Russia's initial market transformation, more economic trouble occurred in 1998. Partially because of the Asian crisis of 1997, international speculation, and falling oil prices, Russia's currency collapsed in August of 1998. The ruble lost 75 percent of its value almost instantly, and as a result, the government defaulted on its foreign debt. In addition, people's purchasing power evaporated, wiping out the emerging Russian middle class, and this problem was compounded by the collapse of businesses and high unemployment. Banks also failed during this time, as the Russian stock market, where the main index had grown five times larger between 1995 and 1997, lost 93 percent of its value in half a year (Meier 1999; Polozhevets 2001).

After the 1998 crisis, the Russian economy recovered and was removed from the list of 'hyper-inflationary' economies (International Bank of St. Petersburg 2002). It was hit by another crisis in 2008, and has now recovered again, albeit twice as slowly (Kramer 2012). Nonetheless it is experiencing economic growth, largely thanks to its huge energy sector.

Post-Transformation Social Values in Russia

Given the consensus that family decay had already begun by the moment of the Soviet collapse and that radical changes were brought about by the decade of economic collapse and recovery which followed, it is fair to ask how the Russian family might have fared during this roller-coaster ride after the collapse of socialism.

There is a small literature indicating the decay of family life in Russia. On the one hand there is much evidence for declining fertility and rising divorce rates (Vannoy et al. 1999), out of wedlock births, and single parent households (Klugman and Motivans 2001). On the other hand, Russians report that the quality of their existing family relationships has deteriorated as well (for the St. Petersburg case, see Swader 2007).

Regarding changing demographic trends, partially because of rampant consumerism and the resulting drive of many to accumulate wealth and material goods, Shlapentokh (1991) argues that fewer people seek marriage in Russia. This negative effect of consumerism on the family formation process implies a deterioration of the value of social relationships compared to individual economic goals. Here, there is an alleged shift toward individualistic and materialist values (Shlapentokh 1991; Swader 2007). On materialism, observers note the growth of consumption, luxury lust, and money's place in terms of imbuing power in modern Russia (Neidhart 2003; see also Humphrey's 2002 account of "New Russians"). Neidhart (2003, 203) explains how "the collapse of the command economy has transformed the *homo-sovieticus* into a *homo-economicus*. The Russian's life has become immensely demanding- full of choices, insecurities, traps, and temptations."

Another reason for an apparent decay in family life is the widespread demoralization alluded to above. For example, entrepreneurs and managers may have converted their values from collectivism to individualism (Grancelli 2002, 109) because they identified the previous system as one of corruption (Kharkordia 1994, 423, cited by Grancelli 2002). Likewise, Kupferberg (1999, 29) refers to a "moral rot" across Eastern Europe as a whole during the transition years but is careful to note the roots of this malaise within the previous communist regime. Neidhart (2003) is less subtle on the demoralization question, noting the rise of the "anything goes" mentality, captured vividly in his book by the title of Chapter 9: "Mafiosi and Prostitutes: The New Role Models."

In recent years, perhaps to counter opposing cultural messages, the Russian state has disseminated pro-family propaganda, intended to promote fertility. Public posters in the subway system proclaimed "Love to the Motherland begins in the family" or "Family—one of nature's greatest wonders." Also, in 2007, Putin began a program to provide cash incentives to mothers for giving birth, and this has been credited as successful in contributing to a rise in Russia's birth rate (Haub 2011), albeit the change worked through affecting the cost-benefit nexus rather than through modifying individuals' intimate valuations of the family.

EASTERN GERMANY[4]

Family and Intimate Relations in the GDR

Mayer (2006, 16) notes two common observations about socialist-era families in East Germany. First the close family served as a counterweight against state and party control in socialist times. Second, families were also an important resource for the acquisition of scarce goods and services during those times. His expectation is that, since families would be less directly affected by institutional disjuncture, they would remain useful during post-communist times. In contrast, Diewald and Lüdicke (2006) also question the fate of social networks due to their changing functions during the transformation years and come up with a different response. They note that East Germany was less individualized than western societies because of material shortages and the comprehensive control exercised by the state over public life; thereby, they describe GDR social networks as close-knit communities formed on the basis of ascribed characteristics, rather than being based on choice and achievement (Diewald and Lüdicke 2006, 191). Thereby, the authors expect the East German networks to become liberated and modern, that is 'individualized' with the transformation.

Another observation concurring with the existence of strong intimate networks in the GDR is that private social relations during the post-1971 Honecker era were able to develop into an intimate "social niche," so long as people toed the ideological line in public (Uhlendorff 2003, 219). Grix (2003, 270) describes these "social niches" in more depth, noting they were made up of face-to-face primary groups: "The society of niches, which embodied the ultimate in retreatism from state politics, was made up of atomized individuals who had close, trusting relations with family members, relatives, friends, work colleagues and other acquaintances," and this society functioned "as a safety-valve with the majority of east Germans using their niches to escape and retreat from the tedious party propaganda and over-politicized daily life of communist society to pursue activities that made their lives more bearable." This retreatism, comments Grix (2003, 271), "actually encouraged the creation of both strong informal social networks built around families, friends, acquaintances and so forth, on the one hand, and networks and patron-client connections in the barter economy, on the other, through which scarce goods/

services could be procured." In a balanced fashion, Grix attributes the close social relations during GDR times not only to barter networks, but also to their being built around social motives themselves, not merely instrumental ones. Diewald describes GDR social networks according to the two above concepts, the "niche" and "Vitamin B" ("B" for *Beziehungen*, or "connections"), in addition to the label of "collective," which he describes as implying not only social control, but also, at the personal level, warmth, understanding, dependability, solidarity, and humanity (Diewald 1995).

It has been alleged that the combination of a malfunctioning economy and the suppression by the police state of intimate private lives caused a sharp distinction between close trustful relationships and weak instrumental ties (Völker and Flap 2001, as cited by Diewald and Lüdicke 2006). A competing hypothesis, however, emphasizes a more encompassing community orientation comprised of solidarity and emotional warmth (Schlegelmilch 1995, cited by Diewald and Luedicke 2006, 194). This is confirmed by evidence showing that, despite the socialist state's use of the firm as a site for control of the population, East Germans were more likely to search for collectivity and camaraderie in the workplace, *even through* discussing sensitive personal and political issues (Diewald and Lüdicke 2006, 194). These data suggest that the East Germans were less individualized, in the sense that they were more likely to turn to their parents, friends and colleagues for support in personally difficult situations; this is interpreted as a higher willingness to help among social ties (Diewald and Lüdicke 2006, 197). The same authors conclude that, "this again underpins the argument of a more widespread community orientation supported by the more comprehensive pattern of the employee's social integration at the workplace in the GDR" (Diewald and Lüdicke 2006, 196). They explained this heightened valuation of personal ties at work as due to values of communal work, long working hours, the multifaceted role of the firms, the low levels of status and career competition, low pressure to work harder, and a lack of workplace insecurity. Meanwhile, strong supportive family relationships within the GDR reflected the higher frequency of familial living arrangements, more time spent within partnerships and families with children, a narrower generational gap, and fewer alternatives to become acquainted with others outside official channels (Diewald and Lüdicke 2006, 198).

Regarding respect of elders, it has also been argued that East Germans, during GDR years, were more likely to speak to their parents about personal difficulties than West Germans. This is said to be due to the fact that "advice from older people gets less devalued than in faster changing societies," and this is "caused by the slower pace of social change and individualization in the GDR" (Diewald and Lüdicke 2006, 198). This information suggests that strong family orientations in Eastern Germany became nested during socialist times. The strength of GDR family values in contrast to weaker valuations of work is well-documented (Huinink and Wagner 1995, 145).

Apparently, however, within the 1980s, there were already signs within Eastern Germany of a bourgeoning individualism, perhaps spurred by growing material resentment. In 1984, Ramet remarked:

> Ironically, individualism has never flourished in Eastern Germany as much as today, whether one looks to the withdrawal and consumerism of the working and middle classes, or to the rejectionism and headlong assertive individualism of those youths caught up in the East German rock scene. (1984, 89)

Meulemann's (1996, 131–132) data support Ramet and demonstrate an early and rapid growth in independence for children as a goal of parental upbringing between the years of 1967 and 1990.

The Post-1989 Economic Transformation of East Germany

Economic and monetary union between the two Germanys occurred on 1 July 1990, while political union was made official on 3 October 1990. The East German transformation was unique from other post-communist states in that it amounted to "unification through system transfer," whereby the institutions from the West were transferred to the East, with the expectation of achieving quick restabilization (Flockton, Kolinsky, and Pritchard 2000, 3). This advantage of the GDR's transformation, compared to others, was that the others "had to repair their sinking ships while still at sea, whereas the GDR was retrofitted in the FRG dry dock" (Offe 1997, 151). The psychic results of the unification upon East Germans however, were less successful than this "refitting" suggests. One group of researchers noted "A decade on, there is no east German sense of **Wir sind wieder wer**—'we are somebody again'—which had buoyed west Germans in the mid-1950s in their bid for normalization" (Flockton, Kolinsky, and Pritchard 2000, 4; emphasis in original).

This perhaps resulted from the limited ability of the colonized to take part in the reformation of their own society (Offe 1997, 151–152).

Yet the starting point for many describing the East German post-socialist transition, as Goedick (2006) noted, is nonetheless that of a 'friendly takeover.' This distinguishes the East German transformation from nearly every other post-communist country. Eastern Germany's *Sonderweg* ('special path') implies transformation and integration at the same time (Kupferberg 1999, 129), although the manner in which it occurred is less ideal than the name might make it sound. For instance, despite the fact that Article 146 of the West German Constitution suggested the adoption of a new constitution upon unification, the ruling parties decided instead to transfer the West German institutions and legal structures directly to the east (Goedicke 2006, 45). As a result, East Germany did not follow the typical neo-liberal prescription of release of currency controls and removing state subsidies (since huge subsidies were given by the West), and many East Germans experienced alienation and frustration at the 'Machiavellian' manner in which the transformation was imposed upon them by West Germans (Goedicke 2006, 63–64). This is a likely cause for a uniquely Eastern German demoralization, that of the 'colonized' as opposed to that of the 'vanquished' in Russia.[5] This demoralization was heightened by a sense of having been tricked by the previous regime. Kupferberg describes how when East Germans came to "get a look" at material life in the West, they realized they had been fooled by socialist claims of superiority (Kupferberg 1999, 164)

Already by the 1980s, there was an economic crisis in the GDR, for reasons such as having to supply the USSR with raw materials, high consumption and low economic performance, and excessive welfare entitlements (Mayer 2006, 32). Upon reunification, the steps of reforming this 'failed' economy, in order to match it to the West German model, were three-fold: macroeconomic stabilization, institutional reform, and privatization (Goedicke 2006, 46).

Central control of prices was abolished in East Germany in the spring of 1990. In July of that same year, the monetary and economic union of the two Germany's became activated, thus introducing the Deutsche Mark to the east. Bad for the competitiveness of Eastern enterprises but good for E. German consumers was the abnormally high exchange rate of GDR marks for the Deutsche Mark, effectively revaluating the East German currency upwards by 300 to 400 percent, thus functioning to sever trade with the GDR's former partners (Goedicke 2006, 46) and allowing Eastern Germans to buy more West German products.

By 1994, the work of the German privatization organization, the *Treuhand*, was completed. In all, it had privatized 53 percent of East German firms, while 13 percent were reprivatized, 30 percent were liquidated, and the rest were transformed into other types of ownership. Its deficit as a result of this work was 230 billion Deutsche Mark and many jobs (Goedicke 2006, 49, as per Bruecker 1995b, 326).

Remarkable in the East German case was the huge influx of funding it received from its West German benefactor. One estimate is that, between 1990 and 2003, 980 billion Euros in public resources were transferred from the West to the East. No other post-socialist society received nearly as much external support in its transition (Sachverständigenrat 2004, 466, cited by Goedicke 2006, 51).

Despite some of the rosy outlines of this economic story, there is also a darker side. The former East German 'employment society' was destroyed, with nearly 90 percent of workplaces being eradicated in industries such as textiles and clothing, 80 percent were destroyed in agriculture, and over 50 percent disappeared in industry. In the early 1990s, Eastern German unemployment was near 30 percent, while, as of 2000, 57 percent of those aged 18 to 59 had been unemployed at least once since 1990 (Dennis 2000, 96–97). Overall, East Germany's shock therapy reduced its labor force by a third (Mayer 2006, 9). One of the greatest populations affected by the unemployment of the *Wende* was that of women, of whom 82 percent worked in the East in 1990, compared with only 56 percent in the West in 1989 (Dennis 2000, 99). The mind-set of the East Germans, after losing the previous state-sponsored security, and now being subjected to market forces, was as "being thrown into the cold water" (Eppelmann 1993, as cited by Kupferberg 1999).

The Eastern German communist state had shielded East Germans from the uncertainties of modern society, so that unification meant the incorporation of a great deal of modern risk, in the guise of unemployment, for example. This riskiness is one their Western counterparts had already experienced for a much longer period and is a great departure from the "employment society" of the former GDR (Flockton, Kolinsky and Pritchard 2000, 5–7). Thereby, the sudden collapse of the GDR regime came as quite a shock, in particular since it was unique in providing a quite high socialist standard of living (Kupferberg 1999, 3).

The Eastern German economy today is still in a rough condition. It has problems with productivity levels, huge public debts, and poor domestic demand caused by enduring mass unemployment (Goedicke 2006). It continuously suffers from its lack of economic resources and its thorough deindustrialization as a result of economic reforms (Goedicke 2006, 64).

Post-Transformation Social Values in Eastern Germany

In addressing social values in post-unification Eastern Germany, some observers note the remarkable continuity in values between the two eras. Kupferberg, for example, says Eastern Germany still possesses the values of an older Germany, as the values of modesty (*Bescheidenheit*), mutual help ethics toward neighbors, and collectivist and egalitarian ideals still prevail. In contrast, this lifestyle no longer exists in Western Germany (Kupferberg 1999, 180). Nonetheless, he notes that East Germans had difficulties in adjusting and experienced "culture shock" during the transformation period, likely because they still "have one foot in the previous system" (Kupferberg 1999, 131, 183).

The clash between old and new values in Eastern Germany is made clear by phrases such as "a wall in the head," the "battle for moral supremacy between two collective identities," talk of the "slowness of Eastern adjustment to Western behavioral patterns," worries of "anomie" in East Germany, and talk of the "lost generation of youngsters" (Hessel et al. 1997, cited by Flockton, Kolinsky and Pritchard 2000, 17). Evidence of a different self-perception is that, in establishing the social identity of the East Germans near the transition time, a 1992 poll demonstrates that "East Germans regard themselves as more friendly toward children, more modest and less greedy than the self-confident and arrogant westerners" (Dennis 2000, 93).

Research indicates an individualization of families in Eastern Germany, in that the population, upon transition, enacted a drastic postponement of first childbirth due to increased labor market options, educational participation, and stronger career options (Huinink and Kreyenfeld 2006, 188–189). On the other hand, family relations between parents and children have remained relatively stable in Eastern Germany after the transition (Diewald et al. 1995, 337; Diewald and Lüdicke 2006, 202). It is also alleged that close families became closer and more important for personal recognition and informational purposes. In this hypothesis, close relations before 1989 served as a coping resource after 1989 (Diewald and Lüdicke 2006, 199, 205). On the other hand, relations with siblings and more distant relatives allegedly weakened (Diewald et al. 1995, 337). Interestingly, family relationship health tends to be negatively correlated with work, as Diewald and Luedicke (2006, 206, 209) found that emotional closeness in relations with children *increased* for the unemployed and downwardly mobile (for similar finding in St. Petersburg, see Swader 2007). In contrast, for siblings and extended family relations, there was a high risk of diminishing emotional closeness for the upwardly mobile, which the authors interpreted as due to diverging life paths (Diewald and Lüdicke 2006, 206–210). However, this may equally be due to the growing materialist and individualist values more directly possessed by the upwardly mobile, which in turn lead to the devaluation of family.

Certain sources predicted that friendship networks should widen as a result of transformation (Diewald and Lüdicke 2006, 199). Yet measurements indicate a deterioration in relationships with friends and acquaintances as well between 1989 and 1993 (Diewald et al. 1995, 337; Diewald and Lüdicke 2006, 202). In addition, the previously strong workplace relationships enjoyed by GDR citizens were apparently devastated because of the disappearance of low competition and high job security (Diewald et al. 1995, 337; Diewald and Lüdicke 2006, 213). Both of these, the deterioration of workplace and of friendship networks were found to be most exaggerated among the older cohorts. Other studies point out that the shrinking of friendship and workplace ties occurred mostly because people mostly "stuck to their old relationships with people they had long known and trusted" (Völker and Flap 1995, 105, as cited by Diewald and Lüdicke 2006).

Shifts toward individualistic and materialist values are indicated today in Eastern Germany (Keddi et al. 2003; Uhlendorff 2003). Meanwhile, other research (cited by Huinink and Kreyenfeld 2006, 175) suggests that, after unification, new leisure and consumption options, supply of hedonistic fulfillment (Linde 1984), and the overall "increase in choice" (Zimmermann

1989) may have played a role in the postponement of family formation (Beck-Gernsheim 1997; Münz and Ulrich 1995; Sobotka, Zeman, and Kantorova 2003), amounting to diminished family values as a result of expanded materialism and consumerism.

In relation to expanded materialist values, Kupferberg has noted the growth in consumerism and private consumption ideals in Eastern Germany after the transformation (Kupferberg 1999, 5). Uhlendorff (2003, 216) reports similar findings using an example from one of his informants: "Mr. B. had to get used to his son's requests concerning his clothing—which has to be produced by certain companies: 'It is no longer enough to have a good pair of trainers. It has to be a leading brand.' His son does not want to wear other things any more." 'Mr. B' then laments "To struggle against material desires, to take up arms against them, does not get you anywhere. You can't change the situation by changing the individual, you have to change the outside conditions." This informant had also experienced the lack of respect the youth have for the older generation:

> His son reproaches him some time ago: "If you had learned something useful, you wouldn't be in this situation now." Mr. B. had put his hands in his pockets and said: "Son, you just can't understand this yet." (Uhlendorff 2003, 217)

Uhlendorff (2003, 218) also demonstrates how increased unemployment threats and work pressures leave less time for focusing on family and education. He further notes how teacher-student relationships were more intimate during GDR times (Uhlendorff 2003, 218). Other research has noted stricter moral sentiments and greater moral conformity in the East compared to the West, as measured by the recognition of institutions of marriage and family and of recognition of moral restrictions; important is that the East has seen a demoralization between 1990 and 1995 in the sense that its levels of morality have regressed toward those of the West because such morality is no longer useful in the new society (Meulemann 1996, 364; Meulemann 1998).

One reason for this moral decline and associated heightened individualism is that both may have served as a form of risk management, a career planning strategy; one that results, however, in a "reduced commitment to marriage based families and a postponement (or even avoidance) of child bearing" (Flockton, Kolinsky, and Pritchard 2000, 6). Kupferberg describes the result of this transformation of intimate relationships:

> The transition to a Western society is a transition to a society where most social relations are treated like contracts. . . . Becoming accustomed to this new way of doing things can be extremely exhausting.

> Basically it is a learning process, often a very tough one, and there is little you, as my friend or my mother, can do to help me. I have to do it on my own. This is the background to the state of coma within personal relations I have sensed lately (particularly in East Germany, where the transformation process has been most dramatic) (Kupferberg 1999, 25).

As a result, the previous "speech communities" that were encapsulated inside the private sphere have ceased to function, and "the citizens have yet to produce or become accustomed to speech communities of a different kind, focused around instrumental, task-oriented issues, rather than heavily emotional ones, based exclusively on trust." (Kupferberg 1999, 25–26)

COMPARING SOCIETIES

Besides economic development, there are, of course, many other potential causes of individualization, such as the degrees of urbanization, industrialization, and technological development. In addition, states attempt to influence values through their ideologies and supporting policies, such as China's 'one-child policy' or the values of the pro-family German welfare state. Or perhaps the styles and speeds of economic transformation themselves have led to changing values. Religions too are major sources of values and potentially may also have substantially impacted social values during the transformation era. In addition, the economic conditions during transformation may be a critical factor of difference. I control for each of these factors in that my three cases differ across them. As a result, any finding of common values across cases may be due to the only factor that is similar across cases, the fact of free-market economic transformation. Key differences between cases may be observed within Table A.1 in Appendix A.

The formidable differences in culture and history also highlight that this is indeed a most-different case design. East Germany was the most modernized of the three countries, riding the wave of European technological, bureaucratic, and rational development until it's culmination in the horror of WWII. After the war, East Germany became one of the most advanced of the USSR's satellite states. Compared to East Germany, Russia was not as modernized regarding the developments of its family, philosophical, and industrial worlds, especially considering its large underdeveloped rural regions. I consider it, at the time of the transformation, less individualized than East Germany, especially because of its sizable rural population. Chinese 'progress' toward modernity was further behind the other two cases. With its huge rural populations and only recent, albeit rapid, industrialization, modernization's influence on China has come later than in East Germany or Russia. Moreover, China experienced the disruptive Cultural Revolution immediately before its economic transformation, whereas the last large scale state-induced family disruptions in Russia were during the Stalin years, and in East Germany as late as the 1980s, as a result of mass Stasi infiltration into society. Thus, the large variation in levels of development and individualization in my three cases also would be unable to explain a common individualization of values during the transformation period.

The cases also differ in terms of the state responses to changing values. China actively encouraged value transformation through slogans such as "get rich first" and "become the first one million yuan family." Russia's response throughout the 1990s, due to the complete collapse of previous state institutions and ideological uncertainty, was largely to do nothing in terms of values promotion, and the German state contributed throughout the transformation period through its regular family-work harmony ideology, typical of the social-welfare state. Thus, with three very different state responses to the values issue, one would expect that any similarity between cases is due to, not state ideology, but rather to something else: the economic structure.

The three cases differ in their economic transformations. Russia's economic shock and collapse of the 1990s contrasts sharply with China's slow steady growth with no collapse. The East German model was different still, with a quick industrial collapse and economic restructuring under enormous West German funding and 'expertise,' thus leading to some economic growth amid massive unemployment. These three styles of transformation, shock, slow and steady, and colonial, would unlikely lead to the same value transformation, unless it was not the *style* of economic transformation at all which mattered so much, but rather the *fact* of economic transformation from planned- to market-economic culture.

Religion and spirituality is another major sphere of variation between my cases. While considerably less religious than West Germany (because of its atheist socialist past) remnants of Christianity, both Catholicism and Protestantism had survived the communist regime in East Germany until this day. The Soviets were even more effective at eradicating religion in Russia, although Russian Orthodoxy has seen a strong resurgence after the transformation, albeit perhaps a somewhat superficial one in the large cities, except among the elderly. Finally, China, without a unifying religion, and even the remnants of Confucianism under assault throughout much of the Communist Party's reign, is largely atheist, although some note the functional equivalence of nationalism in providing a group identity, although not individual morals, to the Chinese people. Therefore, any similarity in values between the three countries could not be due to a common religious background.

Thus, because of the above-noted differences between the cases, it will be assumed that similarities in value change between the three cases are due to their *common* feature, that is the transformation from a centrally-planned economy to a market-economy. Furthermore, when differences in value changes between the cases are discovered, the causes will be sought among the factors mentioned above and from the specificity of the particular case.

By now, I am ready to describe the cross-country findings in value tensions by theme. The next section, Chapter 5, outlines the emergent importance of the values of individualism, ambitiousness, and work.

5 Individualism, Ambition, and Work

S13, let's call him Yang, is a 40-year-old married Shanghai man with a 9-year-old son. He is president of a state-run, yet very much profit-oriented, pharmaceuticals company. His father, S14, here known as Ye Pin, is preparing to retire. Despite their father-son connection, their values have little in common.

While the elder Ye Pin attaches "great importance to the family," his son Yang, when pressed, says he "think[s] more for the enterprise and less of the family." The elder puts family first, and the younger puts family second. This traditional Chinese value of the strong role of the family seems to have missed Yang. The same can be said for the duty of respecting elders, spoken of by Ye Pin but not by his son. In fact, Yang says he had no role models during the transition era, unless you count some famous entrepreneurs he saw interviewed on television.

However, it is a mistake to say that Yang is in every way more 'modern,' while Ye Pin, the father, is simply more 'traditional.' In terms of gender views, for example, their values are the opposite of what one might expect. Ye Pin, the elder, says that family-work responsibilities are balanced between him and his wife, while Yang believes in splitting responsibilities, with his wife being expected to accept that he has to work.

Differences between Yang and his father extend beyond work and family. Ye Pin possesses the traditional Chinese value of thrift and believes strongly in saving money and not being wasteful. Yang also speaks highly of thrift, but he must focus on cultivating his image for his work, which means he is more of a consumer than his father, since he is expected to wear nice suits and drive a nice car.

Finally, Ye Pin's belief that his generation was selfless stands in stark contrast to Yang, who does not speak about helping others outside of his own family. Even for his own family, his contribution, as he sees it, is primarily a material one. His bigger motivation for work has been own ambition for personal achievement.

Max Weber (2003) wrote that hard work, along with a drive to accumulate material wealth, are central to a functioning capitalist system. Without the drive to accumulate profit or the work required to see it fulfilled, it is hard to imagine capitalism at all. Nonetheless the nature of 'hard work' today has changed dramatically since Weber's time. Weber's capitalists were humble; they worked as an offshoot of Calvinist religious convictions. Their hard work was a sign of salvation. Modern work departs from these steady and unassuming Calvinist roots based on stable accumulation. It is fueled by personal ambition rather than spiritual discipline. This ambition is characterized by the drive for self-realization, self-empowerment, fame, and riches. It is familiar to us as the core of the Western individualist ethos.

Individualism and modern capitalism are inseparable. The individualist ethos allows liberal market economies to displace blame for market failures from the political system to the individual. In the meanwhile, success is attributable to the individual's work ethic more than to one's networks of social support. 'Pulling oneself up by one's own bootstraps' is how Americans describe this feat. When the individual alone is responsible for his/her fate within a system where profit-accumulation is encouraged, and without limits, aspirations are unleashed. This fuels ambition to achieve and thereby a powerful motivation to work hard. Individualism, ambition, and work values thereby function in harmony.

When comparing the values of younger and older generations in China, Russia, and Eastern Germany, few differences are as prominent and striking as those in the valuations of independence, ambition, and work. These values are not only central to young business people, but they are also the core values associated with individualist capitalist culture. This chapter will demonstrate this through the words of our businessmen and their fathers and through data from the World Values Survey. I will start by describing quantitative findings across these three societies. Thereafter, I will summarize the cross-country interview material before providing specific interview results for each country.

QUANTITATIVE FINDINGS

An analysis of data from the World Values Survey is presented here, particularly from surveys collected in 1990, 1995, 2000, and 2005 in China, Russia, and Eastern Germany (World Values Survey Association 2009). These data make clear that independence is a value disseminated within younger, richer individuals in modern occupations. Work values, as well, appear enhanced in post-socialist societies. Business people and office workers value work more than those in traditional occupations, such as agriculture. In addition, there is a gap between cohorts and occupations in their valuations of the non-materialistic, ambition-related, aspects of work. This indicates that, in the rise of the phenomenon of the career, work increasingly becomes an end in itself; it is valued beyond the material benefits it brings. Data on risk-taking propensity mirror ambition findings: those who are ambitious must also be able to tolerate potential failures, and so risk-taking is more widely disseminated among younger, richer respondents in modern occupations.

To start, independence is taken as a measure of individualism. Figure 5.1 displays how independence as an ideal trait for children delineates nearly perfectly across birth cohorts, with younger cohorts progressively more highly valuing independence in China, Russia, and Eastern Germany. For instance, of the oldest 1901–1920 Russian birth cohort, only about 12 percent mention independence as an ideal for children, in contrast with nearly 55 percent of those in the 1986–1990 birth cohort. Furthermore, it is clear that independence is valued much less often than in China or Eastern Germany; there is nearly a 30 percent gap, but the rates of growth in independence values between the older and new cohorts are nearly the same in all three societies. Independence is increasingly favored in these three countries, with younger generations widely hailing it as important in comparison to those who grew up in earlier times.

An analysis of occupational groupings reveals that people within modern occupations value independence the most. The differences are moderate in Eastern Germany and Russia but quite strong in China, where 83 percent of those with 'new economy' occupations (owners, professionals, supervisors, and white-collar workers) value independence, compared to only 63 percent of the others (see Appendix B, Table B.1, for T-test results for this chapter). Thus, the new economy encourages 'going it alone' and

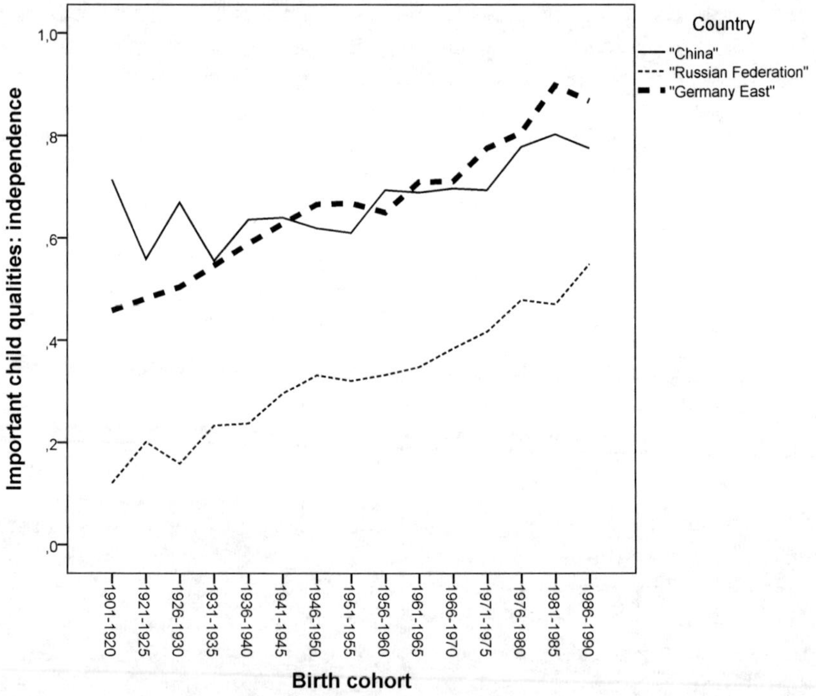

Figure 5.1 Value of independence by birth cohort in China, Russia, and Eastern Germany, WVS 1990–2005.

Source: World Values Survey 1981–2008 Official Aggregate Files v. 20090901 and v. 20090914.

managing oneself as ideals for its new members compared to the traditional norms of group support and group identity.

I have also identified a difference between the richest 15 percent and others in terms of how they value independence. Especially in Russia, where this gap is greatest, about 42 percent of people of the highest income category value independence, as compared to only 30 percent in other income groups. Richer individuals in China are also more independence-oriented; whereas this trend is reversed in East Germany, although the gap is small.

When surveys ask people about the importance of work in their lives within surveys, we see large differences in how members of different birth cohorts answer. As we would expect, we find that those cohorts within the 'work phase' of their life course place a higher value on work. There is a declining importance of work for the oldest cohorts. In all three countries, the youngest cohorts also tend to lag behind in the importance of work, with the middle birth cohorts, born between 1940 and 1976, experiencing the highest work valuations.

Findings indicate that adjustment to work requires considerable adaptation, and that this adaptation is more radical within the new occupational sphere. Indeed, high values of work are held and nourished more by those within modern occupations, meaning those employers, managers, professionals, supervisors, and office workers not involved in manual labor. Across all three pooled countries and four waves, people working within new occupations are more likely to value work (mean=3.44 versus 3.37). Those with higher incomes are also statistically more likely to hold higher valuations of work (mean 3.49 versus 3.36).

Ambitiousness can be measured by the extent to which people value the following non-material aspects as important in a job: respect from others, ability to use initiative, possibility for achievement, and responsibility. We look later at some of the *material* job expectations in the Chapter 6 as a comparison. Birth cohorts in all three countries are also split visibly regarding this non-material form of ambitiousness (See Figure 5.2). In Russia and China, the younger cohorts are far more likely to value these job qualities than their older counterparts; this intergenerational difference represents a potential long-term indicator toward change. Especially the rise of ambitiousness among Russian cohorts that have begun their careers since the transformation is explosive. The East-German generations exhibit a much smaller gap, likely because of the already high level of ambitiousness of the older generations.

Furthermore, ambitiousness is much higher among those in "modern" occupations compared to those in other occupations (mean .36 versus .45). Those in modern jobs are much more likely to value finding a job with a high degree of respect, a job which provides chances

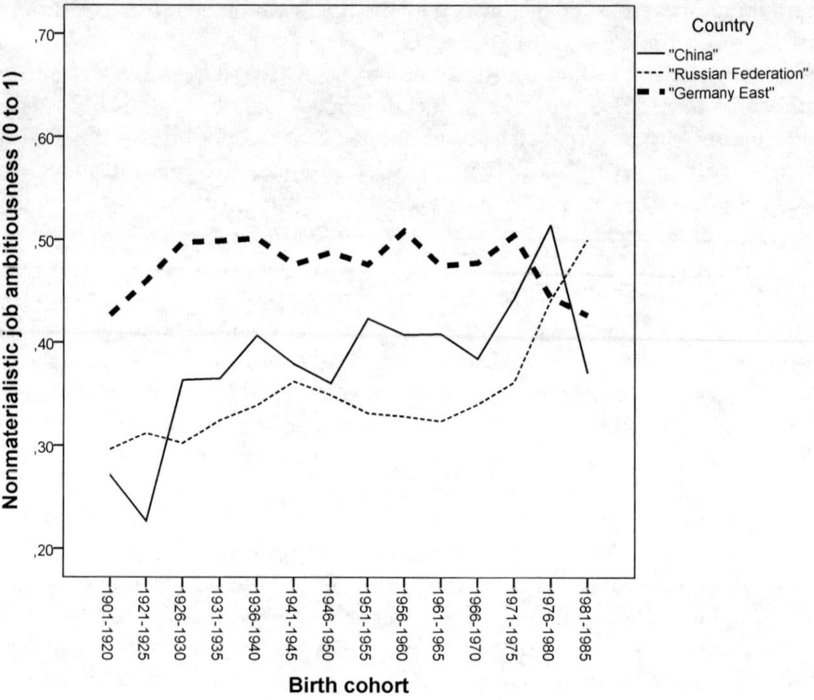

Figure 5.2 Non-materialistic job ambitiousness by birth cohort in China, Russia, and Eastern Germany, WVS 1990–2005.

Source: World Values Survey 1981–2008 Official Aggregate Files v. 20090901 and v. 20090914.

for personal achievement, a job with responsibility, and a job that offers chances to take initiative. This divergence suggests that the economy is supplying new motives to individuals regarding to their willingness to work. Furthermore, it should be emphasized that these non-material job expectations are *not* 'post-materialist' in the sense of heightened sociality. Rather, they highlight the non-materialistic aspects of work, which have a strong correlation with individualism; these job characteristics stress the personal achievement and ambition of the worker. This focus on 'career' correlates well with qualitative findings regarding the heightened 'ambition' among workers and the young.

Finally, we can also report that those with higher incomes, particularly in the top 15 percent, tend to be more ambitious in this sense as well. While insignificant in China, this pattern holds for both Russia and Eastern Germany. However, the difference is relatively small, on the order of about 4 percent higher ambitiousness among the rich.

Chapter 3 reported that 'failure tolerance' is a tool for success in the new economy. In an individualized society, especially compared to a socialist one, those who are ambitious must be willing to endure failures while steering themselves on the personal and risky path toward success. In this way, risk-taking values are a key means for the ambitious to achieve their goals. The importance of risk-taking is also starkly delineated by birth cohort (see Figure 5.3). Here we can see that the most traditional societies—China followed by Russia—are the most risk-averse, but we see a strong trend toward the enhanced valuation of risk-taking among increasingly younger cohorts, as represented by the statement, "one must act boldly to achieve" versus "one should be cautious with major changes in life." Furthermore, quantitative data suggest that those in new occupations in Russia and Eastern Germany tend to be less risk-adverse, although only moderately so, compared to those in other occupations. In China, this relationship is reversed, although the difference is small. In the meanwhile, in all three countries, those with the highest incomes are most likely to believe in taking risks compared to others. Risk-taking thus appears to be another favored value among those excelling in the new economy.

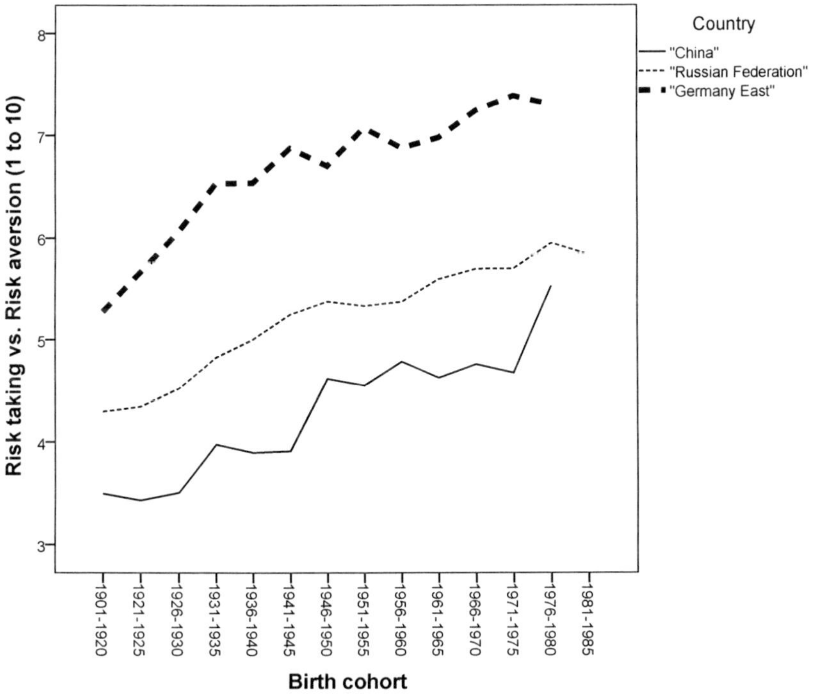

Figure 5.3 Value of risk-taking by birth cohort in China, Russia, and Eastern Germany, WVS 1990–2005.

Source: World Values Survey 1981–2008 Official Aggregate Files v. 20090901 and v. 20090914.

OVERALL QUALITATIVE FINDINGS ON INDIVIDUALISM, AMBITION, AND WORK

Interviews offer a more complex view of the themes that I have just covered using World Values Survey data. Yet the overall picture is a harmonious one. The interviews demonstrate the extraordinary ambition in relation to work, one that is linked to the individualist ethos of self-realization, that drives most of the successful post-communist men interviewed. To begin with, working informants indicate the expansion of their working hours at the beginning of the transformation period compared to socialist times. In China this trend seems to have reversed itself among successful people, with most of my informants reporting they have freed their weekends from work. In contrast, the Russians and East Germans report they have to work much more than they did 15 years ago. The East Germans most readily complain about the costs that their families must pay in relation to work; this attitude contrasts markedly with the Chinese and Russian informants, some of which even refer to work as a "calling" which gives them "moral calm." In parallel to the World Values Survey data reported before, the interviews also reveal a gap in work-related values between the younger working generation, exemplified through its 'work *then* family' orientation, and the older generation's 'work *and* family' orientation. Yet another relationship is clarified; this generational difference is mainly due to the involvement in work culture, because those older informants who had to occupationally re-invent themselves had to also substantially adapt their values.

My analysis identified the temporal phasing of work-family valuations across the life course in China, Russia, and Eastern Germany. While retired persons usually emphasize work and family harmony, working individuals, whether young or old, more often employ a phased valuation of work and family. In this phasing scheme, people justify their heightened work orientations at the beginning of the transformation period through plans to more highly value the family later, once high work values have been fulfilled. Among people across the three societies, this phased valuation of work then family, in contrast to the work-family harmony emphasis, is accompanied with high ambition in work. Material insecurity, a longing for personal achievement, and the establishment of a career usually drive this ambition. Thereby, for younger ambitious informants, work tends to be viewed as all-important, in contrast to the more balanced 'work as duty' orientation of the less ambitious and older informants. A focus on personal achievement and career development among the ambitious appears to be universal across the three groups of informants. Among the ambitious, ambition subsided usually with the evaporation of opportunities for further personal advancement or having achieved 'enough.' Informants then typically transitioned into their 'family' or 'leisure' life phases. However, for some informants, even while money-related and ambition-related motivations have faded, work remains an 'end in itself,' and the informant never transitions to the 'family phase' as he may have envisioned. He continues instead to work, either because of the idea of work as a secular salvation, or does so dispassionately, because he lacks alternative lifestyle possibilities. The 'work-phase' becomes extended indefinitely.

One interesting difference is observed in the predominance of the 'ambitious' type in each country. While the ambitious were a majority among the young Russian and Chinese informants, this type was more rare in Eastern Germany, where it was seemingly replaced by a more family-oriented, less work-centered, type focused more on accumulating material *sufficiency* for the good of the family than on accumulating material wealth, maximizing personal achievement, or building an outstanding career.

Material insecurity is not a dominant theme among the Chinese businessmen, perhaps since China, at the macro-level and among its bourgeoning new middle and upper classes, experienced an economic boom during its transformation years, in comparison to Russia's total economic collapse and East German stagnation. The factor of material insecurity, not found among my interviewees in China, appears to be linked to another phenomenon lacking in China: the presence of 'ambitious' older generation workers. Additionally, the fact that the Chinese transition was slower and smoother would have offered less of an incentive for the older generation to adapt. In contrast, both Eastern Germany and Russia had cases of older generation informants who adapted to the new economic system, presumably due to the shock and poverty of the transformation years.

Russia's severe shock therapy caused "hungry and poor years" and great material insecurity, in stark contrast to China. This deep level of material insecurity made the Russian transformation more radical, thereby also precipitating more adaptation by its older generation, for the sake of material survival. Indeed, within some of our Russian father-son pairs, the father's adaptation was more extreme than the son's, for whom the transformation proceeded more smoothly. This radical flavor of the Russian economic conditions likely contributed to a more extreme ideological adaptation as well. Some Russian informants, for example, referred to work as their "calling" and "salvation," while others came to worship the economy as the ultimate source of value: "Everything else is crap" (M10). In Russia, while the achievement motivation was great, many informants, once they accumulated a comfortable level of material resources, then transitioned to Phase II. For the Chinese and Eastern Germans, this phase more often meant more family time. Yet for the Russians we see something new: the insertion of leisure time competing with family obligations, with some Russians opting for a hedonistic path, enabled by their newfound wealth, rather than a quiet family life. This becomes a source of inner conflict, where the original work versus family conflict is replaced by a conflict of leisure versus family. Some Russians never transition to a leisure or family phase at all, but are instead content from the "moral calm" they receive from working. The Russian case clarifies that the most important distinction is between those *working* and *not working* within the new economy. Regardless of when they were born, those who worked during the transformation years experienced a value shift. Furthermore, for some, later life is dominated by a leisure versus family conflict in place of the work versus family conflict of earlier years. This rising importance of leisure is likely due to the arrival, and widespread acceptance of a hedonistic 'everything goes as long as you have the money' culture.

In Leipzig, many informants dedicate themselves fully to their work only with great reluctance because of the costs of working for the health of the family. Such conflicts are more rare in Russia and very rare in the Chinese interviews. Of course, it was necessary to work hard in order to secure material security in the early transition years, especially in order to support the family. Thus, ambition struck many Leipzigers, and some Leipzig fathers were forced by material needs, like in Russia, to adapt to the economic change and take up employment. What is unique, however, about the Leipzig case is that some businessmen rejected the route of high career ambition for a more relaxed one of material sufficiency; in other words, they worked only enough to secure the basic essentials for the family but desired nothing more. Such a practice was rarer among the Chinese and Russian informants. Among the ambitious in Leipzig, ambition declined upon reaching retirement age or upon securing a degree of material sufficiency. The Leipzig informants also point to how the nature of work changed, with "working at home," on evenings and weekends, becoming more regular. This notion of working at home parallels the Russian and Chinese notion of spending weekends in the office, but working at home opens up more possibilities for family interactions. The Leipzigers are also quite cynical and fatigued regarding the overstretched work duties of the new economic culture, even calling it "enslavement," and they complain that family life and leisure suffer as a result. The following sections report on interview findings for each of the three cities.

The Shanghai Interviews

Retrospective reports in China indicate that the value of work increased at the beginning of the transition, as my young informants worked to establish their own material security in the new economy. Most of the younger informants (S9, S13, S15) are still within this initial ambitious, work-centered phase of their lives. S9, for example, is highly motivated and working most weekends. S13, as well, is highly work- and achievement-oriented. He justifies this orientation as necessary, for it is his duty to materially provide for his family. S15, 32 years old and working 14-hour days, is also highly ambitious and work-centered, admitting that this allows him little time with his family. The ambitions of this young cohort seem tied to the amount that they could achieve and subsided under two conditions. First, they may run out of opportunities, as was the case for S5, who is the director of a state-owned enterprise, and who cannot rise any further in his company. Second, they could achieve a degree of comfortable material wealth, as is the case with S17, who at 43 years old, thinks of retiring soon because he has already achieved what he aimed to and has no need for more. For other informants, however, even after their initial ambitions have subsided, they have not transitioned to the leisurely lifestyle enjoyed by S5 and S17. This is the case with S7, who, at 49 years old and financially very successful, describes his life outside of work as "dull" and seems quite unhappy. None of his current plans involve leisure or family; rather, he aims to establish his own business, perhaps to reawaken his former ambitions. In contrast, some of the informants, such as S11, are less ambitious, and therefore less work-oriented. S11, although not married, still keeps his weekends free for his girlfriend and parents.

Retrospective reports from the older generation demonstrate, not surprisingly, a decrease in their work values over the years, since most of them are now retired. S4, for example, a former newspaperman, recalls changes in his work during this period, as his job required him to increasingly visit clients in order to sell more advertisements for the newspaper, but he soon retired, so he did not have to change substantially according to these influences. S6 notes no changes in his work values over the years. Fifteen years ago, S8, a former employee in the transportation sector, worked almost every day, including weekends, and he is now retired. S14, a former factory engineer, also was a very hard worker until he retired. The question thereby arises as to whether this former work-focus of the elder generation during their younger years has given way to qualitatively different work values today.

Father-son pair comparisons, of which there are three for the Chinese sample, also illustrate the enhancement of work in the younger generation. Take for example S5 and S6. S5 is a 32-year-old president of a state-owned construction firm. His father, S6, is a former manager in the industrial sector. Whereas the father puts family first, and places much emphasis on family harmony, his son mentions that his family members, including his parents, complain that he goes away too often on business. The following excerpt, from young Yang of this chapter's vignette, shows that he sees the family as his wife's domain, while work is his primary responsibility:

> *Q:* If you have emergent things [at work] to deal with at 06:30 a.m., will you get your daughter ready or go directly to the company?
>
> *A:* It depends. If my daughter wets the bed or falls ill suddenly, I will make arrangements for that, such as ringing someone for help. Or I will see what my wife can do and who can settle things for me. I will make good arrangements in a short time so that my wife can cope with everything successfully at home. If under some circumstances she can cope with it, I will go directly to the company.

In comparing S7 and S8's work values, it is clear that work has dominated the son's life, while the father is more balanced. The son, 49 years old and having spent much time working in Japan, has adopted what he calls the Japanese notion of 'work as family'; his company has a cohesiveness that "can hardly be described in words." Nonetheless, he seems unhappy, reporting that "for me, besides work, life is dull and I seldom go out to have fun." In contrast, his father, S8, emphasizes that one should not only work, but should also enjoy life.

The third pair comparison, S13 and S14 from the vignette that opens this chapter, highlights a similar trend. As you may recall, the father, like the other fathers, puts family first, advocating a balance with work, and the son places family second in importance. Thus, once again the son is more work-centered than his father. Interestingly, they both enjoy the same television program, "Life Fortune," a show which spotlights successful people in the new economy, highlighting their various roads to success. It is remarkable that the father and son both find this program attractive, despite their different values. Of course, the son must live these values in everyday life, while the father, a former factory engineer, is retired and may view them from a distance.

A wider intergenerational comparison of cohorts reveals similar results. The role of work, or career, dominates the lives of the working generation. S7 remarks that "maybe the values of my generation are different from those of the previous generation. Since I am in my present position, I have to do my job well. I never have weekends and I think I have done what I should do." Although members of the younger cohort may have a higher drive toward work than their fathers, it is clear that hard work is also highly valued among the older informants. Despite a common focus on work, there is also a difference between the generations, with the older generation focusing more on *work as life* and *work as a duty*, while the younger generation describes work more as a career for the purpose of earning money and making personal achievements. The following are typical work valuations of the older informants:

(S8)

Work is the most important thing in my life.

(S14)

Q: Who was your biggest role model?

A: I had no role model at all. We just worked hard. That was the only principle not only for me, but all the people around me. If someone didn't work hard, he would be told by others not to behave like that anymore. In fact, nobody was taking charge of you. We were self-conscious. Working hard was the only principle that had guided me since I graduated from the university.

Similarly, many from the younger generation also expressed such a valuation of work as a way of life:

> *(S7)*
>
> *Q:* What is the most important thing in your life?
> *A:* Work. Each day's work is almost the same for we are engaged in developing software.

> *(S9)*
>
> I thought the most important thing was to do my job well. No matter what I did, I should do it well. Maybe I had the idea that I might do the job all my life.

The value of hard work is also extended to 'studying hard' in school:

> *(S15)*
>
> *Q:* Let's go back to 1990. What were the most important things in your life? The most important thing for me was to study hard in order to go to the university. My parents were schoolteachers and many excellent students of theirs were enrolled at Tsinghua University, Peking University and Fudan University. So I hoped I could also . . . This was not only the dream of mine; it was also the dream of many parents. It was impossible for us to have other greater dreams at that time.

In contrast to the work as life or as duty approach, passages about work from some of the businessmen show something different. For them, work may be framed as career, as focused on personal achievement. Typical of such passages are the following:

> *(S13)*
>
> But to be honest, I wanted to do some great deeds and achieve success. I began my work as a salesman and I had contributed a lot to many enterprises with one million or 10 million RMB in capital. I could give some useful advice to presidents of the companies who were not experts in their own fields so that they could reach their goals. Company X is a famous Chinese health-care products company. Though its president only attended junior middle school, he managed to develop the company into a large one. After enlarging the company, he had a strong desire for knowledge and wanted to improve himself and therefore he attended training courses in various training centers.

(S15)

Presently in my age, I attach the greatest importance to achieving my goal according to my career plan. . . . Therefore, all the members of my company, including me, have a sense of responsibility. I came to this company last year when it was just founded and made an exact career plan. I hoped that I could get to somewhere in a totally new field and that what I do would be really helpful to the development of agriculture, the society, and the country. So far I still feel that our work is sacred and full of a sense of responsibility. I think the most important thing is doing my job well through my own efforts and the efforts of the company. In fact, it's not easy to do it well for no one knows how to do it and we are just groping our way along.

Another interviewee links his work not to a general principle of working hard, but rather to the salary he makes from it and the expectations that arise from earning that money:

(S11)

Q: Which ideas make you work hard and improve yourself?
A: There are no specific ideas. I should work hard since I receive a salary. If you receive a salary and work carelessly, you will be fired sooner or later.

Although "career" and its relation to earning status and money is more common among the younger group, some individuals in the older generation also have an admiration of the status aspects of career. S6, for example, most highly admires those who are both successful in their careers in terms of prestige and who possess a strong moral character:

I have always been impressed by those who enjoy a good reputation for their career success and for their character.

In summary, there is an agreement between generations that work is valuable, although the younger informants more readily value work instrumentally for status and money rather than as a simple duty. Also, in comparison to the older cohort, the younger generation has lost the balance between the value of work and value of family, with work now tending to dominate its value systems.

The Moscow Interviews

Interviews with the Russian informants also allude to the expansion of work-focus at the beginning of the transition. M5 notes that work came first for him during his period, while M1, another informant, refers to the growth of work as a "calling" for him during those years. The expansion of these work values, also reported by M9, is likely due to the material insecurities brought about during this period in Russia, which M7 calls the "hungry and poor years." M5, for instance describes his extraordinarily high work regimen at the beginning of the transformation years, and the effects this had upon his family:

> The reason for losing my first family was that I worked a lot. I mean that I spent whole days working, and the children did not see much of me. Additionally my wife stopped taking care of them and lost interest in me as well. Generally, the family fell apart. That is why currently I have limited influence on the children.

This heightened work focus continued until enough material resources were accumulated, as was the case with all young informants except for M9 and M11. M9 is not as wealthy as the others, while M11 is extraordinarily achievement-oriented and has not yet fulfilled his material and career goals. Once their material well-being was achieved, informants then transitioned into a second stage of life, with some taking time out for family (M7) and others devoting their lives to leisure (M5). However, some informants, such as M1, never transition out of this work stage, even when they have enough. Instead, M1 continues to devote all his time to work without reassigning his priorities to family or leisure, as work for him brings "moral calm."

In contrast, most of the older informants—M6, M2, and M12—did not experience an expansion of their work values during the early transformation years, since they were retired. The two older informants who continued to work during these years also illustrate that, despite their age, they experienced enhanced work valuations at this stage of their lives. This is the case with both M10 and M8, the latter of whom is a workaholic valuing the family only "by default."

Comparing the generations as pairs leads to the same conclusion, with the younger cohorts experiencing adaptive expansion of work values in comparison to the older generation. One piece of evidence for this is that time diary data indicate that most of the young cohorts work at least one weekend day per week, as opposed to their fathers, who reported having their weekends free during Soviet times.

One father-son pair that fits the expected pattern is M5 and M6. For the father, M6, work was his "second love," second to his family. In contrast, at the beginning of the transformation, work became first for his son. Now the son is in an advanced stage of success, where the business functions on its own, but he does not spend his extra time with his family. Rather, he is torn between spending his money, which he calls "leisure," and spending time with his family.

A similarly contrasting pair is M1 and M2. M2, the father, barely speaks of work at all, even when referring to the past. In contrast, M1, who is content and lives in material comfort, works quite hard and long hours, but he is ambivalent on *why* he values work. At first, he says his interest in working is for the love of the job itself, which he calls the "protestant ethic," which is related to a sense of "moral calm" which he feels while working. Later, he notes that the job is for making money, after all, and that is his primary interest in it. He speaks of work in a complex way: it is something he started to do in order to make money, for material security, and in so doing he found a sense of moral calm within, a secular "calling." Now he sees the money as a side-benefit of doing what he likes.

M11, like most from his generation, feels compelled to work a lot, both for material security and the well-being of his family, while his mother M12, although she was a hard worker in Soviet times as a single mother and sole wage-earner, is fortunate to now be a retiree supported by her son.

A contrasting case would be M7 and M8, where the younger values family more than his father, and the father is a workaholic who values the family on the side. Both are similar in that they work a lot in order to provide for their families. The main difference is that the father had to undergo extreme adaptation with the transformation in order to rush to commercialize his new business, while the son's transition appears to have been smoother. Stronger adaptive pressures led to the father's enhanced work-orientations, thereby facilitating his success within the new economic system at the expense of making his familial values more latent.

Likewise, M9 and M10, both working, the son in design and the father in technology sales, report working harder since the transformation began. The son complains that he has to occasionally work on Saturdays in his present occupation, while his father works even more, having only two free days *per month*, on average.

The Leipzig Interviews

Like their Chinese and Russian counterparts, many Leipzig informants recognize an increase in their work valuations over the years, but most of them display some reluctance about this high work focus, especially in regard to its impact on other life spheres, such as the family and free-time activities. All of the informants were faced with material and job insecurities in the early transition years. Each of them reacted in a way to secure work in order to take care of their families. For most, this work came with initial heightened ambition at the beginning of the economic transformation (L2, L4, L3, L12, L7, L8, L9). L3 describes how ambition is greater early on in the professional career:

> Of course, if one is just at the beginning of his life, well, at the beginning of his professional career, things like financial security or simply

> the profit you get out of your work are certainly of great importance, right?! Even today, one also tries to get, I will simply say, an appropriate income out of the work one is doing in order to support his family, in order to make certain things possible for the family, right?

This "early career ambition" seems to have affected the working older informants as well. L4, L3's father, for example, rushed to learn about western practices relevant to his business and to educate himself with new skills, such as how to use a computer, so as to remain up to date and successful in work. This ambition was usually accompanied by a drive for 'success' and recognition in work, the building of a career, and a desire for material accumulation.

However, some informants have rejected this path toward achievement for one of sufficiency: they desired to work enough to support their families, but not more (L1, L5, L6, L11) (see Schwartz et al. 2002). L5 remembers his desire then to secure an existence in order to provide a good start for the kids, while L6 values the mere fact of "having" work, which is quite different than a focus on success and achievement in relation to work. Among those in the ambitious group, these ambitions subsided in a number of ways. For some, only retirement brings a diminished focus on work (L2, L4, L12). Sixty-nine-year-old L12, for example, is still working and can only vaguely imagine a day when he works less, for work is his main source of satisfaction. For others (L3), work values diminish once the "appropriate" amount of income is earned for the family. Yet other individuals remain heavily work focused even though they are no longer ambitious; with dullness they continue with their lives in a work-centered manner although it apparently gives them little satisfaction (L7, L8).

Many of the new jobs allow for more personal independence than did those under the previous regime. Such jobs require more responsibility and out-of-work contributions. L2 notes, for example, that although the amount of time he spends at work and at home is roughly the same as before, he brings more work home nowadays, since he is a freelancer. In contrast, his son is less work-focused because he has chosen a profession where he is not in a position to earn big money like his parents.

L3 and L4 were both quite work-focused in the early years of the transition but became less so over time. The father naturally withdrew from work because of retirement, while his son stepped back from his high work focus once a sufficient level of income was earned to support his family.

L5 and L6 speak about work similarly. For the son, L5, work represents a secured existence, a "good start" for his kids. For his father, work is seen in a similar light, as a crucial activity *for* the family. To *have* work is the central factor for L6.

Both L7 and L8 work very hard and admit that their family lives suffer as a result. Both wish for more free time as well. The father will retire soon, while the son, L7, doesn't wish to be anymore "enslaved" by self-employment. Like many others, L7 also notes that work has become more important for him over the years. He complains that the expansion of work has caused his involvement in other activities, such as volunteering and participation in sports clubs, to wither. As a result, one of his goals is to enjoy life more than he does today.

Similarly, both L11 and L12, who together own a family business, were very business-oriented at the beginning of the transition, trying to build a fresh start. Both seem to be worn out from their routine, longing to eventually take a break from everyday work and enjoy some free time. L12 describes his status as a "family manufacturer:"

> Work, too. independent manufacturers . . . means basically: once a manufacturer, always a manufacturer. This is independent from the system of society, isn't it? I mean, our business has existed for over 100 years. One has to realize that we have survived five social systems. Didn't we? Beginning with the Kaiserreich, the Weimar republic, National Socialism, GDR and the Federal Republic- And I mean, when the family remains the center, a social system can come and go, but the family manufacture remains.

In this family-work mix, he says that, despite his lack of free time, family is "the center." Work brings him satisfaction.

At the beginning of the transformation years, L9 was quite ambitious. During those years, he wished most for economic independence and wealth, such as having his own island by age 40. He imagined that family would come later than it did. Although he started a family earlier than he would have liked, he has incorporated it fully into his plans, as his goals today include long-term happiness, encompassing both family life and a successful business. He hopes that, by a certain age, he will be financially successful enough to have enough free time and money for hobbies.

Although many of the value conflicts in post-communist societies are linked to the story told in this chapter, the marked importance of an individualist and ambitious focus on work, this is only the beginning of the story. People want more than just status, or even fame, for their work in the new economy. Many want to 'get rich' and stay there, and to enjoy the privileges and luxuries that money can buy.

6 "Get Rich First!" Materialism and Consumerism

> This is civilization. Formerly, men worked in the open air only as much as they liked. Now thousands of workmen meet together and, for the sake of maintenance, work in factories or mines. Their condition is worse than that of beasts. They are obliged to work, at the risk of their lives, at most dangerous occupations, for the sake of millionaires. Formerly, men were made slaves under physical compulsion. Now they are enslaved by temptation of money and of the luxuries that money can buy.
>
> —M.K. Gandhi, *Hind Swaraj* [Indian Home Rule] (1946, 26)

> Money means only a number for me now and the process to make money is the process to manifest success. The number is indicative of the correctness of one's decisions.
>
> The winner is the king and the loser is the servant.
>
> —Shanghai informant, S13

"Igor" (M5) is 47 years old and lives a luxurious life as a wealthy marketing executive. He has been married multiple times and has many children. Although his business is based in Moscow, he lives both there and in another major European city, where his family lives. His father, "Sergei" (M6), is a 77-year-old retired engineer. The contrast between them is great.

The father is non-materialistic. He speaks with admiration of contemporary writers who refuse to put materialism first. His attitude toward material goods is that they should not be "turned into idols." The son, in contrast, speaks often of money, both as a means of fulfilling his "entertainment" needs, and earlier in the transformation period, as a necessity for taking care of the family. "Everyone would like to live a nice life," and being rich enables this, he says. While Sergei views non-materialism as an ideal value for children, Igor complains that his own son (Sergei's grandson) is completely materialistic and lazy. Ironically, Igor wants to ease his son out of these traits by inducing him to attend college through buying him a new car.

Sergei highly values honesty and mentions it as a value he would like his grandchildren to inherit, but Igor does not mention honesty, and, by his own admission, got his start in business through mafia

> and criminal activity. This value gap between them seems to extend to morality in general. Sergei believes there should be moral constraints on one's behavior; it shouldn't be "live how you want to live." In contrast, Igor spends his time in Moscow, away from his family, involved in hedonistic pursuits, such as "drinking, night clubs, and lechery."
>
> Sergei and his son Igor also have very different opinions of Russia's oligarch class. While the elder Sergei despises Khodorkovsky—the oil tycoon imprisoned by Putin ostensibly for tax evasion because he "took everything valuable [from the country] and did not give anything in return," the younger Igor idolizes Khodorkovsky. Igor admires films about the Russian oligarchs, while Sergei says such films are mostly about criminals.
>
> Finally, Igor is also more conflicted than his father. He realizes that there is a tension between his two lives, one in Moscow and the other with his family in the other city. This is a conflict, he says, between family and entertainment needs, going out drinking and clubbing, for which "having more money is all that is needed."

Gandhi's (1946) is among the most acute critiques of Western civilization, particularly of an imperialist capitalism he saw as destroying the spiritual roots of Indian society. His critique extended to modern technology, Western science, medicine, and the state. His claims were first and foremost shaped toward accomplishing real social change in India. In his quotation above, noting that men are "enslaved by temptation" of wealth and luxuries, Gandhi communicates with streams of thought related to the Marxian veil which alienates modern individuals from one another, from nature, and prevents them as well from seeing their true class interests. Similar ideas are found among the Frankfurt School critical theorists.

Adorno and Horkheimer (2002), in writing about "The Culture Industry," are especially focused on the ways that the economy controls both consumption and political preferences through the production of culture. The culture industry makes individuals more alike while offering them superficially different products, and a result of this process is primarily to 'dumb down' people, making them privately content and politically uncritical. Along these lines, it was Edward Bernays, the nephew of Sigmund Freud, who did much to cement the scientific tools of mass economic and political manipulation. The disciplines of market research and public relations achieved their success by using Freud's theories to manipulate emotions for economic and political gain. "If we understand the mechanism and motives of the group mind, is it not possible to control and regiment the masses according to our will without their knowing about it? The recent practice of propaganda has proved that it is possible, at least up to a certain point and within certain limits." (Bernays 1928, 47; see also BBC 2002).

Among the Gandhian and critical theory takes on material temptations and control over individuals through their engagement in consumption practices, there are two broad findings useful for my argument here. On the one hand is the value of money, consumption, and luxuries; we could call this material temptation. This material temptation is prominent among successful people in the post-communist world. On the other hand are the effects of these temptations on the political sphere: specifically apoliticism. This chapter will deal with the first issue, material temptation, while the second, political values will be handled in Chapter 8.

In a related vein, Thomas Veblen's (2004) critique of business focuses on the conspicuous consumption, and waste, of the leisure class. It extracts profits in order to consume luxuries, thus displaying its status to others. Such status display is prominent among post-communist business people as well. This chapter also discusses how they cultivate their images in order to project and achieve success. I will first present findings from representative surveys, followed by results from qualitative interviews.

QUANTITATIVE FINDINGS

I demonstrate materialism trends in China, Russia, and Eastern Germany by using statistical results on the value of thrift, good pay in a job, the belief that wealth accumulation is zero-sum, the belief in 'easy money,' and the value of job security.

World Values Survey respondents were asked to name the values that should be taught to children. Figure 6.1 demonstrates how the value of thrift, or saving things or money, is increasingly devalued by younger and younger cohorts in all three countries. This may be because it is being challenged by modern values of consumption as will be indicated within the qualitative interviews. Excessive thrift may also be opposed to modern notions of financial risk-taking and investment. Across three countries, in the oldest cohorts, 68 percent of people claim thrift as an ideal value, compared to only 43 percent in the youngest cohorts. The overall levels of and rates of decline for thrift across these three countries are very similar.

As a clue for the reason of thrift's demise, in all three countries, it is highly undervalued by those in modern occupations compared to others, and the gap is large (See Table B.2, Appendix B, for all T-test results pertaining to this chapter). For example, of the pooled East Germans, 49 percent of people in modern occupations chose thrift as an important value for children, while 63 percent from other occupations did the same. Among the Chinese, 51 percent of those in modern occupations chose thrift as an ideal, compared to 63 percent from other occupations. Among Russians, the overall difference between these groups is less extreme, 52 percent in modern jobs compared to 57 percent in the traditional occupations. Each of these

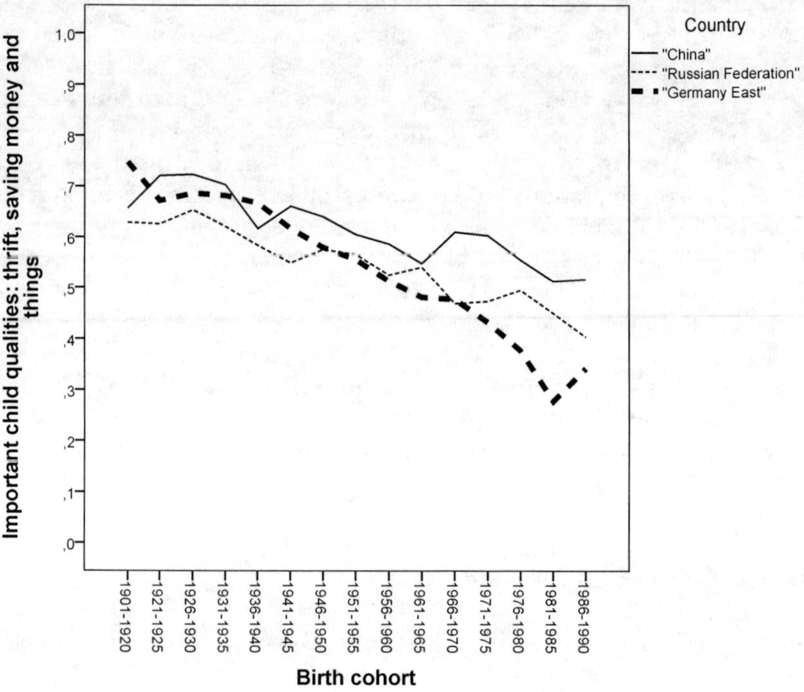

Figure 6.1 Value of thrift by birth cohort in China, Russia, and Eastern Germany, WVS 1990–2005.

Source: World Values Survey 1981–2008 Official Aggregate Files v. 20090901 and v. 20090914.

differences is highly statistically significant and demonstrates that thrift is not a favored value for those participating in the modern economy.

Similarly, thrift is also highly devalued among the rich. Those in the top 15 percent of incomes, representing those who have achieved "success" in modern capitalism, value thrift less in Russia and Eastern Germany. The difference is greatest in Russia, where 45 percent of high-income respondents value thrift compared to 57 percent among those with less income. In China, where the overall level of thrift is higher than in the other two societies, the difference is not statistically significant between income groups, although it is in the same direction.

In comparison to the earlier presented findings, in Chapter 5, on how non-materialist job ambitions were highest among younger birth cohorts, we find the same regarding materialist job expectations, indicating that the younger respondents are overall more emphatic about *all* ideals related to work. On "good pay" within a job, younger birth cohorts are progressively more concerned with it than the older cohorts (see Figure 6.2). The overall concern with "good pay" among Russians is higher than among the

Chinese or East Germans, but in each country, younger cohorts value it more than do older cohorts. Overall, 69 percent of the 1901–1920 cohort named good pay as important compared with 83 percent among the 1981–1985 birth cohort.

Likely because of their higher incomes and lower material insecurities, fewer in the 'new occupational field,' including management, ownership, and office work, value good pay in a job compared with workers in other occupations (77 percent compared to 81 percent). This difference is strong and significant in Eastern Germany, with only 66 percent of modern occupations valuing high pay compared to 78 percent in other occupations. The other countries have smaller occupational differences in this variable. My qualitative findings will help us explain this fact since the Eastern Germans tend to be less 'ambitious' and are more oriented toward material sufficiency and basic satisfaction of needs than their Russian and Chinese counterparts. Thus, it is possible that the Eastern Germans know when to say "enough is enough." This may be also because of the overall comparatively high level of development in East Germany, compared to China or Russia. As such, those in modern occupations already earn more than others and may be more likely to shift their focus toward more family time once these

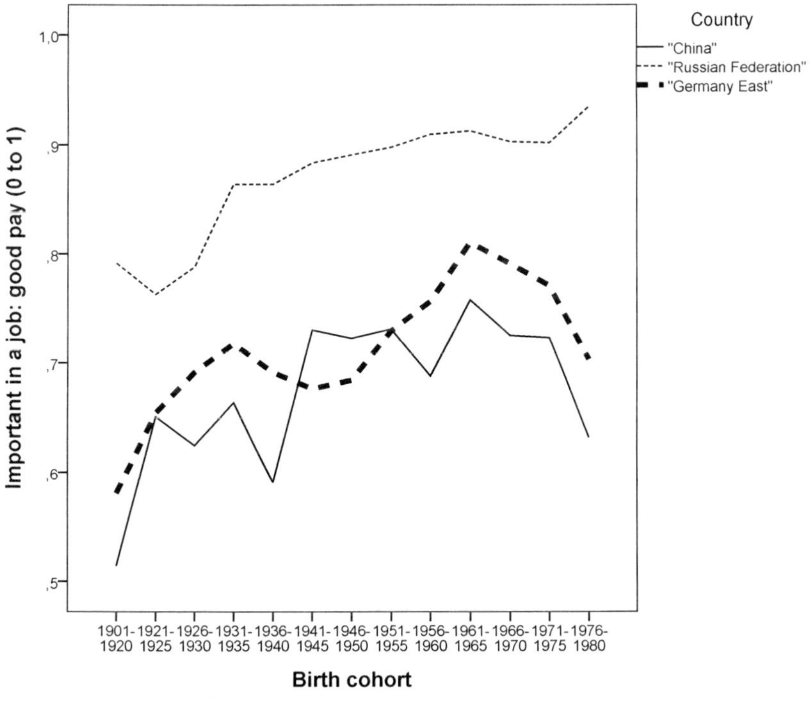

Figure 6.2 Value of good pay by birth cohort in China, Russia, and Eastern Germany, WVS 1990–2005.

Source: World Values Survey 1981–2008 Official Aggregate Files v. 20090901 and v. 20090914.

basic needs are met, in contrast to the more consumerist Chinese and Russians who may rather opt for earning even more money. People with higher incomes, in each of the three societies, are also less likely to value high pay. While statistically significant, this difference is, however, minor (78 percent versus 80 percent).

In 2005, the World Value Survey asked people whether or not they consider it important to be rich and have material things. An intergenerational comparison (Figure 6.3) reveals a very strong trend across all three countries by which younger cohorts are consecutively more focused on being rich and having material things than are the older birth cohorts. The Russian youth are most materialistic in this sense, followed by the East Germans and Chinese, who are at equal levels.

Results comparing the value of being rich between modern and other occupational groups are inconclusive. In China and Eastern Germany, those in traditional occupations value "being rich" more than others, whereas the opposite is found in Russia, albeit each of these differences is moderate in size. In Russia, counter to post-materialism assumptions, the richest 15 percent value "being rich" significantly more than other income

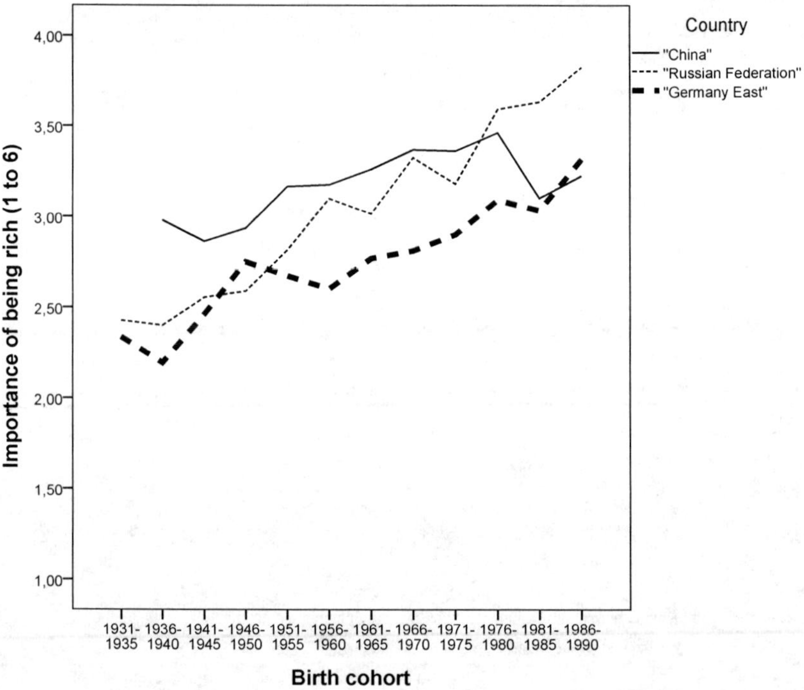

Figure 6.3 Value of being rich and having nice things by birth cohort in China, Russia, and Eastern Germany, WVS 2005.
Source: World Values Survey 1981–2008 Official Aggregate Files v. 20090901 and v. 20090914.

groups (mean of 3.6 versus 3.0), and this difference is found in Eastern Germany as well. The direction of influence in China is reversed, but the gap between is very small.

A question in the World Values Survey asks respondents to rate whether or not "people can only get rich at the expense of others" versus "wealth can grow so there's enough for everyone." I investigate answers to this question because of claims among my informants that "Wild West" capitalism is exploitative 'by nature.' A fascinating finding is that this belief is held especially among younger, more adapted people in Russia and in Eastern Germany. In contrast, no significant intergenerational trend can be seen in China. These findings appear to harmonize with our qualitative findings reporting enhanced dissonance and ideological demoralization in Russia and especially Eastern Germany during transformation years (Chapter 3). People in modern occupations are also more likely to believe that wealth growth is exploitative rather than egalitarian. In the meanwhile, top earners in each of the three societies are slightly less likely to believe in the exploitative nature of the accumulation of riches.

Materialism may also be measured by the extent to which individuals believe in the justifiability of 'easy money,' which is the moral acceptability of receiving money without working for it. This is seen as opposed to Weber's original and disciplined capitalist ideal and more in line with Veblen's notion of a hedonistic and parasitic leisure-class. While Western biases assume that socialist systems collapsed because of the 'handouts' they gave to their lazy and 'entitled' populations, data indicate otherwise. For example, especially in Russia and China, belief in the acceptability of 'easy money' is greater among younger, not older, cohorts. However, there is no significant difference between modern occupations and others in the valuation of 'easy money.' In the meanwhile, top earners are less likely to highly value this notion compared to others, and this difference is most prominent in East Germany (mean 2.70 vs. 2.95).

A further measure of materialism, one discussed in the interviews as well, is concern about job security. Analysis indicates a gradual expansion of job security worries among younger birth cohorts especially in Russia and Germany. These results concur with the qualitative finding that many individuals, especially at the beginning of the transformation, experienced great material insecurity and were thus especially likely to look for secure jobs, especially in Russia, where the economic shock together with the lack of unemployment benefits combined to produce crisis. Analysis of these values by occupation tell us that those in the modern occupations are less likely to have job security worries, since they have successfully adapted to the new economy, and perhaps to the notion that job security is a thing of the past. This gap is small but significant in Eastern Germany (71 percent versus 78 percent), quite large in China (48 versus 65 percent), and small but significant in Russia (59 versus 62 percent). In their valuation of job security, the differences among those with the highest income and others is negligible.

OVERALL QUALITATIVE MATERIALIST VALUES

The interviews reveal the enhanced role of materialist values due to the new material culture. Through adopting practices such as image cultivation and profit calculation, people adapt to this culture in order to achieve success. This new materialism is exemplified through consumerism, a focus on money, and worries about material security.

In all three countries, people felt an enhanced material insecurity in the early years of the transformation. They responded to this situation by becoming fixated on material needs and survival. In this way, they tended toward a survivalist materialism. For some, especially in Russia, this survival focus was accompanied by temptation by the allure of a new consumerism, entailing luxuries and money lust. Compared to Russia, such consumerism was more muted in China, perhaps because the traditional Chinese value of thrift stood in the way. There was also disdain toward this luxury consumerism among the Eastern German informants, often because of professed Christian values and social welfare state ideologies. The East Germans, while being quite focused on the "material situation," more rarely allow their values to digress into luxury lust. Situations in which money is both 'needed' and 'lusted after' reflect a state of high material aspirations and low degree of actual material action, which could be characterized as *wishing for* money and material goods. These interviews also help explain our quantitative findings that younger generations increasingly value being rich, yet this value is lower among those in new occupations and the rich, because they work and live with money rather than 'wish' for it.

Later on, this way of thinking about money in terms of needs and luxuries became rather a focus on *working with* money, the inculcation of a materialist habitus, and sometimes without the strong conscious insecurity and luxury focus of the past. This transformation of values between the time of high material aspirations and the time of their fulfillment is described well by M8: "This period could be compared to thirst. If a person is thirsty, he thinks of water. When there is no thirst, he thinks of water less even though he drinks it maybe even more than before." This is a state within which the value of money and material things becomes active and clearly visible in behavior, although the person may not constantly strive after them as much as before. One outcome of the development of this materialist habitus may also be seen in the World Values Survey finding introduced above, whereby younger generations, the rich, and those in modern occupations have a diminished value of thrift, as consumer spending becomes more important.

During the transformation, the interviewees seemed to have learned quite early on that "thinking about money" and profit is a necessary tool of success at work. They built their businesses based on discipline and a skill in dealing with money, which varies from the high levels of careless consumerism they pursue while at home, especially in Russia. It is as if the capitalist and consumer classes are united, in many cases, within the same individuals, requiring alternatively, disciplined calculation at work and hedonistic fulfillment at home.

Just as profit calculation becomes a key to work success, image cultivation is another key skill to be developed by the successful worker within the new economy. Informants in all three countries refer to this need to look good and 'successful,' although some of them refer to it as a merely instrumental concern, while for others, it becomes inculcated as a value in itself.

In each of the three countries, there is a sense among the informants, young and old, of the dominance of the new consumer culture. In China, this is posed in opposition to, and detrimental to, the traditional value of thrift. In Russia, a sense of loss of "intellectuality" is noted in relation to this newfound materialism, while in Eastern Germany, material culture is more often posited as in opposition to religious beliefs.

Now that I have covered quantitative findings and overall qualitative results, detailed information about the interviews in each of the three countries will be provided in the sections below.

The Shanghai Interviews

Interviewees remember a high level of material aspirations at the beginning of the transformation in China. S5 for example, had a strong drive to attain material security during this period. S11 also was highly materialistic at the beginning of the transformation, as he came from a poor background. Similarly, S15 says he is less materialistic now than in the early 1990s because now he "has owned what [he] should own." S17 is less focused on material wealth now than before, since he has already accumulated a good deal of wealth, and now he is happy to "live a simple life" and focus on health and family.

A shift from high material aspirations and low consumption to low aspirations and high consumption forms a pattern in Shanghai. For example, S17, who plans to retire early, notes that he is happy to live "the simple life," but this means retiring at age 45 and spending the rest of his life in leisure and travel. S5, now that he has become materially comfortable, spends large amounts of money on treating his daughter to toys. S11 also consumes a lot, appropriate to the level of his income, but he no longer has the lack of material security which drove him before. In contrast to this pattern, S13 was also materialistic at the beginning of the transition, but has not lost his material ambitions:

> *Q:* How did you think about money and material things in the past? And how do you think about them now?

A: In the past, I had a friend in Guangdong who was the same age as me. After graduation from college, he worked as a salesman in a joint venture. He knew how to entertain himself and he had a high income. When we went out together, he would ride a motorcycle. I admired him very much and I wanted to ride a motorcycle too. I told him that: "I earned 72RMB in 1988 and if I can earn 10,000RMB each year, I will be very happy." He replied: "it's very simple to earn 10,000 RMB." Later on, he went on to do business as a merchant and earned several million RMB. I was very impressed by what I saw when I went to visit him in his company.

Q: His deeds impressed and encouraged you greatly?

A: It didn't play a crucial role but only influenced me gradually.

Q: Do you think more about money and material things than you did before?

A: I want to make money through my creativity and the added value created by me for the company. My current 200,000RMB annually is not my whole income. My income also includes bonuses given by the leaders according to the market situation by the end of each year. What I am thinking now is whether I can succeed. I think that you can get much after you succeed. "The winner is the king and the loser is the servant."

S7, in contrast to the others, indicates he has not become more materialistic with the transformation, but he complains that his daughter's generation only cares about money. Like S7, S9 says he has resisted becoming more materialistic, although he indicates the importance of profit-oriented thinking in business in the following excerpt:

> I think, in my line of business, everyone is almost the same as the others, and we think little about money and material things. We can meet life's basic demands and think little of our individual lives. As for the enterprises, the more the profits are, the better, which is absolute.

Important here is the split he introduces between profit-oriented thinking at work and non-materialism outside of work. Also in relation to materialism at work, S13 notes the importance of money for maintaining one's image:

> I can't dress casually as I am the president of the company. I didn't pay much attention to my image in the past but now I can't do that anymore. I have to think carefully about clothes, consumption, and the brands of products. To tell the truth, I won't buy things from stands along the streets nor will I go to have dinner in a small restaurant. I think a western suit worth several thousand RMB is acceptable, but I will think it a waste of money to buy a suit worth tens of thousands of RMB.[1]

S15 is similar in linking money with status. Although he claims to no longer be materialistic, he declares with a sly smile that "money indeed represents success."

The retrospective reports of the older generation informants indicate that they have not changed at all in terms of their materialistic values. They each highly value thrift and tend to look down on the materialism of the younger generations. For example, S4 reports that "the society has become too commercialized and I'm not satisfied with it." S8 decries the effects of gambling on society, and sticks to his old values because of his lack of need to adapt:

> Even now I still stick to the traditional values such as diligence and hard work, thinking of others before myself. One reason for this is that I am quite old now. The other reason is that there is no need for me to enjoy the high-level of consumption. To meet the basic demands of life is enough for me. These were also the traditional values I held in the past.

S6 and S14, without openly condemning the materialism of the younger generation, nonetheless have maintained their traditional valuations of thrift.

Father-son pair comparisons also demonstrate a trend of expanded material aspirations in the younger generations, which is especially notable considering the high traditional valuation of thrift in China. While S6 highly values pragmatism, thrift, and de-emphasis of material accumulation, his son, S5, focuses excessively on possessions, for example, in his purchase of toys for his daughter "every two to three days:"

> *Q:* Since your daughter is still small, she won't ask much from you.
> *A:* No, she has high requirements and I have to buy toys for her.
> *Q:* Do the toy costs make up a large proportion in your expenditures?
> *A:* I think they make up a medium proportion, from 500RMB to 600RMB[2] every month.
> *Q:* What is your principle in deciding to buy a toy for her? How do you decide whether to buy toys for her or not? Or you buy her toys whenever she wants?
> *A:* Uhmm . . . no principles.
> *Q:* Do you meet her reasonable requirements?
> *A:* I will meet her unreasonable requirements as well. (He laughs.) Usually, I buy her one thing every two or three days.

While S7 does not reveal much materialism in his own interview, his father (S8) complains about the materialism of the younger generations and of his son and his daughter specifically:

> The youngsters hold different opinions, that they always consume and enjoy life in advance. When we were young, we were told to be frugal

> and we held the opinion that we should enjoy life after we struggled. Even now I still cannot change my mind. How much money I spend totally depends on how much money I own. I will never spend my next-month's salary. So we fall behind the young people . . . oh no, not the young people, we fall behind the current society and cannot catch up with it. In that time we were frugal and never spent more money than we had. What could we do if we lost our jobs? How could we pay the debt? I also worried about it. But now, the youngsters have different experiences and opinions . . . Now things have changed. The economic level has been improved a lot. For example, my daughter and her husband are working in Japan and earn a lot of money. My son also gets a good salary. However, I often say to them, "even when you are rich, you shouldn't spend all the money you have. You must think of the future and the resources."

The difference between S13 and S14 is less notable. Although both father and son demonstrate high thrift in their interviews, as previously noted with his need to purchase expensive suits, the son engages in high consumption for the purpose of maintaining his image.

A comparison between the generations as groups within my interviews also demonstrates the tension between the traditional Chinese value of thrift and modern consumerism and heightened materialism among the younger informants. First, thrift remains a core value among several of the Shanghai businessmen we interviewed. However, several of the businessmen (S5, S9, and S11) did not mention thrift at all, while every one of the older interviewees spoke of it as an important value. The following is a typical valuation of thrift by the older generation:

> *(S4)*
>
> Nowadays, my wife and I still flush the toilet with water that we have used to do the washing. It is stressed that rubbish should be sorted. So we have done this. There are lots of newspapers in my house. We sell them so as to save resources by recycling.

Some from the younger generation also refer to thrift within the interviews:

> *(S13)*
>
> I will make a balance and I will take control of my consumption. I will set an example for others and seldom attend dinners and parties and therefore I don't spend too much money. . . . When I worked in company X, I couldn't spend the several thousand RMB I earned each month. I don't like to waste money.

However, some businessmen do not mention thrift at all, and, among those who do, there is a noticeable tension between the traditional value of thrift and the modern value of consumerism, as was noted in a previous excerpt, where a smiling S15 reveals that money indeed represents success. A similar assessment is in the following excerpt:

> *(S9)*
>
> I am not particular about consumption, and don't have higher requirements. I think there is a link between success and consumption, but it's not necessarily always so. A person doesn't mark his success by means of consumption. I personally think success is to do what you should do well. Of course, I don't deny that sometimes consumption is a criterion for success, for example, you can go on a holiday when you have time, etc.

A growth in materialism is indicated between generations, where I have found that, for our informants, the younger businessmen are much more materialistic than their fathers. For example, each of the older informants expresses low material aspirations to the extent that they do not desire more than they need or more than they can afford:

> *(S8)*
>
> I have no demand of material things. I don't regard money as so important. But there is a premise: how much money I spend depends on how much money I have. I think there is no need to save money. I'd like to spend the money that I have. But I have no other extra demand. For example, my wife wants to travel to the United States, and then we went there. We could afford the costs, so why not? If we cannot afford it, there is no way for us to demand more.

In contrast, several informants from the younger group express their high valuation of materialism and wealth. The following is an example:

> *(S13)*
>
> I appreciate the following words said by Jiacheng Li: Money means only a number for me now and the process to make money is the process to manifest success. The number is indicative of the correctness of one's decisions.

It would give a false impression to say that all of the businessmen we interviewed could be considered "materialistic." S15, for example, seems to be non-materialistic in private life but admits that money still represents success for him, and at work he is expected to focus on profits and value money above everything else:

> *(S15)*
>
> I had an early start in my present field so I concern myself little about material things. However, I care about material things for my company and my business.

As shown before, some of the material and consumption pressures arise from work requirements. However, some of them arise from within the family. These businessmen consider it their duty to "provide for" their families:

> *(S13)*
>
> *Q:* Do you have any plans for going on vacation?
>
> *A:* Basically, I will have a plan for each long holiday, but I didn't go out during this National Day holiday. I will go out with my family. I think as a successful man, you should be kind to your family members and make sure that they don't feel the pressure of life.
>
> *(S15)*
>
> I hope my family members will be all healthy in the future. I want to let them be happy through my efforts. For example, if they want to visit foreign countries, they can just go ahead and do what they want to do without concerning themselves about the material things.

The Chinese interviews reveal three sources of enhanced materialism among the younger generation: the necessity of consumption for cultivating a professional image, the need to focus on profit calculation within the business, and a focus on the family's material security.

The Moscow Interviews

Similar to the Chinese, the Russian informants also actively speak about materialism, compared to other topics they might have addressed. The economic devastation of Russia's transition years brought a powerful and motivating sense of material insecurity to many people. This material insecurity appears to have generated both enhanced cost-benefit thinking at work as a necessary tool of success and enhanced consumerism and money lust privately as individual aspirations begin to mirror the limitless possibility of the new material sphere.

An older respondent illustrates the first part of this transition well. M8, says that, in 1990, he was focused on material survival, but his values had to broaden as he had to "commercialize" within his business in order to stay afloat. He came to the realization that "money is needed" in work; in his mind, the meaning of money transformed from a basic commodity for survival into a way of life.

Money as a way of life means that the expansion of cost-benefit thinking occurred as a necessary tool of success within business. This mode of action requires the establishment of strict monetary boundaries and the notion of profit calculation. M11 describes this:

> First, [thinking more about money nowadays] is connected to what I do. In my opinion, a businessperson who does not think about money and material success cannot engage in business. Among my acquaintances and the people of my age, only few are engaged in establishing and running their own business.

Paradoxically, in contrast to the rational cost-benefit calculations at work, materialism in private life appears to have become liberated from boundaries and tends to a form a passive consumerism. M1, for example, illustrates this pattern. He thinks of expenses for the office, but in his private life, his consumption has become second nature:

> The last and single thought that I have today is how to pay for the new office. I'm tired of thinking about that—how to turn over my money. Frankly saying, neither me nor my wife, we cannot even make some savings. My wife has said it well: "Look, everybody thinks how to buy a car, how to manage all around it, but we . . ." All my thoughts about the BMW lasted exactly 10 minutes. Honestly. Just dully went and bought it quickly. I even didn't choose a model. I had just a clear and bright opinion that one should buy a BMW, that's all. But I can say that we just do not have an example, so I can't compare. I see it, as my brother thinks about some themes in a detailed way. But I'm too lazy to spend my time for it.

M1's thinking in the office is dominated by concerns about costs and profits, while his home life is the opposite as he transforms into the unthinking consumer, perhaps as a retreat, as he is "tired of thinking about how to turn over his money."

Related to this consumerism is the expansion of the general attraction to material wealth. For the older generation, money was valued for survival purposes only, whereas for the younger generation it becomes the major focus. For example, in pair M5-M6, while the father is anti-materialist, his son is wealthy and materialistic, throwing his money around to satisfy his needs for "entertainment." Similar is another pair, M9 and M10, both of whom started their own businesses and both think about money more now than before, albeit the father refers to money still more in terms of survival and the son in terms of wealth. The father, although a workaholic, remains nonetheless quite family oriented. In contrast, the son, more money-centered, is divorced and estranged from his family. At times in his interview, the son ostensibly downgrades the importance of money, saying he desires wealth, but not "luxury." However, he is unable to hide the allure of wealth for him, and his dismissal of luxuries appears to be a self-soothing mechanism since he cannot afford them. For example, he mentions "of course I could say that a Ferrari is nice, but it is anyhow inaccessible for me." Although he admits that wealth doesn't bring happiness, he still wishes to have more. At the beginning of the transition, he was striving in academia, a pursuit he abandoned, apparently for material reasons. He notes that there are more temptations and possibilities to spend money nowadays, such as a greater variety of consumption options and leisure activities. At the same time, the costs of everyday expenses have increased as well, as one must manage the apartment and other survival-related expenses. He has a sense of uncertainty in how to deal with money; it is unclear how to save and invest, even if one has money. These facts lead him to note that he thinks about costs and money much more than before. Even M9's less materialistic father M10 is somewhat attracted to the ways in which the oligarchs 'made' their money, because he understands "in what a brilliant manner the money was stolen." Money has a sheen in the new society, even among those who turn their backs to it.

Another pair, M11 and his mother, M12, is also an illustrative comparison for the materialism theme. M11, at the beginning of the transition, valued intellectuality and says that he was "disgusted" by the goal of making money during those times. However, prodded by material insecurity, he soon realized the "reality" of the necessity of making money to survive and then created his own business. He has now learned to accept these new values, and writes off his earlier aversion to materialism as due to the "maximalism of the young person." However, his mother M12 still possesses those very same values and is exasperated by the changes. She notes that there were fewer chances to be materialistic before, since it was so hard to locate scarce goods. One could therefore not plan for them:

> *Q:* And when you had to look at prices, what influenced your choice? Was that influence bigger earlier or now?
>
> *A:* Of course that was bigger before. But conditions were different then as well. One couldn't buy something good then, one had to manage some unbelievable searches. And probably occasionally you could find something good, but you couldn't plan it. There wasn't anything good, especially as a present. That's why . . . I search, choose, look now, but within some reasonable limits. I can pay several thousands but of course not many thousands.

Now, in contrast, she notes that boundaries should be erected in regard to money, for the market itself does not prescribe boundaries in the same way as during Soviet times, where scarcity was very real, and to acquire something special, one had to launch some "unbelievable searches." It is these internal boundaries that are lacking in her grandson, according to his father, M11:

> When I observed my son and his friends, I found out that it is much easier for them to give their toys to each other as presents. They give each other different games, Gameboy, that is, the small amount of property they possess.

The father does not understand why the son has no concept of something being too expensive or the idea of not needing something; paradoxically, this also allows the son to part more easily with his many possessions, such as his video games. This shows materialism both as a form of high aspirations and habitus in regard to material possessions and also as a simultaneous low degree of internalized boundaries regarding the scarcity of material objects.

The elder M12 also sees modern materialist values as having a negative impact on other spheres, such as in education. Based on her former work experiences in the government education ministry, she laments:

> Now everything is different. There is a new generation now. Teachers have changed, if we observe secondary education. They have to make money; they have to think always about that. It's hard to bring back the old things. Maybe they'd like to, but they can't do it another way. It's the old generation who had the feeling of duty. The young generation already counts [money].

Her impression is that burgeoning aspirations and survival incentives negate moral duty, a point to be returned to in Chapter 8. Her son M11 describes how the collapse of the Soviet Union led to this new materialist ethos:

> The reason for this was that everything around collapsed, the whole old system . . . You see, it was very hard to talk about this. In the newspapers it was widely discussed that the majority of the young people believed that there is no point in studying if you have a street-stall near by the Kursk train station for selling Coca-cola and beer. This would mean that you have achieved everything! Or for example in case you had a 10-year-old BMW, leather jacket, and golden chain, this meant that you have reached the top. Everything was measured with material values.

Even some members of the older cohort have been affected by this transition from valuing intellectuality to valuing materialism. For example, M10, who owns a computer business, notes that at the beginning of the transition, his role models were creative scientists. In contrast, now he only thinks about "economics," because "everything else is crap." Calling it "a certain human logic," economics becomes reality for him, a state of nature, which has caused him to think more about his and his family's material needs, a focus on simple survival:

> *Q:* Do you think nowadays more about money and material goods than before?
>
> *A:* I have to think more about them because there is no future in front of us. During the communist times there were good prospects and stable wages, which we received no matter what. Of course, one was supposed to work for them, but the whole thing happened in a different way.

The Leipzig Interviews

Like businessmen from Shanghai and Moscow, many young Leipzigers report a rising focus on material survival since the beginning of the transformation. L1, for example, says he thinks more often about money and material things for the purpose of survival: "Well, I do think about them more often now, not because I'm materialistic, but because it's just . . . necessary."

In contrast, his father, L2, says that he was more focused on material *survival* at the beginning of the transformation, but now thinks more about the material *situation*, such as pensions, health care, needs arising from growing old. This transformation is one from material survival to material administration. L5, introduces a similar distinction between "wishing for" and "working with" money:

> *Q:* If you would have to compare today with 15 years ago, how much do you think today of money and material things, as compared to the past. More, less . . . ?
>
> *A:* That would have to be distinguished. In the sense of wishing, less, so to say, than in the past and in the sense of handling it, working with it, more. As a student, of course money did interest me as well but these were those wishes to have lots of money sometime or to have money and to have an existence, to be able to buy a house or something, they did of course exist and worried me, but the actual situation to need money, that did not worry me so much. And today I have to take care of a family and I have a house that I invested in, so today that is much more important but less in the sense of wishing for money. I could also live with considerably less. I would have to change but that is not. . .the situation of wishing for more money, of course, it happens every once in a while, but that doesn't worry me a lot.

L2 also notes that he has come to think more of costs and benefits "in order to get along." This difference between generations could be one of lifestage, since the son may have more pressure for material survival now because of his family. The material values of some informants have apparently changed little. L4, for example, writes off his lack of materialism to the fact that he is "well-off," noting that his material views did not change since he was also doing financially well in GDR times.

More radically than the others, L9 thinks more of money now than in the past. He remarks that he must think about money more nowadays as a practicality, because of image cultivation at work:

> When [commercials] communicate it like that, so that I accept that for my image . . . simple example, cars. Although one isn't alone saying that a car has to drive from A to B reliably. But where one is also judged from the outside: Is the business alright when he is driving such an old wreck? Or, when the car is too big, the customers say, "we're all paying for that" as well. One has to have certain influences from the outside that guide one searching for a car and the commercials of the producers is of course a means, that shapes the image and that one orientates oneself after.

Intergenerational comparisons reveal that both the younger businessmen and their fathers have enhanced valuations of material administration and material survival in relation to the necessities of adapting at work. However, most appear to disdain materialism in the sense of luxury or money lust. Pair L1 and L2 exhibits this trend, as mentioned above. Regarding another pair, L3 and L4, both are focused on their family's financial security and education but consider themselves unmaterialistic. L3 notes, "It is important to me that my son doesn't solely live out of commerce but that he directs his life by such things as friendship." In comparison, his father says that while money is important in life, it is "not the most important thing." Similarly, L5 and L6 both also devalue money and materialism. L5 also tries to communicate to his children that "money isn't everything," while L6 complains about the "greediness for money" that is presently in society:

> What bothers me most is that . . . this greediness for money, which did not exist in our times because there was not that amount of money and the crimes that come with it. There is hardly any sense of solidarity, hardly any. Everybody tries to find ways of making money, of ripping somebody off, or of attacking somebody in order to get money. And that's the worst thing we took over when the Wall came down. The worst thing. Crime, greediness for money and hardly any sense of solidarity, hardly any. Because everybody somehow tries to get money. Today, people are robbing an old lady for 3.60 Euros. I mean, in the GDR we also had crime, that I can say, but it was not in this way because it just wasn't necessary.

L7 and L8 both think of money more now than in the past, but for L7, this means in terms of material activity or "working with money." His father, L8, tells that he became quite materially oriented at the beginning of the transformation, but now regrets it. During those times, he longed to establish a business, create new jobs and lasting products, but now has grown more cynical about his society. For example, he says that, in the past people worked more for idealism, whereas now, it is only for money. Nonetheless, he boasts that he and his wife have owned five pieces of real estate.

Both L11 and L12 say that they think about money more today than in the past, largely because of business requirements. A businessman, L12 says, knows cost-benefit calculating "from the cradle." He says:

> Yes, one is forced to think more about money now. You have to. During the GDR, You got your money for what you did, there was no need to hurry after your money. It was a totally different moral of payment, what you put on the invoice was paid. Today that's different. And neither was there haggling or something. That's different today. And that's why you have to talk more about money and contractual things. It all moved more into the foreground. During the GDR the prosperity wasn't as high as today and we had no possibility to make big money or something. And to think about money, that all went automatically. Today you have to be careful not to be cheated and buy insurance or something or to be lured by the stock market where the money is gone or something.

While his business focus is similar to his father's, there is something different about L11. He has another type of materialism as well: a hunger for luxuries. For example, he hints that he would like to indulge in a nice BMW or Porsche for himself, had he the money, and fantasizes about building a villa:

> *Q:* What you want to accomplish in your life, what you wish for . . .
> *A:* Let's say, but that's now more of a fantasy, Villa Toscana, that is, building a house in a Mediterranean style.

Thus, for businessmen from all three societies, the importance of material things, money, calculating profit, and material habitus moves into the foreground with the expansion of opportunities and a new money culture. Now we come to an important question: how do changes in work, ambition, individualism, materialism and consumption affect the main topic of this book, the interpersonal sphere? The following chapter deals with the growing latency of family values and the instrumentalization of friendship.

7 Family Relationships and Friendship

> I am comprised of two different persons. One of them is a family type. When I go back to [the city where my wife and children live], I am a devoted family person: I clean my little children's behinds, I kiss my children, I take them horseback riding and to play tennis. These things bring me enormous pleasure. The other person is the Moscow one. This means lechery, the night clubs, et cetera.
>
> —Moscow informant, M5

"Christian" (L7), is 34 years old, and has just taken over the family business, a print shop managed during GDR times by his father. He has a 6 month old baby with his live-in girlfriend. His father, "Gerhardt" (L8), is 62 and still works part time at the business he used to own.

Gerhardt reports having had no role models during the transformation years. Christian reports that, as a former swimmer himself, some famous swimmers—and even David Hasselhoff from "Baywatch"—served as role models for him. However, Christian does not report his own father as a role model, even though he was in the same family business. Their father-son relationship appears strained from working so closely together for so long.

Regarding their 'materialist' values, both report thinking about money more often today than in the past and say that the degree of exploitation has increased in society. Gerhardt reports that such exploitation, within "a brutal capitalism," is "totally normal. A worker will never make money using his own money. He will always make money using your money."

As a result of their high focus on work, both have grown weary. Christian, for instance, remarks that, even in comparison to his relationships, "work by now has become pretty much the center of life." In another section of the interview, Christian expresses the wish that he would be no longer "enslaved" by self-employment. His father Gerhardt had long ago grown tired of work and wishes to retire soon.

Both value their work very highly because of their motivations to take care of their families, but they mention that the family suffers as a result of these efforts. They say that they have "chosen" work over family but feel nonetheless conflicted about their choice. Christian says this problem is due to the lack of time in the day. Gerhardt implies that the problem is more fundamental, that the family had to suffer from building a business. Going further, Gerhardt says that it is "normal" that one's work makes the family suffer within capitalism.

The personal relationship is the medium for normative transmission and control. The family and friendships are the core, primary, relationships that provide emotional support, well-being, and this social integrative function. Although family relationships undoubtedly remain the greatest niches into which to escape from the stresses of work, they are also profoundly sensitive to competing demands for time, alternative values, and alternative ways of thinking that are promoted by working life. Work-family conflicts are therefore a dominant problem to be solved by successful workers in the modern economy. One of the key solutions is 'delaying' the active valuation of the family until after retirement. Friendship undergoes change as well, especially as it becomes useful, instrumentalized for business purposes. This cues us in to a fundamental feature underlying valuations of close personal relationships; they are intrinsically and intuitively valuable, rather than rationally calculated as valuable. As was explained in Chapter 3, this mode of valuation is threatened by more rational, calculative modes, where individuals may become means to an end rather than ends in themselves.

This chapter proceeds by first presenting the quantitative survey findings, followed by a summary of interview results, followed by country-specific interview findings.

QUANTITATIVE FINDINGS

Survey data indicate the differentiation of the value of unconditionally respecting parents and especially of parental willingness to sacrifice for children by birth cohort. The relative importance of family is also substantially lower among the younger birth cohorts, the rich, and those in modern occupations. Friendship, however, appears to be a modern value, as its valuation is higher among younger people in modern occupations.

Figure 7.1 represents a strong trend, whereby each younger birth cohort consecutively cares less and less about sacrificing for its children. Within this question, informants could agree with one of the following statements: "Parents have a life of their own and should not be asked to sacrifice their own well-being for the sake of their children" or "Parents' duty is to do their best for their children even at the expense of their own well-being." Across the three countries, which are similar in values (albeit the rate for Russians is somewhat lower), 77 percent of the oldest cohort, born between 1901 and 1920, is likely to agree with parental sacrifice, while the same is true for only 45 percent of the 1976–1980 birth cohort. To reiterate, each new birth cohort, including those middle cohorts in the 'parenting phase' of the life course, is less likely to believe in parental sacrifice.

We may also look at the value of parental sacrifice for children through the perspective of occupation (See Table B.3, Appendix B, for this chapter's T-test results). These differences are significant across all three countries. The Eastern German (63 percent of new occupations versus 70 percent of others)

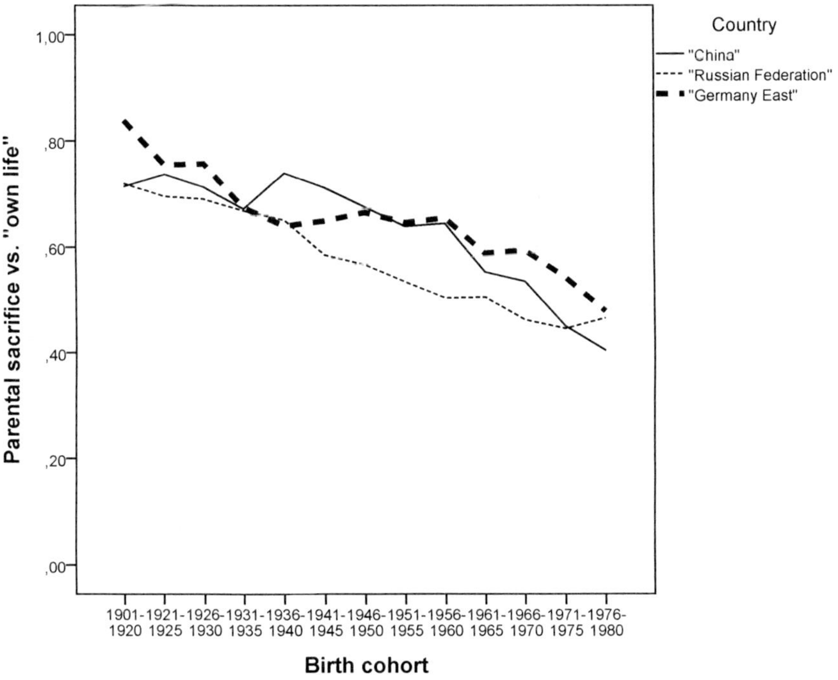

Figure 7.1 Value of parental sacrifice for children by birth cohort in China, Russia, and Eastern Germany, WVS 1990–2005.
Source: World Values Survey 1981–2008 Official Aggregate Files v. 20090901 and v. 20090914.

and Russian cases (55 percent versus 58 percent) display smaller variations within this dimension, but the differentiation in China is huge, with those working within the modern economy, as office workers, managers, and owners, 15 percent *less* likely to sacrifice their own well-being for their children.

In Russia and Eastern Germany, the richest 15 percent of people are also 3 to 4 percent less likely to believe in sacrifice for their children. The difference in China between the rich and the others is insignificant.

In regard to whether or not one should love and respect one's parents unconditionally, this also appears to display an overall decline by birth cohort. Especially in Eastern Germany, the older cohorts place more and more value on respecting parents and the younger ones are more likely to say that parents should "earn" their respect. In China, the change across cohorts is relatively flat, while in Russia, a gradual decline with younger cohorts is visible.

The new occupational groups, being less traditional in theory, also are less likely to embrace unconditional respect for parents. This difference is greatest in China and more moderate in Russia and in Eastern Germany.

Across all pooled respondents, 78 percent of those in the modern occupations embrace unconditional parental respect for parents, compared with 84 percent in other occupations. Results comparing the rich to other income groups on this value are mixed. In China, the rich are more respectful, in Eastern Germany they are moderately less respectful, and the difference negligible in Russia.

A problem with the main World Values Survey question on the importance of family is its lack of variability. For nearly everyone, family is "important." For this reason, I made a relative scale that compares the value of family to the valuations of three other known values: friendship, leisure, and work. In this way, we can see how the value of family measures according to other competing values. Figure 7.2 demonstrates that this value drops strongly among younger birth cohorts groups. In Eastern Germany, where this drop is the strongest, family is valued 80 percent more than the average of competing other values among oldest birth cohorts, whereas for youngest cohorts, family's 'edge' over other values approaches 15 percent. This drop is much more moderate in Russia (from 85 percent higher valuation to 60 percent higher) and is the smallest in China (from 80 percent higher to 63 percent higher).

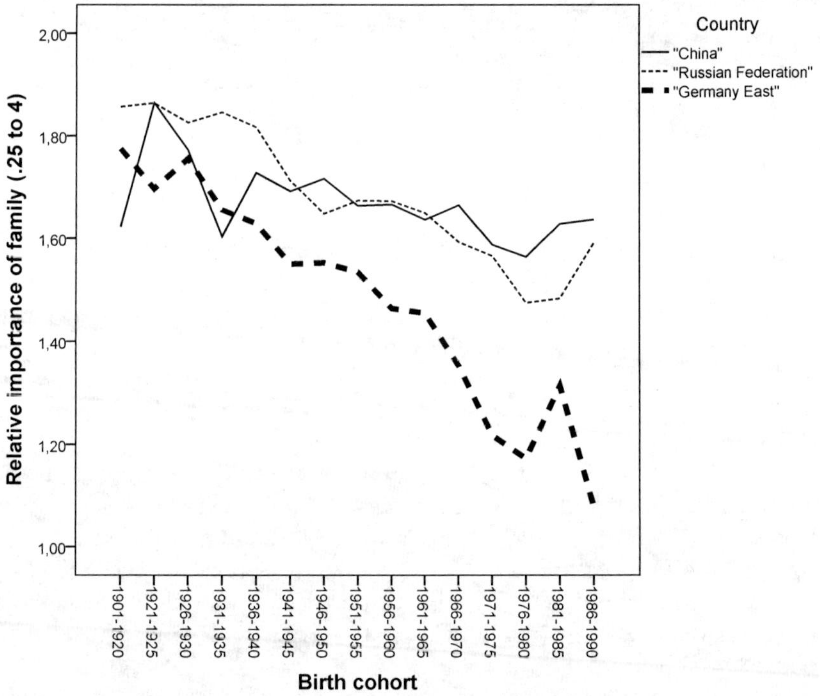

Figure 7.2 Relative importance of family compared to work, leisure, friends by birth cohort in China, Russia, and Eastern Germany, WVS 1990–2005.
Source: World Values Survey 1981–2008 Official Aggregate Files v. 20090901 and v. 20090914.

Among individuals in modern occupations, the relative valuation of family is moderately, albeit significantly lower than among those in traditional occupations. This same trend is found among the richest 15 percent; they have a lower relative valuation of the importance of family.

Within the WVS, the value of the importance of friends in life varies nearly perfectly by birth cohort (Figure 7.3). Each newer birth cohort is consecutively more friendship-oriented in each society. Across all years and countries, the oldest cohort (mean=2.98) is less friendship-oriented than the youngest cohort (mean=3.52).

When viewing friendship values through the prism of occupations, it becomes clear that high friendship values are focused within the privileged occupation group. Across waves and country samples, employers, managers, professionals, supervisors, and office workers (mean=3.21) have a significantly higher value of friendship than the other combined (mean=3.09) occupational groupings. Thus, the expansion of friendship values appears to proceed in tandem with the economic transformation, perhaps because of the importance of 'contacts' and weak ties, the instrumentalized relations mentioned by the interview informants. In China and Russia, those with the highest income are also more friendship-oriented, albeit moderately so, but the difference between income groups in Eastern Germany is negligible.

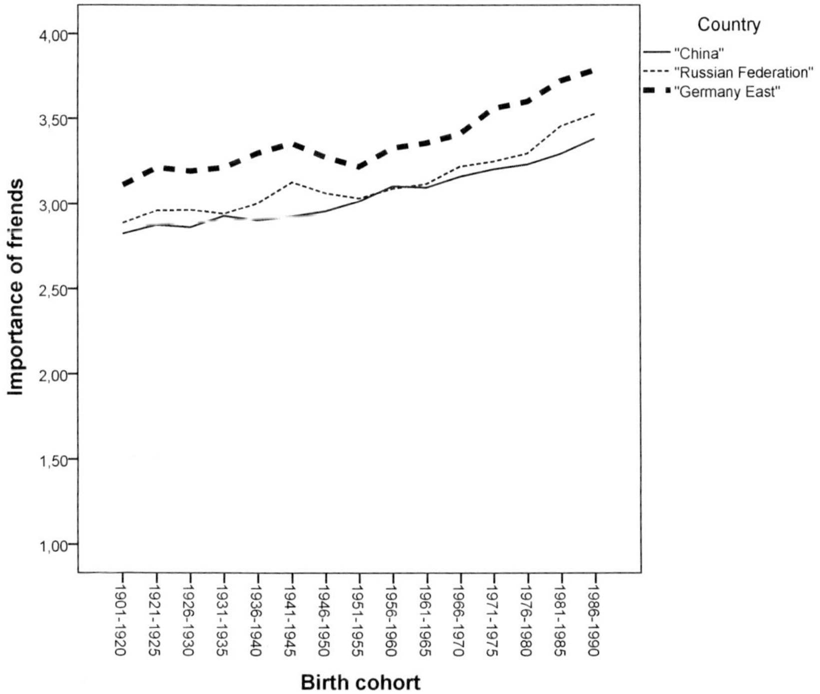

Figure 7.3 Importance of friends by birth cohort in China, Russia, and Eastern Germany, WVS 1990–2005.
Source: World Values Survey 1981–2008 Official Aggregate Files v. 20090901 and v. 20090914.:

OVERALL QUALITATIVE FINDINGS

In parallel to the quantitative analysis reported above, interview data indicate that family values appear to be challenged by enhanced values of work. Two pieces of evidence especially support this trend: the mal-adaptation of the older generation to the transformation and thus diminished respect for it, on the one hand, and the individualization of the socialization of children, on the other.

Family valuations closely follow work valuations across all three countries. Typically, when informants are ambitious, in terms of both self-realization and material goals regarding their work, they are devaluing the family in tandem. The quantitative results above harmonize with this interview finding: younger cohorts are less likely to believe in sacrifice for children in lieu of living their 'own lives.' Furthermore, the relative value of family compared to other values sinks rapidly in younger cohorts. In the interviews we find that those who are ambitious in the early years of their working lives tend to put off high family valuations until their work lives are complete, until their retirement years. Work valuations are variable across the three cases, and we find a parallel variation in family values. For example, a reluctance in sacrificing the family for work becomes quite apparent in Leipzig, whereas this is rare among the Shanghai- and somewhat limited among the Moscow informants. The younger informants are usually more ambitious and less family centered, while older informants were usually more family centered. The Leipzigers were exceptions to this trend in both directions: the younger Leipzig informants were more family-centered than the younger informants in Shanghai and Moscow, while the older Leipzigers tended to be less family-centered than other older informants, presumably because they worked during the transformation years.

Regarding the respect of the elder generation, it is clear that, across each of the three cases, the working generation's respect of its parents has become challenged because of the perceived mal-adaptation of the elder generation. This trend is especially noted in China, followed by Russia and Eastern Germany. While the Leipzigers may tend to emphasize this value more than the others, questions still emerge regarding the successful transmission of this value to the younger generation. Quantitative indications reported above have shown the diminishing respect for elders among younger and younger cohorts, especially in Eastern Germany.

The value of socialization of children among those within the parenting generation seems to be challenged in similar ways across societies. Among those investing energy in thinking about the socialization of their children, the entrance of individualist values, such as independence and ambition, is apparent across the three societies. However, some informants have also adopted an individualist approach to their children's upbringing in another way, preferring to let them be socialized 'naturally' rather than imprinting them with any specific values. Confusion and contradiction regarding the parental child-rearing role also becomes apparent, especially among the Shanghai and Moscow businessmen. Especially among the Muscovites, the role of material values seems to conflict with the transmission of traditional values to the new generations. While Moscow and Shanghai informants clearly have trouble spending time with their children due to their strong focus on work, Leipzig informants tend to rather highly value their children at the expense of work.

Another difference between qualitative cases is that the Chinese informants report the expansion of their friendship networks during the transformation period, while the Russians and Eastern Germans report that their friendship circles contracted. The latter informants spent less time with friends usually because of their attempted focus on family alongside their demanding work schedules. Presumably, since the Chinese report that informal social networks remain quite important to how they do business, and they spend very long hours at work as well, this strong friendship focus may come at the expense of family. While representative quantitative data do not report upon the size of friendship networks, it does tell us that the overall valuation of friendship is higher in consecutively younger cohorts in each of the three societies.

Quantitative findings and an overall summary of interview data have been presented on the topic of family and friendship values. More detailed interview results for each of the three cities will be presented in the following sections.

The Shanghai Interviews

We find qualitative differences in how the younger and older cohorts in Shanghai reflect on their families, and these differences are directly connected to their valuations of work. This intergenerational variation could be summarized as the transition from 'work and family' harmony in the older cohort to a 'work then family' ideal in the younger. To clarify, 'work then family' does not imply a postponement of *family formation* as it might in Europe but rather the establishment of a family and the postponement of *qualitative participation* in family life.

To be sure, some from our young cohort of Chinese businessmen do value the family very highly. For example, S5 reports, "The most important thing for me now is my daughter." Another informant, S9, also rates his family as quite important, although in second place behind personal achievement, in the following passage:

(S9)

Q: Which values are important to you?
A: The first value is to devote myself to the cause I love and make some achievements. The second is that family is very

important so that a person's mood will be happy and therefore I value family very much. The third is how to make myself happy. That is to communicate more with friends and make more friends, which I think is very important. And those are my values.

Despite the two cases above which value family very highly, the dominant trend among the businessmen we interviewed in Shanghai is a conflict between the family and work, as illustrated in the following exchange:

(S15)

Q: Do you think some of your values are in conflict with others'?
A: Yes. Take my family values for example. I think family values are very important while my family members and friends don't think that I regard them as important. Nowadays I don't spend much time with my family members for I have little time to do so.

Other informants apparently experience less of a conflict because they clearly value work over family. This is the case for S13, who explicitly says that he solves conflicts by valuing the enterprise over the family. His wife understands when he has to miss dinner because of working late.

In one case, Interviewee 7, who has been heavily influenced in his life by Japanese enterprise culture because of time he spent in Japan, has very weak relations with his family and, at the same time, considers his workplace *as* his family, suggesting the possibility that, for him, one has replaced the other:

> I have no communication with my daughter. There is a deep generation gap between us. . . . I value the enterprise culture, which is like a family conception. What you do is for the company. Of course, you can leave the company but we usually won't do so for the company has a cohesiveness, which can hardly be described in words.

The retrospective reports of the young informants indicate, as was reported above, a phasing of high family valuations within the life course after the high work valuations of their younger years. Such informants tended to be highly career oriented in their youth and middle years, and they transition, income and values allowing, to a leisurely 'family-first' phase of their lives thereafter. This is the ideal pattern—in the sense that it seems to lead to an ideal outcome for them—followed by two of our informants (S17, S5). Three informants (S9, S13, S15) remain in the 'career' stage of this pattern, and it remains unclear whether they will progress into the family stage or not. Another informant S7, who is 49 years old, has seemingly failed to make this transition. He no longer has the motivation of his younger years, but he also has no strong family to turn to. Instead, he describes his work as his family, since his life as dull, and his personality has seemingly dissolved within his work:

Q: What is the biggest goal in your life?
A: My personal biggest goal is connected with the company's goals for there is no use separating company goals from individual goals. The company has its three-year plans and five-year plans. In the IT industry, especially in a modern enterprise, there are no individual goals to speak of.

A final young Chinese informant, S11, is unique in that he is not yet married and did not yet have a family. Despite this, or perhaps because of it, if material insecurity is indeed a major motivating factor, he has very low career ambitions compared to his peers; he almost never mentions his job or his goals.

It may be tempting for some readers to see the above patterns of values as natural, since the informants are in the 'work phases' of their life courses; thus, a high valuation of career would be expected. However, keep in mind that each informant, except for S11, has a child, their ages ranging between 2 and 19 years old. In other words, these businessmen are *also* within the family-phase of their life courses, so why do their work ambitions trump their family duties?

In strong contrast to these businessmen, there is much less ambivalence and conflict for the older generation when they refer to their family values:

(S6)

In my opinion, family is the most important. The Chinese people always attach great importance to the harmony of family. You will feel it is a pity if you don't enjoy a harmonious family, even though you have an excellent job and earn a lot.

The other older informants also attach great importance to the family and report that this is normal for their generation. Retrospective reports from the four older informants highlight two important points: they were also highly work-oriented during their younger years, but they were not work obsessive to the extent that their family lives suffered. S14 illustrates this point clearly:

Q: How do you coordinate work values with family ones?
A: There is no big problem. Every time when I was on a business trip, I would ask my wife to spend a little more time at home. Sometimes she went to other cities or countries for business

> reasons, I had to spend more time at home. Usually we didn't leave home for a long time at the same time . . . So we always took turns and tried to find a balance between work and family. Sometimes both of us had to be on business trip, and then I would postpone my leaving date, because the time was not fixed and could be changed. In such circumstances, my colleagues would leave Shanghai earlier than me. After I finished seeing to matters at home, I went and traveled to the place as well. We adjusted the work to the time. All of us were purehearted, so the work just went through smoothly.

In marked contrast to the younger generation, none of our older interviewees ever devalues the family, is ambivalent about family, or is conflicted about family. This fact is also emphasized within the above father-son comparisons, where in each case, the fathers were considerably more family oriented than their sons.

Corresponding to the intergenerational enhancement of work at the expense of family, I have found a gap among the informants in filial piety, or respect of parents and elders. Whereas Chinese culture traditionally has placed filial relations as the core of Chinese social relations, only our older informants speak about filial piety when asked about their values. For example, in response to the question about whether any specific principles guide his actions, S6 reports the importance of ethics and morality in the family, such as respecting and being filial to parents and the elders. This man also attempts to pass these values on to his children and grandchildren. S14 reports on his filial values in a similar way:

> Be respectful to parents and others. Now my children are very respectful to us. I think this is because I am very respectful to my father. They see it and remember it. Then they are also respectful to my father and me. We are respectful to each other in the family. You know, family is the smallest element of the society. If you can't manage your family well, how can you work well and manage other people?

Both of these older informants highly value traditional Chinese filial relations and try to pass this value onto the newer generations, and the second man implies that this value-transmission has been successful. However, the interviews with the younger generation show that not only do these two particular informants' sons not mention filial piety as a value, but our younger informants almost never mention filial relations. One exception is S17, who notes the importance of elders in the following passage:

> However, if an old person celebrates his ninetieth birthday, it's impossible for you to postpone it. In this case, I will lay my work aside. As a result, I will do those things first which can't be changed.

The near total silence of the younger generation on the issue of respecting elders is also noticed by some informants. S7, who himself does not seem to value filial relations, laments that his daughter and her generation are no better: "They won't express thanks to their parents and they won't learn from their parents, either." Perhaps explaining some of the declining respect for the older generation, many in the younger generation express that they had no adequate role models during the transition years, since their parents lacked the requisite knowledge and skills to succeed. S5 notes this fact:

Q: Who set the most important example for you in your life?
A: Do you mean when I was a middle school student or before then?
Q: Fifteen years ago?
A: Finally, you've got me to say things about 15 years ago. (He laughs.) My father was my example. However, after I entered college, I found that he wasn't above me in many aspects. In the college, I had no example to follow.

S13, like many of the informants, took his role models from popular culture, rather than from his family:

> I haven't had any definite role models. The "Life Fortune" program and the guests interviewed by the "Chinese entrepreneurs" [television programs] are all my role models. I want to combine all the strong points of every successful entrepreneur together and learn from them.

One of the exceptions is our 'social' S11, who learned much from his parents, but admits that they have perhaps become a bit outdated:

Q: What values do you learn from your teachers and parents?
A: I have learned almost nothing from my teachers as to how to behave, but I have learned much knowledge from them. My parents have a greater influence on me in values. And I have learnt much from them. They are farmers, honest and upright. I am honest and upright too, which I sometimes display to others.

The older informants, of course, recognize that they do not earn the respect that they perhaps believe they deserve:

> *(S4)*
>
> People care more and more about themselves and feel less and less responsible for the society. Take my wife and me as an example.

Nobody will give up his seat to us on a bus. This was not the case in the 1950s and the 1960s when we were young. We often gave up our seats to the old. Even now, if we have seats, we still give them up to those who need help such as pregnant women or women with babies in their arms.

Thus, there seems to be a tension between the younger cohort members and their parents. How are their relations with their own children?

It is important to ask whether or not parents are inclined to engage in the work of value transmission to their children, especially considering their high work valuations simultaneous to their fatherhood. Within the interviews, this issue is specifically inquired about through the question of "which values would you like to transmit to your children or grandchildren?" In every case, our older informants give examples of the values they try to transmit to the younger generations. Here is an example:

(S8)

Q: Which values did you try to instill in your grandchildren?

A: I told them how to behave. I told them to live morally straight. Those who were studying should study hard and those who were working should work hard as well.

... Everyone should make more contributions and ask for less. I just told them such kinds of things.

... But modern social values are different from ours. Now when I talk to them, they would always say, "you lived in such a period that you are bound to undergo a hard life. Now it's time for us to enjoy life." Our values are totally different so my communications with them work little.

In sharp contrast, most of the young informants (with the exceptions of S9 and S15) do not, or cannot, name values that they would like to pass on to their children. Some informants are noticeably caught off guard and are unable to answer the question. The following exchange is an example of this:

(S5)

Q: Thanks. Now your daughter is nearly three years old and she will attend preschool soon.

A: It's too early to talk about such things. She is not old enough to go to preschool.

Q: Two or three years later?

A: Yes, three years later.

Q: What values and principles do you require in her?

A: I haven't thought of such a question. You are requiring me to think of the problems of 15 years later. (He laughs.)
Q: Don't you think she should develop some values and principles from an early age?
A: I think I will let her lead a princess life for raising a daughter involves more money than raising a son. We have to find opportunities to let her broaden her mind, buy nice things for her and take her to go on holidays abroad regularly so as to heighten her horizons. Then, we will find a good husband for her. After that, we don't hold much responsibility for her. The reason for broadening her mind is for the fear that she might choose a husband who isn't suitable for her. It's the main reason for doing so.

Another pattern is that the businessmen consciously choose to not impart any specific values into their children and rather preferred to let them develop naturally and independently:

(S11)

Q: You are not married yet. When you get married and have children, which values will you instill in your children?
A: I won't instill anything in him purposely. The qualities of my girlfriend and me are enough to influence him gradually and there is no need to do so. I will let him develop and express himself freely and I won't care too much about him. My only wish is to have more kids. (He laughs.) I shouldn't spend too much time on my kid for he can develop in the direction he chooses.

In one case, S7 expresses the irrelevance of the question for him, for the generation gap between him and his daughter is too big. Instead, he turns inward as a reaction against this alienation between him and his daughter:

Q: What kind of values and principles will you instill in your children?
A: I don't know how to tell her those values and principles for I have no communication with my daughter. There is a deep generation gap between us. Children today have no gratitude for the family except for the sake of money. They won't express thanks to their parents and they won't learn from their parents, either.
Q: Have you ever tried to change this situation?
A: I won't do that for I am tired of this phenomenon. There is no need to do so and there is no possibility of success. It will be better to think only of myself.

In contrast to the other businessmen, interviewees S9 and S15 are unique in that they can easily answer the question about which values they would like to pass to their children:

> *(S9)*
>
> For children, I think the most important thing is to instill a certain value in them. That is to be open-minded to everyone and everything. . . Other values? Maybe it's being good at communication. Children should be good at communication. And they should know to show love to others and be sincere to others.

However, for S15, it becomes clear that a real-world time conflict between work and family interferes as he tries to implement his ideal values in his son:

> *(S15)*
>
> *Q:* Are these conflicts a source of anxiety or do they make you feel bad?
>
> *A:* No. Generally speaking, the conflicts won't make me feel bad except conflicts in the family. I remember several days ago when I went back home, my son was very naughty so I spanked him. My wife complained, "Why did you beat him? You have spent so little time with him." I replied, "All of you are kind to him, there should be someone who is strict to him. I just spanked him and yelled at him." However, I feel guilty about spending too little time with them.

Concerning father-son pairs, S14 has successfully transmitted the value of independence to his son, but the son, S13, has not echoed the father's valuation of thrift, respect for parents, or family. In other words, he has exaggerated the message of independence and self-realization above the other values. In another pair, S5 and S6, S5 does not know which values he wishes to pass onto his daughter aside from hoping she finds a good husband and is not a burden, despite the fact that his father has emphasized the values of filiality and hard work. Another informant, S8, emphasizes thrift and social contributions as values he has tried to pass to his children, but his son S7 has not tried to implant any specific values within his daughter 15 years ago, and now he says the gap between them is too great.

Friendship is valued more highly in the younger compared to the older Shanghai generation. The older generation members also spend time with friends, as evidenced by the time diaries, but they do not speak of friendship nearly as often as the younger as an ideal.

Typical of the younger generation is S9, who, according to his time diaries, spends a considerable amount of free time with his friends. He says one of his goals "is to communicate more with friends and make more friends, which I think is very important." S11 is also quite friendship-oriented, and he drinks tea, plays cards, billiards and badminton with friends during the weekends and had a similar arrangement 15 years ago. Interestingly, S11 limits the size of his circle of friends to 5 or 6 people. His reasons for doing so seem to be over a fear of being exploited, or used, by his friends. He notes, "In our society, some people need to reach their goals by personal relationships. I like making friends but I don't like to and am not used to succeeding through personal relationships." He says, instead he makes "friends for the purpose of making more friends, which doesn't involve economic benefits or other purposes. I have many friends but few best friends." He distinguishes between two types of friendship relations: those for common work goals and friends who do not use one another for gain. His non-instrumental friendships are initiated, he says, when it is clear someone appreciates him rather than merely wants to use him.

S13 is ambiguous in that he says he refuses to allow his friendships to become instrumentalized; he refuses to have dinners with customers, for example, because of potential conflicts of interests. 15 years ago, he says, he did this more often. Today, he rather spends much free time with his non-work-related friends, playing tennis, and eating dinner with them. On the other hand, he notes:

> If you have to do business, you have to get help from others. If not, others will ask for your help for you can't run a business all by yourself, as the division of labor is more and more obvious nowadays. For example, if a friend asks me to do business with him, I will give him a chance if he has a good character and strong ability. My principle of making friends is that I will surely help you if I can and you should lend me a hand when I am in need, too.

Also he notes that he bends the rules for his friends in contrast to his earlier claim that he does not mix business and friendship:

> My friend asks me to provide a job opportunity for his child. My requirement is that you should have the ability to do the job. It's just like taking an exam. You are required to score 60 to pass it. If you score 55 or 50, I will let you pass; if you score only 30, I won't let you pass. You should at least meet my requirements and conditions.

Noticeable both with this informant and the last is their sensitivity regarding exploitation and instrumentalization within friendships; they find it necessary to clarify how they personally are different.

Also, there are indications that work puts a stress on these intimate friendships as it did family. S15 notes that "I hope I will keep my relationships with my friends all the time. Sometimes devoting myself to work too much makes me communicate with friends less and less. But I hope I will always be able to keep my personal relations and friendship with them."

However, other informants maintain instrumental friendships that are closely tied to work and mutual gain. These instrumentalized friendships do not appear to suffer the same stress as the non-instrumental ones. S9, for example, spends much time with his friends and has no problem with using these networks for instrumental purposes:

Q: Compared with before, do you think people more often use you for money or material gains?

A: If I can make contributions to my company through my personal relationships, I will definitely do so and in fact, I have done much work for my company. Can I say it in detail? For example, in terms of assets, I will turn to my friends and long-term cooperative partners for help.

Nonetheless, S9 possesses what might be called modern friendship ideals, with mutual understanding being a key value between him and his friends.

For S17 as well, instrumentalized friendship networks are considered normal. He considers a "good group of friends" one of the most important things in his life and maintains a small group of 3 to 5 "best friends," with whom he gets along with well. His friends come from diverse backgrounds, from his community and business as well, and he views helping his friends in need as a duty:

Q: Compared to before, do you think people more often use you for material gain?

A: I'm glad to do so. We have made use of others when we started our company.

Q: Do more and more people make use of you?

A: If my friends ask me for help, I will do whatever I can.

Q: Compared to before, is it more tempting for you to think about using others for help?

A: It's the same as before when it comes to turning to friends for help. However, such kinds of situations are very rare and more and more people come to me for help.

For older informants making use of personal networks and helping out their friends is also quite normal. S4, however, notes that society has become more "merit-based," and that it is less common to obtain benefits merely through relations:

Q: Are there any relatives of friends who want to find a good job through your help?

A: Yes. It was much easier to do so in the past. Now things have changed. How good a job you can obtain depends on your ability. (He took out a CV.) You see, he has majored in sociology and graduated from "X" University. He wanted to find a job in Shanghai. I once talked with [my friend,] the chairman of the sociology department in "Y" University. The chair said an undergraduate with average ability is not well-accepted, even if he or she is from a prestigious university. So I said to my relative that he should continue his studies to get a master's or even a doctoral degree . . . Later my relative found a job in Ningbo on his own. . . . Generally speaking, I'm glad to help others. I often help others through recommending them. For the most part, I help others to look for good hospitals and excellent doctors.

Several informants rarely address friendship within the interviews. For two older informants, S8 and S14, they spend much time with their friends, but apparently did not feel the need to address the friendship in the interview when asked about values. For another informant, the younger S7, he mentions once the importance of his childhood friends, but his time diaries reveal very little contact to people outside of his "boring" company life. S5 does not mention his friends at all.

It is clear that friendship, in both its intimate and instrumental forms, is a key value among the younger generation in comparison to older informants, who rarely mention it. However, no notable patterns between valuation of friendship and the valuation family and work can be found, except that extraordinarily high valuation of work may stress intimate friendships more than instrumental ones.

The Moscow Interviews

As was the case in China, family values appear to negatively correlate with the work orientations of the Moscow informants, with the more work-centered informants the least family-centered, and vice versa. In terms of staging, the older informants appear to have embraced a 'work and family' philosophy, while the younger function more on a 'work then family' basis, intending to delay their qualitative time spent with the family until the process of material accumulation is complete.

One pair that meets this pattern is M9 and M10. Although both of them established their own businesses during the transition, the son's family and friendship orientations became challenged:

> I just recall myself in the 80s. The opinion of classmates was important for me then. But I didn't care about it after 91, as everything had

> collapsed. A kind of mind individualization had happened. I realized that I do not need to count on anybody; I can count just on myself, maybe partly on my parents and a couple of friends. All the rest was not important.

This "individualization" was not one experienced by the father, as he remained 'family first' during the transformation years, stating "The most important thing is the family. I cannot think of something else."

A similar case is the M11-M12 pair. The mother, now retired, is family-centered, in that she cares much for her son and grandson and speaks often of them in the interview. In contrast, M11 notes that his goals are:

> Success, material satisfaction, influence. I am forced to say that the family comes last, but this is because of internal problems. I have such problems in my family that I need . . . how to say it . . . for the security and the well-being of my family I have to work a lot. Currently, the situation is not quite normal . . .

Here, even though his striving for material security is partially in the name of the family's troubles, both of these are trumped by his striving for personal success and "respect from others." Note here that the family is not actively devalued, but is rather devalued as an indirect consequence of focusing on personal achievement and material accumulation.

The M1-M2 pair is exceptional on two counts. First, the younger M1 does not appear to strive toward greater family participation even at some point in the future. Second, his father is also more individualized than other members of his cohort. The work-centered M1, whose time diaries indicate he spends very few days at home (3 per month), says this time is "enough," and appears to not be overly interested in family participation, even in the future. The reason for this appears to be his is extreme attachment to work as a source of peace and calm. In contrast, the father (M2) does speak a bit more of family, in the sense of the value of respecting elders and helping with family when he can, but his orientation, rather than being family-centered, is more toward the nation and the state of the overall society.

The M7-M8 pair is also unique in that the son is more family-centered than the father. M7 is an exception within the younger cohort in that he remains family-centered despite his hard work. He claims this as a life-stage effect, in that he "naturally" became more family focused when he had children; this should be viewed in contrast to the claim that work 'normally' comes first at this stage of life. Nonetheless, even this comparatively family-centered informant admits that his father is less a role model now than he was before. As noted before, M8, the father, is also the exception in the older generation in that he values family less highly than his son. For him, family is reduced to "a life condition":

Q: A lot of people put family values in the first place. What is your attitude towards the family?

A: It is a life condition. There are factors and there are life conditions. The impact of the factors depends on their scope and the conditions are necessary by default. Well, the family is such a condition.

The father-son pair M5 and M6, also greatly contrasts in regard to family. While M5 ostensibly places family first, noting that, in terms of importance, "the first thing that comes into my mind is the family. Second comes entertainment and the third place is most probably for work," this contention is challenged by statements in other portions of the interview, such as his contention that he is divided into two competing personalities. One of his halves is the family man, while the other is engaged in hedonism back in Moscow. His father M5 values both the family and the country quite highly, but he is absent of the apparent 'Dr. Jekyll and Mr. Hyde' split in family versus non-family personality possessed by his son.

Among many father-son pairs, there is a clear tension between generations concerning the socialization of the new generations. The younger generation has the intent of letting its children grow up more independently, while its high valuation of materialism appears to unintentionally affect its children.

For M1, a clear individualistic tendency is noted in comparison to his father. M1 expects his daughter to handle her problems herself. "If it's her problem—then it's not ours," he notes. He is ready to help only if she needs it. 15 years ago, when she was just a toddler, he says he never thought about ideal values for her, whereas now, he wishes for her to be diligent and independent. The teenager's grandfather, M2, lists a variety of ideal values for her, for example she be decent, responsible, and preserve the family's honor. He says that if she needs help, he will drop everything and do all he can for her, apparently in contrast to her father's tendency to let her first learn to solve problems for herself.

M5, the marketing executive, hopes that his children learn to be creative and productive, to earn money through helping others, and to avoid being mere consumers. M6, his father, identifies honesty and non-materialism as ideal values for children. Evidently there is some difficulty of actually implementing or transmitting these ideals to the youngest generation, for M5 regrets the currently lazy and materialistic attitude of his son, but seems unable to break it down. In this interview, the son's socialization is impeded by the father's high valuation of work and the comfort brought by his high income. Here, the father admits his addiction to work:

> Previously the only thing I had was work; now I have a family. I am very grateful to my current wife for her struggle with my tough character because it is really tough. I am grateful also for the fact that

> she teaches me values and the necessity of cuddling with my children, which I lacked before. The problem for me is that my whole life is focused on business.

However, he reports that is son does nothing, only plays computer games all day long and acts as a consumer. His strategy to get his son to change perhaps contradicts his aim to make him into more than a consumer:

> *Q:* Do you think you will succeed in [making your son more active]?
> *A:* I think so. I showed him the possibilities of a beautiful life. Further, if it is not possible, so be it. I suggested that he comes to me under my auspices and does a lot of things I would like him to do. There is a reward however. He will receive money for a driver's license and for his own car to drive, but he will have to drive it to the university.

Another example of the businessmen passing new values on to the new generation comes from M11. He wants his child to have its own opinion, defend his beliefs, and to see the value of "being remembered," *either* as a great evil or great good. His mother, M12, wishes the grandchild would become intelligent, well read, kind, not aggressive, and decent. The father, however, complains his son expects too much in terms of materialism:

> My child does not understand that some stuff should not be bought for some reason. He knows that we cannot buy luxurious house or change the apartment. Nevertheless, he cannot understand for example, that we do not buy this dictaphone just because we do not need it or he does not deserve it. This is in relation to material things.

Other informants seem to maintain quite a social set of ideal values for their children. M7 and M8, for example, both say that "loving others" is important for youth. In the meantime, M8 places "analytical thinking," a critical work value for him, as crucial for youth as well. Similarly, M9 sees Russia's new common values at the beginning of the transition as being "energetic, cosmopolitan, enterprising." Now, he supplements these ideal values for his children with the values of respecting others and critically perceiving the world. However, he laments that he is unable to influence his child now because of his divorce. His father, M10, in contrast, partly refuses to answer, noting that this young generation really has it tough. He says that it is not "useful" to try and teach his values during the new capitalist period, as "other values apply here." He goes on to say that he wishes his grandchildren lived in another country.

Aside from questions of family, two of the Moscow informants refer directly to their friendship circles, alleging that they have weakened. M9, for example, speaks of this issue:

Q: Let's talk about relations with your friends. How have these relations changed through the years? Have the relations become more tight or weak? Which transformations happened?

A: I think they became weaker. There's less free time now, and more time is spent for the job, for business. That's why they become weaker. Communication becomes more virtual. It's either by phone or Internet. There are fewer real meetings. It's hard to gather a big crowd even for birthday party. One-third of all invited people can't come even though they really wanted to. . . . I think they will help in critical situations. Those friends, with whom I talk once a year, who I know from the past . . . they will come if I call and say that I need help. I understand that.

Another Muscovite, M7, alleges that these friendships have faded from the scene because of his heightened family orientations. M11 also says that friendships collapsed alongside other relations, but claims they have started to reconstitute themselves again:

> However, I must admit that 15 ago everything collapsed, including families, friendships, relations. There was this stratification. Emotions were valued with the help of money. Nowadays, this trend starts to disappear.

Although friendship may be strained within this younger generation, the older informants tend to mention it readily. M6, for example, notes that "probably, the most important thing would be to have good friends with whom you share common ideas and understandings and with whom it is nice to interact." This informant has found it very important to maintain the old friendships he formed during the Second World War.

The Leipzig Interviews

In strong contrast to their Shanghai and Moscow peers, despite their strong focus on work, many of the Leipzig informants have nonetheless remained quite family-oriented. Many of them rejected a 'work then family' orientation in lieu for a 'work and family' or 'work for the family' orientation. In the life course, education and work came first until children arrived, at which point many Leipzig informants devalued their work ambitions in order to focus on the family. L3 is a representative of the 'work and family' orientation, whereby work is envisioned for the family rather than in competition with it:

> Thus whenever someone says "the prioritization has shifted," this only refers to the stage of life someone is in at that moment. Of course, I had different interests as a student; I was less occupied personally and didn't have as much responsibility as I do nowadays, right? My wife

> and children are simply . . . of different responsibility. The set of values itself however remained the same.
>
> Regarding interpersonal relationships though, of course, I set a higher value on them or I attach great importance to them. Nowadays I have a different point of view because of my family. I personally set a higher value on time that I can spend with my son and that is one of the problems for example I didn't have before.

In contrast, L7 remained heavily work-centered throughout the transition period despite having a family:

> *Q:* First of all, I'd like to ask you which values are the most important for you in your life.
>
> *A:* I have to think for a second. . .well, it's hard to put it in an order but basically it's health, family, work . . . while work by now has become pretty much the center of life . . . then friends, that is, relationships with one another, companionship is important as well of course . . . some kind of prestige . . . respect, actually it doesn't matter from what side, that one is respected in what he does, in his achievements . . . yes, these would be the most important things.

While certainly the family remains important to him, he admits that it has become trumped by the high value placed on work.

The father-son intergenerational comparisons, among the Leipzigers, display remarkable similarities. For example, L1 and L2 are both family-oriented; both emphasize "Christian" values and charity.

L3 and L4, as well, are also both family oriented and Christian. L4 describes his family duties as "self-explanatory," while L3 describes what is most important to him: "at the moment, it is definitely my son who is one and a half years old. Thus family is an important value to me."

Like the others, L5 and L6 both are highly family focused and aim for family-work harmony. L6 describes how he managed simultaneous family and work responsibilities 15 years ago:

> Well, the family was more important to me. That's for sure, but you can't just separate both. You can't separate work and family. If I wanted to offer something to my family, back then as today, I had to work. If not, I couldn't have afforded things for my family. And if . . . I mean, this problem never arose in our family. Nowadays there's sometimes the problem that people say that our wives always had to work and our children missed out. That isn't true.

A similar pair is L11 and L12. Both try to achieve work-family balance, and both emphasize Christian values. L12, however, attempts to balance family together with work though the concept of a family business:

Q: How much can you arrange work and family today?
A: Well, that is actually . . . that is, you don't think about that anymore, that's a habit, which has been worked out since the beginning. Work and family . . . Now my son runs the business, but also in the past as a child, the family or my wife were integrated in the work so that they found support, so to say, in a family business. They have helped there. That's the situation.

His son is the same, stating that "if the business is well, the family is well." Their work-family harmony appears to be achieved through the rationalization of the business *as* the family.

In contrast, another family business seems to have strained the personal relationship between father and son. L8 volunteers about his son, L7: "Children never are as their parents want them to be." He and his son avoid each other on weekends since they already spend together six days a week at work. It is as if working together has made their relationship mainly a professional one. L8 says his family had "to pay" for the fact that he established a successful business.

In contrast to other Leipzig informants, L9 has come to devalue his family. He has placed his family time in the same conceptual compartment as his hobby time; you can do both when you have "free time." In this way, L9 is typical of the work first, family and free-time second ('work then family'), view. He makes time for his family on the weekend and works during the week:

Q: How do you justify the mentioned values, that is, family, job, if you get into conflict?
A: Hm, yes, I don't know if that is justifying. It's more weighing up.
Q: Hm, how do you weigh up?
A: Well, I have a certain deal with the family that during the week, work comes first and on the weekends family comes first. With exceptions of course in both directions.
Q: Insofar it's no problem if during the week a business appointment comes between?
A: Then I have to organize it, but basically, it's no problem.
Q: Okay, and how do you feel when these conflicts emerge?
A: ***I*** can handle that relatively well. It's rather the family, I'd say, that has ***its*** problems. [emphasis added]

There is remarkable agreement between the interviewed East Germans regarding their valuation of socializing the next generation, although the older generation indicates at times that the success of this transmission is questionable. Furthermore, the value of children among the Leipzig informants is, for the most part, self-evident. When children exist in the household, the Leipzigers tend to automatically shift their value priorities from work toward the family. A comparison of the Leipzig generations illustrates this trend.

L1 mentions Christian values, such as forgiveness and other-centeredness as ideals for his children, as well as charity, helpfulness, and tolerance. In comparison, his father, L2, mentions the family, personal relationships, and charity as key values. Materialism and ambition, he says, "should not be the most important thing."

L3 lists quite an ideal set of values for his children, among which are honesty, perseverance, humility, and a strong stance against nepotism and materialism. The father is less specific about ideal values, but more generally emphatic about the importance of Christian values, such as the 10 commandments.

In pair L5 and L6 the elder focuses on listening to and respecting one's elders as a key value to be transmitted to children. He describes his values through this story:

> *Q:* What do you think is the reason for the fact that [your values] didn't change?
>
> *A:* This is because of my parents and my education. I was raised as . . . I want to give you an example: I was a young boy, I am Silesian, not far from Breslau. My father had been an estate inspector there. One day I went to the fields with my father, we had a small carriage and a horse pulling it, so we went onto the fields and there were the women, they were over there. I didn't say hello to them. In front of the women my father slapped me and said: "Remember this for your entire life: You are the younger one and have to say hello." I have never seen my dad not being the first one to take off his hat and say hello to people. And these values I kept for all my life.

The son, also focused on value transmission to the younger generation, emphasizes family, friendship, commitment, and diligence for children. These values appear compatible with the elder's, but the father still implies that the grandchildren are not, in fact, developing the value of respecting one's elders.

L7 mentions determination, openness, tolerance, courage, and the family as important values. L8, in comparison, was quite taken aback by the question, stating:

> Life has to [socialize them]. That does not serve any purpose. You can be an example for him. What I want to have for my grandson, what he cannot buy anywhere is time. And that is also today, with 6 months, very important. When he needs me, I want to have time for him.

While he displays difficulty vocalizing his ideal traits for his grandson, he shows nonetheless high dedication toward his upbringing.

L9 also briefly refers to "Christian values" as ideals for his two children, but he seems to keep his reference quite generic, without providing a more detailed account:

Q: Which values are you trying to communicate your kids?
A: Well, many values can be summarized, I'd say, under the aspect of Christian values. That is, things like, like charity or like, a certain honor, and fairness.
Q: Something else, no?
A: Well, those were pretty huge ones already.

L11 and L12, who care after the family business, highlight the importance of duty to this family business to their children. In addition to transferring this business to the next generation, L12 highlights the values of education and a "humane character." His son, L11, wants to eventually hand over the business to his own children, but complains that now young people only chase commercials or glamor. However, his own goals of owning nice cars and a villa are glamorous as well in comparison to his father's.

Furthermore, several informants report on the deteriorating value of friendship because of heightened family and work foci. L1, for example, as a result of new demands at work, has sacrificed his secondary relationships, such as friendships, in order to spend more time with his family. L4 also notes that his circle of friends became smaller, as many moved away and followed work opportunities. Unemployment among some friends may have also created relationship stressors between them.

The price of ambitious adaptation to work appears to be tension with family life. By constraining ambition and materialist values, and by cherishing competing ultimate values, quality family time can be bought by successful post-communists for the cost of increased cognitive dissonance (see also Chapter 3). Or businessmen may resolve this tension by emphasizing the family less, for example, through the postponement of family valuation until retirement. Yet expanding work and materialist values reported in the previous two chapters produce effects beyond the work-family conflicts reported in this chapter. Tensions have also expanded to a broader sphere, to morality in general and to the valuation of the wider community.

8 Morality, Religion, and Politics

> . . . But today in the FRG everyone is responsible for his own actions. Now it is more important to assert oneself. Well, whereas at the time I would have criticized my son because of egoistic behavior, I now say: "You have to learn to cope with it." In this society, a sheep can't do anything against wolves: he must be a wolf himself.
>
> —Eastern German man Interviewed by H. Uhlendorff (2003, 216)

In October 2011, in China's prosperous and rapidly developing southern region of Guangdong, home to cities such as Guangzhou, Shenzhen, and neighboring Hong Kong, a event occurred which subsequently enraged Chinese people and shocked the world. A video camera in a back-alley taped a two-year-old girl being accidentally hit by one, then two cars. More surprising is what happened afterwards. The camera recorded as about 18 people passed the bleeding toddler without offering assistance. She was finally rescued by a 58-year-old good samaritan, a 'garbage scavenger' by trade. Later, the toddler died in the hospital. The Chinese and world Internet was abuzz with shock at the state of moral apathy in rapidly changing modern China (CNN 2011).

Part of what makes us uncomfortable about this story is that the little girl was ignored by busy traders, shop owners, and passing shoppers and helped by a desperately poor woman. Is there a pattern in this? Is moral apathy part and parcel of economic development?

This chapter reports on a trend that some may find disturbing. Morality is not found to be useful among the successful people we have interviewed. It appears to limit the ability to 'make a sale.' Beyond morality, people's general orientations toward the community and politics are atrophied among younger generations. Evidence for this will first be presented quantitatively, followed by overall interview findings. Finally, detailed interview findings will be presented separately for Shanghai, Moscow, and Leipzig.

QUANTITATIVE FINDINGS

Quantitative findings in this chapter indicate that older people and those in modern occupations and the rich most highly value politics. Results on the importance of god and religion are mixed, with religiosity more common among older people in Eastern Germany, and to a lesser degree, Russia. However, in China, younger birth cohorts are more religious and more highly valuating god. I have also found that younger, richer people in these three societies are more morally flexible, believing that good and evil are relative. Furthermore, younger and richer people are more likely to believe that telling lies is justifiable.

Figure 8.1 displays how the importance of politics is differentiated by birth cohort, with the older cohorts in Russia and Eastern Germany tending toward a higher valuation of politics than the younger birth cohorts. In China, the intergenerational difference is modest. Politics is least important in Russia, followed by Eastern Germany, and finally by China, where politics is more widely seen as important.

In addition, in all three societies, those in the privileged occupations (mean=2.49; see Table B.4, Appendix B), because of their location at the center of the new occupational structure, are somewhat more politically oriented than those of other occupations (mean=2.39). Furthermore, politics are rated as being more important by the rich compared to by other respondents (mean=2.57 vs. 2.39), although this difference is insignificant in China. This suggests that the demoralization and cynicism I will report on among our occupationally and financially privileged interviewees is likely much greater among other groups.

As religion for some is an important source of moral reasoning, I report here on two related indicators: the importance of god and the importance of religion. Data indicate that the "importance of god" and of religion decline

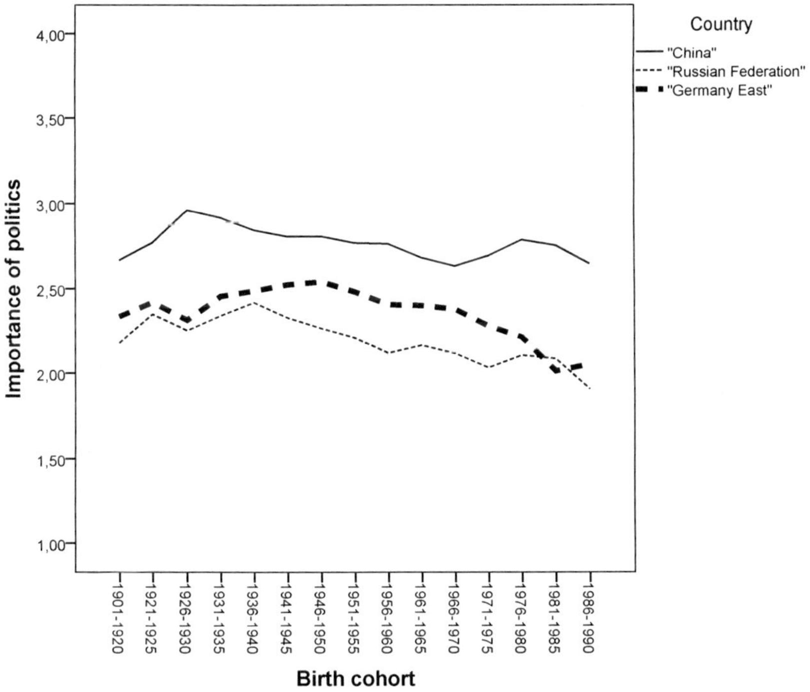

Figure 8.1 Importance of politics by birth cohort in China, Russia, and Eastern Germany, WVS 1990–2005.

Source: World Values Survey 1981–2008 Official Aggregate Files v. 20090901 and v. 20090914.

slightly across birth cohorts in Russia. Each of these declines even more in Eastern Germany. In contrast, in China the value of religion, and especially of god, rises steadily with younger birth cohorts. The Russians are by far the most religious and 'god-valuing,' followed by the Chinese and the East Germans.

There is no significant difference in the importance of god between people in modern occupations and others in Russia or Eastern Germany. However, in China, people in modern occupations value god slightly less (mean 2.2 vs. 3.1). Results comparing the richest 15 percent of individuals to others are less straightforward. In China god is much more important for the rich, whereas the opposite situation holds true in Russia and in Eastern Germany. Regarding religiosity, those people in modern occupations are very slightly, but significantly, more religious across the three societies. In contrast, top earners are less religious in Russia and Eastern Germany, but the difference in China is insignificant.

One particular question of the WVS is a useful indicator of morality. It asks the respondent whether he/she believes in "absolutely clear guidelines" about good and evil. Alternatively, the respondent may answer that there can never be such absolute standards, but that good and evil depend on context. A cohort analysis on this item (Figure 8.2) shows that moral absolutism is lowest

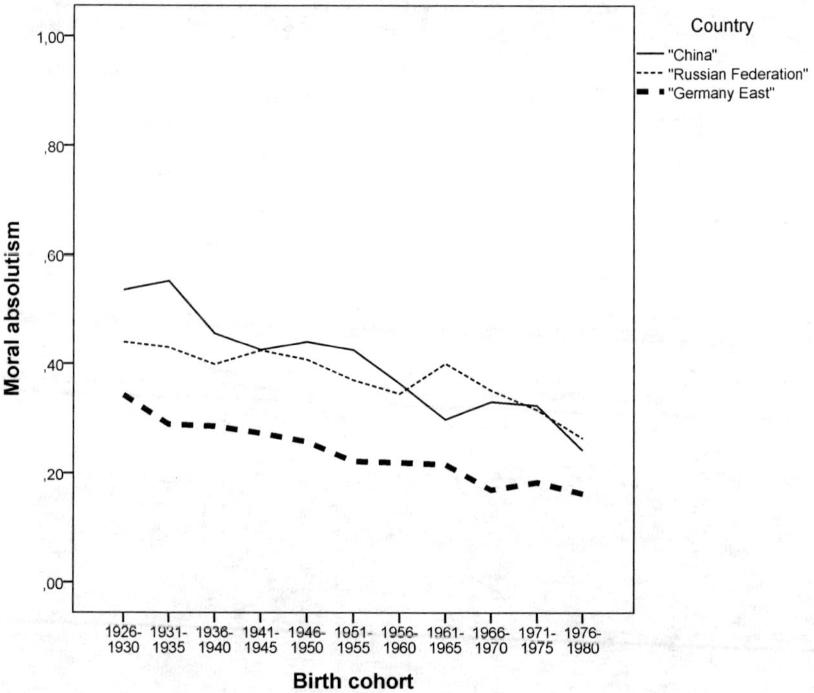

Figure 8.2 Moral absolutism by birth cohort in China, Russia, and Eastern Germany, WVS 1990–2005.
Source: World Values Survey 1981–2008 Official Aggregate Files v. 20090901 and v. 20090914.

in the youngest cohorts and highest in the oldest cohorts. The gap is indeed very wide on this question. For instance, while 42.6 percent of respondents in the 1926–1930 cohort believe in moral absolutes, only 23.3 percent of respondents in the 1976–1980 birth cohort believe the same.

Respondents within privileged occupations do not adhere more strongly to moral absolutes. In Russia and Eastern Germany, there is no significant difference between those in modern occupations and others on this question. However in China, those in modern occupations are less likely to believe in moral absolutes. In all three countries, top earners are also significantly less likely to believe in moral absolutes; this gap is widest in Russia, where 40 percent of the non-rich believe in moral absolutes, compared to only 30 percent of the rich. Across all three societies, the rich are 7 percent less likely to believe in moral absolutes. These data parallel the qualitative finding, to be introduced below, that those who became rich may have become so partially by making their moral principles more flexible.

Quantitative data also show that the justifiability of lying grows consecutively higher with younger birth cohorts across all three societies (Figure 8.5). This feature is especially prominent in Russia and East Germany, where this justifiability rises from about 2 (out of a 1 to 10 scale) among

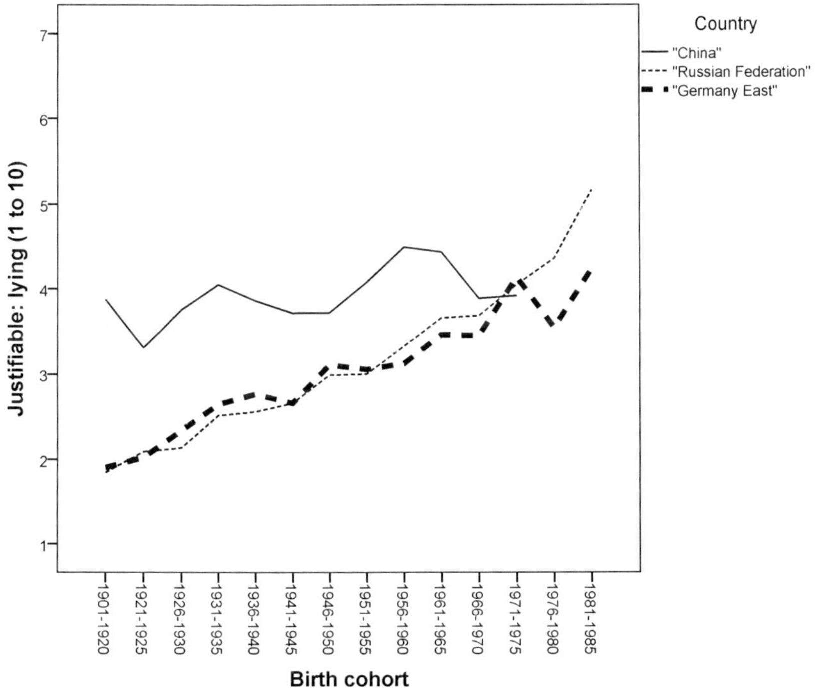

Figure 8.3 Justifiability of lying by birth cohort in China, Russia, and Eastern Germany, WVS 1990–2005.

Source: World Values Survey 1981–2008 Official Aggregate Files v. 20090901 and v. 20090914.

the oldest cohorts, to 4 for the youngest cohorts. In China, while a slight rise is noticeable, the overall levels of the justifiability of lying are roughly the same as in the other two societies. Younger cohorts are more likely to believe that dishonesty is okay compared to older cohorts.

Dishonesty cannot statistically be shown to be linked with one's membership to "modern" versus traditional occupations. However, top earners more likely to believe that lying is justifiable, a difference which is especially pronounced in Russia (mean 3.7 vs. 2.9) and China (mean 4.5 vs. 4.0, although insignificant). Although the gap is smaller, this trend is also significant in Eastern Germany (3.2 vs. 2.9). These findings on dishonesty correlate with what our interview partners told us, that honesty and morality are not beneficial traits in the new economy.

QUALITATIVE OVERALL FINDINGS

In parallel with the quantitative finding that politics are undervalued in younger cohorts, Interviews from all three countries display an intergenerational gap regarding valuation of the outside community and nation. In China and Russia, members of the younger generation are much less nation-centered than their patriotic fathers. In Russia, this gap is linked to the fading of idealism associated with the disillusionment of the early transition years. The East German informants are less focused now on the wider community than they used to be earlier in the transformation years, and a similar disillusionment to the Russian case seems to have occurred because of the failed promises and material insecurity ushered in by the transformation.

There is a contraction of political outlooks among informants from all three countries, especially later in the transformation years. At the beginning, there was a sense of euphoria in Russia and Eastern Germany because of the respondents' hopes about building new democratic and free societies. However, this optimism quickly shifted into pessimism as the true faces of economic and political transformation became known. The resulting social disruption, poverty, political corruption, and crime transformed some of my informants' hopes into cynicism. In China, a broad depoliticization did not occur as there were no widespread expectations of political change in the first place, especially after 1989. Rather the Chinese businessmen's thoughts came to focus on building their businesses, supporting their families, networking with their friends, and taking part in the expanding consumer society. In Eastern Germany and Russia as well, the distractions of daily life, such trying to survive materially, taking care of the family, and consumption, also contributed to the downfall of the initial excitement at the beginning of the transformation.

Younger informants are not particularly concerned about 'contributing to the nation.' This is especially true in Eastern Germany, while some Russian and Chinese businessmen prefer to frame their business contributions as their way of contributing to the overall society. In contrast, other businessmen openly state they do not care about contributing to society. This ambivalence is a contrast to the strong political orientations of the older generation, whose members often framed their personal experiences in terms of their relation to the country.

All three countries display evidence of rising exploitation within close and distant relationships with others, with the worry that relationships become more instrumentalized. Interestingly, the Chinese report that those relationships which are explicitly instrumental seem to suffer less from work-related stress than those that are intimate, implying that the instrumental relationship is more amenable to the needs of work.

Related to this exploitation, the East Germans and the Russians especially expand this discussion into one about morality. Informants from both countries report a trimming-down of morality in association with adaptation to the capitalist economy. In other words, there is a sense that those who were most successful did so by partially abandoning their morals, such as honesty. The older informants lament this moral shift strongly. It is important that this moral flexibilization also makes it yet easier for people to exploit their relationships. Among the younger informants, only the Eastern Germans consistently worried about the moral flexibilization they saw as a necessary adaptation to the new economic situation. These worries surface especially as informants' value conflicts, discussed in depth in Chapter 3. Also, as discovered from some of the Eastern Germans, religiosity appears to be strongly linked to the maintenance of morality and high family valuations within the new economy. If religion is indeed a bastion of morality for many, then the quantitative decline found in religiosity and the importance of god among younger Russians and Eastern Germans may be problematic, unless replaced by secular moralities.

In the following sections, evidence from the qualitative interviews is presented for each of the three cities under investigation.

The Shanghai Interviews

In terms of their orientations toward the country, there is an intergenerational gap between the Chinese interviewees. The older generation consistently speaks of the country as a whole and the importance of helping society. S4 remembers:

> When we were young, we were very vigorous. We were vigorous for our country and hoped the country would become great. We took whatever orders the party gave. Maybe we thought in a very simple way at that time. . . . We always hoped for a better country and a progressive society.

S8 had, and has, an equal level of idealism:

> Frankly speaking, in old China, I strove for a society in which nobody would starve and be out of work. As a 20-year-old young man, I worried about the people who suffered from starvation. I joined the hunger march and anti-Civil-War march. Our biggest goal was to overthrow the social system that oppressed the people. We have fulfilled our goals today. New China has been founded and the society is better than before. Basically, China's state of being poor and dropping behind has changed, though there is still little employment. The society is much better than before although all the people are not well-off. This is my biggest goal.

Another older informant, S14, is equally nation-oriented:

> Since the adoption of the reform and opening up policy, China has undergone tremendous changes in many aspects. In the 16th National Congress of Communist Party of China, we Chinese set the goal that in 2010, the gross domestic product should be doubled and an all-round well-off society should be built up.

In contrast, many of the younger generation do not orient themselves in such a nationalist way. S7, for example, notes "I want to leave this country. I can't change the situation and the only way is to get away from it." Others simply do not care about politics or the country, such as S5:

> *Q:* Then what is your final goal?
>
> *A:* It's the same with what I have just said. In fact, it's quite simple. I don't think of helping people frequently, nor do I think of making great contributions to the country. Many people have the same opinion as I do.

The biggest reason for their lack of concern about wider society again appears to be their focus on business and enterprise. S9's biggest goal in life, for example, is a competitive one, "to develop my enterprise into the best one in China."

There are exceptions to this trend. S15, for example, links his business pursuits to the nation's well-being by hoping that his business will aid the development of the nation's agricultural sector. Another younger informant, S11, is quite politically and nationally oriented. As a child, he dreamed of becoming the vice mayor of Shanghai. Today, he still admires those involved in bettering the country:

> *A:* I admire those who have a great influence on our state politics and economy and those who promote progress and development, such as Wu Yi (vice premier of the state department) and Wu Dawei (vice foreign minister).

Q: What do you admire about them?
A: Their comprehensive qualities: knowing what to do and how to do it while safeguarding our country's advancement.

Nonetheless, S11 is an exception to a trend of the younger cohorts being less nation- and society-oriented than the older generation.

The Moscow Interviews

Moscow findings are parallel to those from Shanghai. Older Russian informants tend to speak at length about the state of their country, in stark contrast to the younger generation, which barely touches issues of the nation or the 'generalized other' at all.

Take the pair M1 and M2 as an example. The son is not at all country-oriented, whereas his father is concerned about the society at large. In contrast, the son never mentions society or contribution; instead, his "own mood" is the most important thing for him. Similarly, M6 places the nation first on his list of priorities, while his son, M5, discusses 'country' a bit, but does not rank it near his personal business, entertainment, and work priorities.

This disinterest in national affairs, however, appears to have arisen from a very different situation, the high level of political excitement and activism at the *beginning* of the transition years. Informants note that they were hopeful (M7) and optimistic (M10) about the collapse of the Soviet system and "rebirth of democracy" (M11). M11 notes that his spirit then was "for changing the world":

> Back then, we saw how the whole empire collapsed. Therefore, because of all the meetings and the perceptions of the establishment of future democracy, life and our understanding of life was not so self-centered. There was the spirit that we are ready for great acts, for changing the world. This is something that interests me now less than before.

This optimism quickly faded into cynicism and disillusionment toward politics (M10 and M11) as high ideals faded. M11 blames this shift on aging, as his youthful idealism faded, to be replaced by a growth in "self-centeredness," in his own words. M9 addresses the issue more in depth, saying that previously, he used to care about others' thoughts, whereas now "I don't care about their opinions," largely because of the "mind individualization" that he reports resulted from the collapses. Ironically, this blasé attitude at the same time also made him more "tolerant and respectful," he says. In other words, he previously had idealistic morals, which caused him to judge others. Now he is has dropped these morals, making him more tolerant, since he doesn't care what others do.

An interesting emergent theme in the Russian interviews is the instrumentalization of interpersonal relations, especially in relation to materialism. A variety of respondents reports that the level of exploitation in society has increased. M2, for example, says that he has become less trusting because there are too many "swindlers" around. There are no more "decent" people, he complains, and as a result, "We cannot trust anyone anymore." He reports that, during Soviet times, such swindling was limited by people's fear of the central government. M8 also feels more exploited. He notes, "I turn into a plunder for those who would like to benefit from me." He claims, however, that he personally does not exploit others so much. M9 says that exploitation has become more common because people have become more "mercantilistic." This is because money has become the most important thing for people, especially for the youngest generation, he claims.

In particular, in certain cases it appears as if relationships became increasingly instrumentalized by those eager to reap profit from them. M5, for example, complains that his ex-wife, even after their divorce, used his relationships for her personal profit:

> She used to come and say to me: "Introduce me to that person, he is your friend. There is someone who is willing to sell an old painting and your friend may buy it. I can earn something from being the link between them."

The morality theme turns out to be a major difference between the generations in Russia, and one closely related to intimate relations with others. In the first pair, M2, the father, highly values honesty and decency. He indicates that his value of honesty *was* stressed slightly by the transformation, but he says he kept it and made it through by maintaining certain boundaries and values above all others, especially not by not 'selling out' on his values of family and country. In contrast, the son became demoralized, and says he does not hold "romantic" principles regarding his work. He says that there is no need to fight for what he believes in while at work.

Between M5 and M6, the vignette pair, there is even a greater contrast. The father highly values honesty, while the son has been involved in criminal business activities. Where the father believes in boundaries, the son is a hedonist "entertaining" himself when away from his family through the power his money gives him.

Like M5, M11 also explicitly refers to Khodorkovskii as a success, even though he believes he is a criminal and his capital is "amoral." For M11, it is *fame* that is important, regardless of its nature; recall his desire to teach his child to "be remembered," whether "as a great good or a great evil." In contrast, his mother, M12, is very moral, stressing biblical values and kindness, and believing in boundaries and limits. "Everything is available. But this everything should be in some reasonable limits," she advises. Her grandson, living in the same apartment, seems to have missed out on her values, as the father complains the son knows no limits. M11, however, is perhaps not as amoral as he makes himself out to be, as he admits he feels a conflict between, as he puts it, his "humanism" on one side and money and a running his business on the other.

We are given an important clue as to the genesis of this amorality among the successful. For M7 and M8, both father and son express a deep-rooted cynicism. The father's is directed toward commercialization and modern values. The son is cynical as well, but rather toward the government. The father has reluctantly accepted what he calls the "new behavior" but not the values that underlie it. This example suggests that the cost of maintaining one's morality amid these changes in Russia is to simultaneously *not* adapt to the new economic system, as illustrated also by M10:

> *Q:* Tell me whether your moral principles have changed now in comparison to 15 years ago?
>
> *A:* The trouble is that they have not changed. If they have changed, I would have changed as well. This is partly the reason why we did not become wealthy people. And we did not become wealthy because we were not given the chance to become such. The young people are predatory because they do not have moral values. They are ready to do everything for money. We have never followed such path of behavior.

In other words, M10 infers that if they had given up their moral scruples and stolen money in a brilliant manner like the oligarchs did, they too would be rich. He continues:

> I did not cheat myself in the respect that during the period of the wild capitalism I could have switched to lying and stealing. I did not turn into a criminal. I found inner strength to oppose this fast way of getting wealthy.

In contrast, M10's son M9, like most of his generation, does not address morality, despite his father's strong focus on it. Another from the younger cohort (M7) recognizes growing numbers of people that:

> almost do not have principles and that is why they try to use any kind of method to accomplish their goals.
>
> . . . Those who had almost no principles are the wealthiest ones.

M11, another from the younger generation, also talks about how the old ideals must exit as one adapts to the new system: "As you see, I have adapted, so . . . I accepted the new rules. In my case, all the communist ideals I cherished collapsed."

Of course, a claim that Russians during Soviet times were thoroughly 'moral' would be an absurdity. For example, M2, a pensioner, also had to sacrifice honesty for his work during Soviet times:

> Even sometimes it was necessary to tell a lie. In business interests, it happened sometimes. It is not necessary to be truthful in the last instance.

Rather, an understanding of corruption and immorality in the Soviet era ever more highlights the nearly universal recognition among my respondents that *nonetheless*, the modern economy has ushered in a tangible stripping-down of morality in comparison.

The Leipzig Interviews

Like in the other two cities, there is not a very prominent focus on the wider community or nation among the East Germans we interviewed. For instance, L1, a highly social Christian, notes that he used to be more focused on both politics and charity when he was younger. The reasons these values declined in importance was because of the need to support his family. "To do good for other people is only second," he says. L4 similarly notes that his worldview contracted toward the intimate family and work, and away from the wider community, during the transformation years. L4 and his son have very different role models. While the father is still somewhat politically and morally motivated despite his perception of a shrinking community orientation during the transition years, he still mentions transition-era politicians and the Pope as role models; in contrast, his son, L3, admires the director of Porsche.

Notable among the Eastern German informants are the moral tensions that seem to have become more acute during the transformation years, coupled with a moral gap between the generations.

One pair, L5 and L6, illustrates how the new economy calls honesty into question. Both of them highly value honesty, but the younger, L5, has problems maintaining it because of his job. He says that "honesty counts less now in society" because it has been replaced by intrigue. He elaborates on the issue:

> Well, for instance, 15 years ago as goes for honesty I would have been honest by all means. That is something that I would tell my kids to be careful with because that is very dangerous. That is a social factor, that's how it is, and with honesty by all means you risk your neck. And insofar today honesty requires a lot more sensitivity. Maybe it was like that 15 years ago as well, and I didn't recognize it, but back then I was considerably more relentless as regards this value.

During the interview, he indicates that he is disturbed over putting his honesty to the side.

L9 is more pragmatic with the amorality of business. He introduces us to the concept of "trader's honor," and when the interviewer misunderstands, he quickly corrects:

Q: Can you remember if there were any moral principles guiding you back then [in 1990]?
A: I believe they weren't much different than today.
Q: Hmm, that is, also honesty, trust . . .
A: Hmm, did I say honesty? I don't think so.
Q: Not exactly, no. I did . . . you said those . . .
A: Traders honor. Yes, that is something else. That I keep the word that I have given. Being 100 percent honest at all times, I claim, isn't possible and isn't good either. Because one would hurt people too often if one would say things that have no relevance at all . . . Not in the sense of lying but rather in the sense of not having to say anything.
Q: Then maybe you could elaborate that a little further. I obviously haven't understood it correctly.
A: Well, if I say, reliance, trust, honor then this could also mean that, in order to either protect or not hurt a partner, I don't say certain things because one knows how the other works and if he's maybe sensitive to certain things. . . . Honesty, I think, is a thin line. That is, when does one begin to lie. He should . . . there is a difference between lying or saying things or maybe stretching the truth. Well, on the other hand, lying is a critical thing because when statements are made they have to stand straight. That is, a consciously made false statement, that's not possible because then trust would disappear.
Q: Okay and you were conscious of that also back then, you'd say?
A: Well, maybe not that clearly.

Honesty as proactive openness in this setting is replaced as an ideal by "keeping one's word." This is equivalent, says the informant, to the difference between lying and stretching the truth.

Other informants also have difficulties with morality. L7, for example, while viewing Oskar Schindler (the historical figure within *Schindler's List*) as a role model because he risked his success, is "not sure if I could do that, honestly." Recall his statement that he is "enslaved" by work. Nonetheless, he is unwilling to risk it, even for what he deems worthy causes. This illustrates well the creeping importance of work over the moral sphere.

Another informant, L12, is cynical, saying that he believed more in moral values during GDR times, because today, society's respect for manufacturing, his profession, is even worse than it was back then.

Leipzig informants also reported enhanced levels of exploitation in their society since the beginning of the transformation. L1, for instance, reports that he is 'more used' by other people because money plays a greater role today since there are more goods on marketplace: "Back then you might have had a lot of money but that didn't mean that you were able to buy a lot of things, money was not worth too much, in that sense." He elaborates, connecting the issue further to exploitation:

> Now things have changed. Nowadays, if I have money, I can do a lot of things, or I can do a lot more with it, and that leads people or makes people do things they shouldn't do, using people for example . . . that's why the risk is greater [now than it was before].

Like his son, L2 also sees rising exploitation. He says that "something new arose" in this regard, with people trying harder and harder to exploit his business:

> *Q:* That means this problem didn't exist 15 years ago?
>
> *A:* No . . . actually not, or sure enough there are always situations when somebody tries to make one's way by taking advantage of someone or whatsoever, but 15 years ago this was a different situation. Certainly there were people who tried to shirk working a bit, but not financially like it is today. It's a different dimension nowadays.

Likewise, L5 feels that he is exploited more now than in the past, but he notes that perhaps this is a lifestage effect, since he has more money nowadays than when he was a student:

> Yes, considerably more than in the past . . . ok, that might be due to, as a student typically you have no money, there is nothing to enrich . . . of course the position was a bit different back then. For instance, I had a car back then, an old Russian car, and this was driven by the whole seminar class. You could call that taking advantage but it wasn't. I mean, they didn't enrich themselves but they drove with it and me as well and when something was broken then I said it needs to be repaired but then they were all here and we made a great party in the backyard with some beer and then repaired the car. Insofar, it wasn't taking advantage at all. Today I see that slightly differently. You have to be careful if you work with someone if he isn't exactly doing that. And you have to think very carefully if you give someone work what he'll do with it. Is he really doing only what he is supposed to or is he taking something to a competing business, something is laid down in a paper or in a document, is he going to peddle with it or is he selling it as his own. As regards this, today I think certainly that this happens more. Sad, but that's how it is.

For some, rising exploitation is society is not surprising. L9 notes that it is "of course" more common today than in the past, "but I don't know if that is to demonize. They make a living of that, it's their job." Similarly L7 and his father, L8, agree that exploitation has increased in Eastern Germany compared to the past, but the father says this is "normal" in capitalism.

Chapters 5 through 8 have argued for emergent work-family and money-morality tensions in China, Russia, and Eastern Germany as a result of the transformation to capitalist economic culture. You might be thinking: "I feel these tensions too. They are hardly uniquc to post-communist societies." My point has been to locate some of the roots of these tensions. More specific than 'modernity' at large, and more specific than assuming value conflicts of this type are natural, I claim that these specific conflicts are linked also to capitalist culture. The post-communist transformations have been a convenient natural experiment that allows us to illustrate this. If this is indeed the case, then surely we should be able to document comparable individualization trends in other societies as well. The following chapter attempts to do this.

9 The Wild West?

> I am not sure that I will be able to teach [my grandchildren] these values and moreover in the time of world capitalism I am even not convinced that this is useful. Other values apply here. I have often visited the U.S. and talked to people who went there with the first, the second, and the third emigration waves. I see all the negative sides of the American capitalism. Nevertheless, our capitalism is even worse than the one in the worst times of the Wild West.
>
> —Male from Moscow, 61-years old, works in technology sales, M10

The findings that I have presented thus far indicate fault lines along which post-communist value tensions are emerging. Younger, richer people in modern occupations in China, Russia, and Eastern Germany tend to be more individualistic, ambitious, work-oriented, focused on wealth, less family oriented, less political, and even less moral. As a result of it all, they are more internally conflicted, unless they have already resolved these conflicts in favor of economic values. These are aspects of individualization, driven by economic change, developing in these societies. Do these findings hold across all post-communist societies? In fact, couldn't we claim that these traits are found in all 'modern' societies? Similar internal Western critiques have been made, for instance, of America's 'narcissistic' nature (Lasch 1979), its hyper-individualism and "wilding" (Derber 2001), de-prioritization of the family and care (Folbre 2001), or declining social capital (Putnam 2000). How do the post-communists compare to the rest of the world?

There are at least three ways my claims about post-communism could be interpreted in view of these societies' positioning compared to the rest of the world: the economic culture argument I have been forwarding in this book, a pendulum-effect notion where the post-communists overshoot the rest of the world, and a post-materialist hypothesis (Inglehart and Welzel 2005). According to the *economic culture hypothesis,* for which I have argued for in this volume, if it is truly capitalist culture driving the types of value tensions previously noted, we should find that the developed world is more individualized compared to post-communist societies, and the developing world would be less individualized. Alternatively, if the speed of change in the post-communist world has been great, the post-communists may be equally individualized as those in the developed world, and the developing world should still be behind. The second idea, the *pendulum effect hypothesis,* posits that post-communist societies, because of the radical and ideologically charged nature of their transition, have over-adapted so that they are more individualized than western societies, and developing societies are the least individualized. Third, if the *post-materialism hypothesis* is correct in its pro-sociality assumptions—those who grow up with higher material well-being are able to focus more on non-material values, such as their social relationships—we may find developing societies to be the most socially 'backward,' with the post-communists in the middle, and the OECD countries at the head of the pack.

So far, I have not been able to conduct comparable qualitative interviews in Western or developing societies on this theme, so I cannot systematically know how social values are actually understood and dealt with among these populations. Moreso, because of the lack of appropriate qualitative data, I cannot compare my core findings on post-communists concerning the central thesis of this book, on value tensions and cognitive dissonance, with people from other parts of the world. Yet, the geographical reach of the World Values Survey can help to display how the values I am interested in are arrayed across the world. In this chapter, I will directly compare individuals from almost all countries of the World Values Survey on the same values questions I have covered in previous chapters. Primarily, I will look at how these values are distributed across birth cohorts among all post-communist societies, compared to OECD countries, compared to developing countries. Where a society is both post-communist and an OECD member, such as Slovakia, I have classified it as post-communist. Furthermore, I have removed four societies from the dataset, because they neither classified as post-communist, OECD, or developing: Andorra, Taiwan, Hong Kong, and Singapore. My results cover four waves of the World Values Survey: 1990, 1995, 2000, 2005, and the sample includes people from 28 post-communist societies, 20 OECD countries, and 37 developing countries (See Appendix A, Table A.7).

Individualism represents the character trait of individualization, deposited in individuals in the form of self-focus. As in Chapter 5, I measure this by whether or not a respondent mentions "independence" as an ideal trait for children. In comparing persons from different societies, this valuation of independence is highest among OECD individuals (Figure 9.1). Among older cohorts born before 1970, those in OECD countries value independence the most, followed by the post-communists, followed by those in developing countries. Among youngest cohorts, the post-communists become slightly more independence-oriented than those in the OECD, but the difference is negligible. The average levels of this value are approximately the same in the OECD and post-communist countries. In contrast, those in developing countries are significantly less independence-oriented compared to the others. Yet the value of independence robustly increases everywhere with younger and

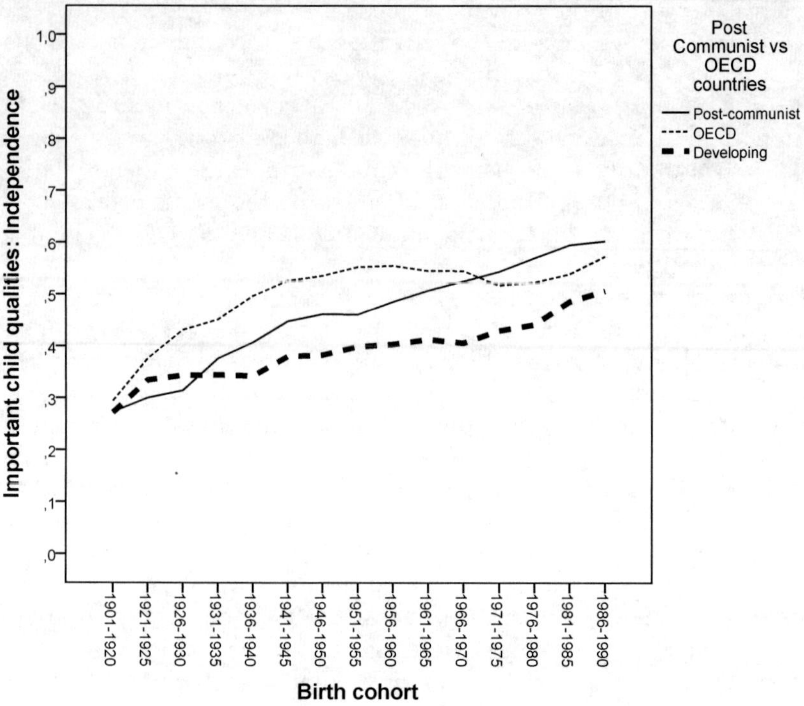

Figure 9.1 Value of independence by birth cohort in post-communist, OECD, and developing societies, WVS 1990–2005.
Source: World Values Survey 1981–2008 Official Aggregate Files v. 20090901 and v. 20090914.

younger birth cohorts. For example, in the 1901–1920 birth cohort, 28 percent of people mention independence as an ideal value, compared with 54 percent in the 1986–1990 birth cohort. These findings support the economic culture hypothesis, whereby contemporary capitalist culture favors independence as a value in new generations, and overall levels of this value are higher among OECD and post-communist individuals compared to those in developing countries.

Risk-taking propensity is critical for ambitious capitalists, since it is important both for investment culture and is also necessary in a society where complicated risks must be managed by competent individuals who are responsible for their own careers and self-realization. My findings indicate that risk-taking, as opposed to risk-aversion, rises moderately in all three groups of societies (Figure 9.2). The trend is nearly identical to that of the value of independence. OECD and post-communist countries are essentially neck and neck in the distribution of this value over birth cohorts, albeit the OECD is slightly higher. In the meanwhile, developing societies are more risk-adverse, although their risk-taking propensity also rises

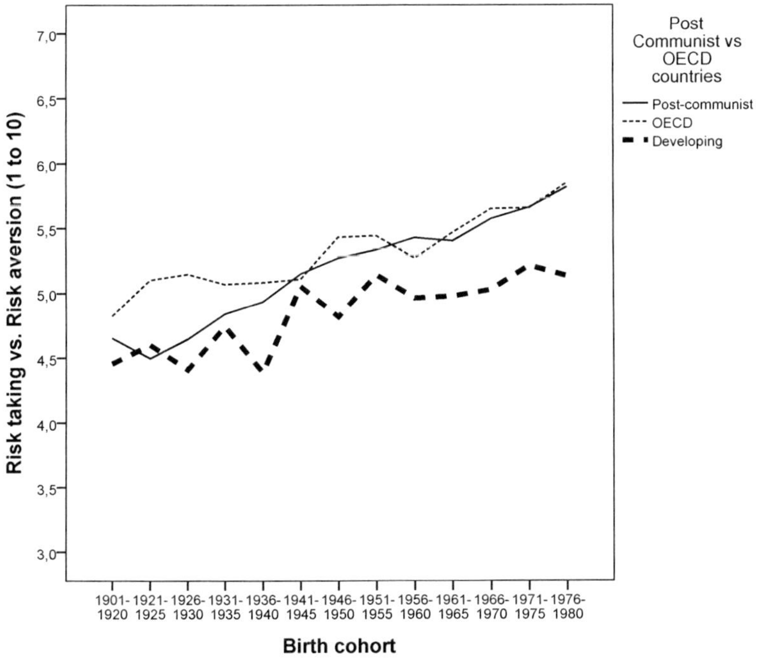

Figure 9.2 Value of risk-tasking by birth cohort in post-communist, OECD, and developing societies, WVS 1990–2005.

Source: World Values Survey 1981–2008 Official Aggregate Files v. 20090901 and v. 20090914.

in younger birth cohorts. These findings also support the economic culture hypothesis. OECD countries and post-communists are roughly equal in their value of taking risks because of their full exposure to capitalist culture, while its penetration is more limited in the developing—in many cases, still industrializing—world.

I measure thrift as the value of "saving things and money" as a representation of the entrenchment of consumer and investment cultures, since excessive savings inhibit both practices. Comparing people in different societies yields surprising findings on this issue. I have found that post-communists have the highest average valuation of thrift and saving things, whereas those in developing societies and the OECD have lower and roughly equal levels of thrift (Figure 9.3). Furthermore, we can find that this valuation among post-communists becomes much smaller with younger birth cohorts and rapidly approaches the level of developing and OECD societies. For instance, 58 percent of the oldest post-communists mention thrift as an ideal value, compared to only 40 percent of the youngest. In comparison, 33 percent of the youngest OECD and developing society respondents value thrift in this way. The value of thrift among people in

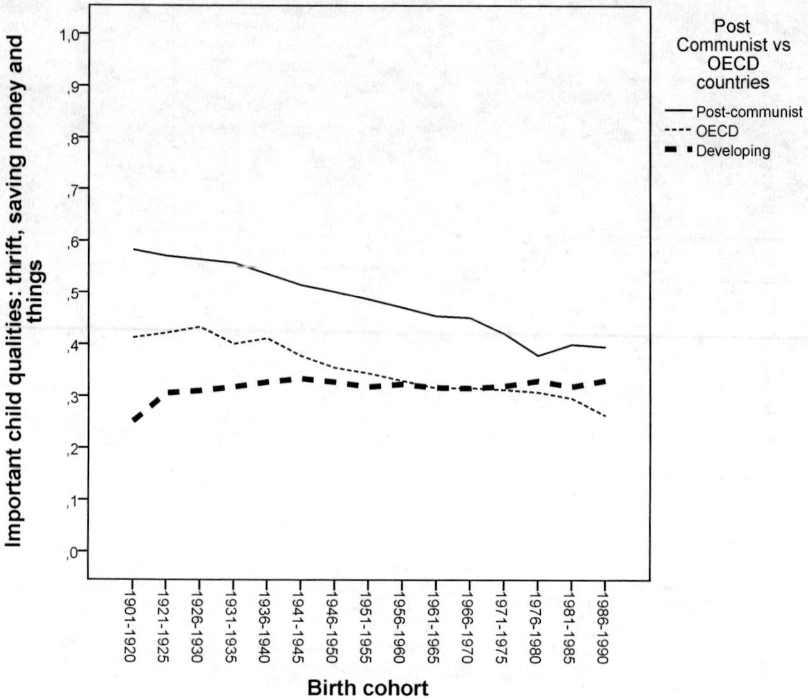

Figure 9.3 Value of thrift by birth cohort in post-communist, OECD, and developing societies, WVS 1990–2005.
Source: World Values Survey 1981–2008 Official Aggregate Files v. 20090901 and v. 20090914.

developing countries remains stable across birth cohorts at around 35 percent, whereas it is moderately devalued among consecutive OECD cohorts, mentioned as an important value for children by about 40 percent of oldest individuals compared to 30 percent in the youngest birth cohorts. These findings are not straightforward to interpret. The economic culture argument would expect thrift to be highest among developing societies, since they have not yet adapted fully to a consumerist anti-thrift capitalist culture. The pendulum effect may presume post-communists to be the least thrifty of the country groups, having become over-consumption-oriented, and therefore less thrifty. Furthermore, like the economic culture argument, the post-materialist hypothesis would presume developing societies to be the most thrift-oriented and OECD countries the least, because of their opposite locations in terms of material conditions. It is clear that none of the hypotheses neatly explains these findings.

My explanation is that post-communist societies are moving away from an industrialized yet shortage-based, hoarding economy for consumer goods, which explains the higher overall level of thrift. Scarce material goods had to be sought after and saved. Yet the strong intergenerational difference can be interpreted as part of a shift toward a more efficient consumption-oriented economy. In contrast, developing societies do not experience a shortage of goods so much as a shortage of money and material means; saving money and hoarding goods is not realistic until basic needs are being met. This overall level of poverty may explain both the low level of thrift and also the lack of intergenerational variance in thrift among those in developing countries. Consumer culture cannot dig in without individuals first meeting their basic material needs. In turn, falling thrift values in younger OECD generations can be explained by the further entrenchment of capitalist investment and consumption cultures.

Focusing for a moment away from economic conditions to economic ideals, we come to the value of 'being rich.' This value represents materialism at the psychological level. Analysis shows that younger individuals in all three groups of societies increasingly strive "to be rich and have material things" (Figure 9.4). While this strong growth in materialism is relatively the same across country groups, the overall levels of this value differ. Those in

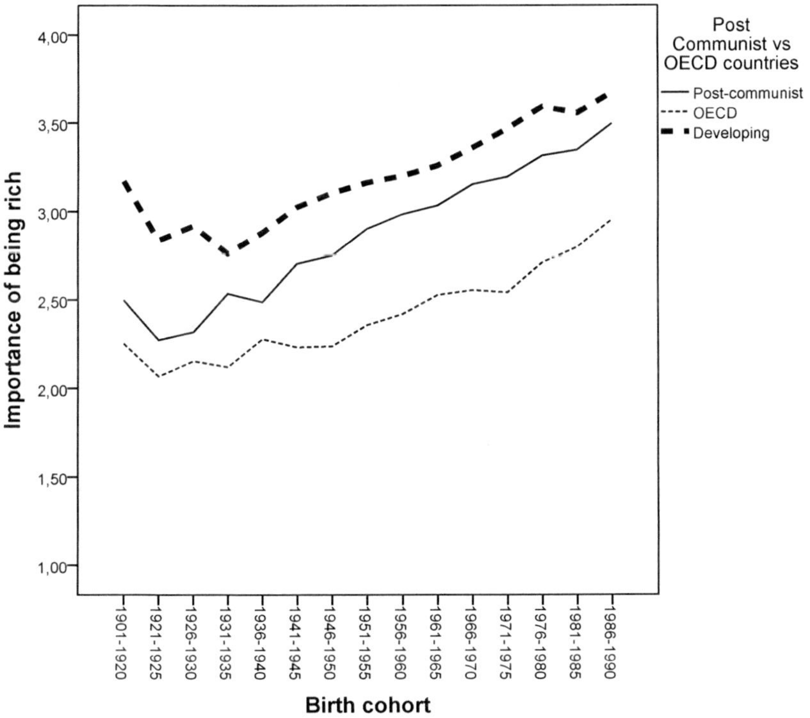

Figure 9.4 Value of being rich and having nice things by birth cohort in post-communist, OECD, and developing societies, WVS 2005.

Source: World Values Survey 1981–2008 Official Aggregate Files v. 20090901 and v. 20090914.

developing societies wish most to be rich, followed by the post-communists, followed by those living in the OECD. For instance, people from developing countries of the 1955 to 1960 birth cohort value being rich by roughly 10 percent more than the post-communists, and 35 percent more than those from the OECD. These average levels can be neatly explained by the post-materialism hypothesis. Those from rich countries value 'being rich' less than those from poor countries. At the same time, the steep rise of this form of materialism in younger and younger birth cohorts in all parts of the world can be explained by the increasing penetration of materialist culture.

One way to make sense of the way that family might compete with an enhanced value of the self is whether or not parents believe they should sacrifice their own development and well-being for their children. Post-communists are slightly less likely than those in the OECD, across all birth cohorts, to believe in parental sacrifice for children, versus the individualist proposition that parents have "their own lives" (Figure 9.5). However, this value moderately decreases in consecutive birth cohorts. Approximately 80 percent in older birth cohorts adhered to this notion,

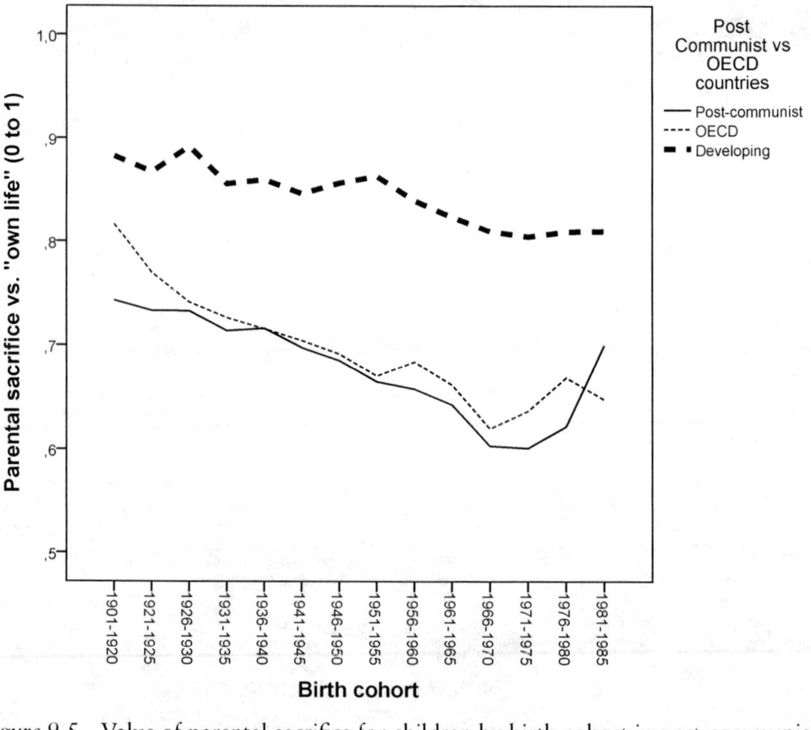

Figure 9.5 Value of parental sacrifice for children by birth cohort in post-communist, OECD, and developing societies, WVS 1990–2005.
Source: World Values Survey 1981–2008 Official Aggregate Files v. 20090901 and v. 20090914.

compared to only about 76 percent in younger birth cohorts, although the drop is steeper among OECD and post-communist individuals. The Post-communist and OECD lines on this value are nearly identical. In contrast, about 15 percent more people in developing societies value parental sacrifice compared with those in the OECD or post-communist world. However, there is also an overall slight decline with consecutive birth cohorts in developing societies. With post-communists and OECD respondents equally individualized in this dimension because of their exposure to post-industrial capitalist culture, compared to those in developing societies, this finding is well explained by the economic culture hypothesis.

In a comparable finding, my data also show that the relative value of family, compared to the average values of friendship, leisure, and work, declines across younger birth cohorts in all society groupings (see T-test results in Appendix B, Table B.5). Furthermore, this value is lowest in OECD countries, followed by those in developing countries, then by the post-communists. The oldest post-communist cohorts are more family-oriented than even those in developing societies, but the deterioration in the relative value of family in younger generations is more pronounced among post-communists than among others. Nonetheless, overall low OECD levels and the OECD intergenerational deterioration in this value result in average relative family values being the lowest in the OECD in every single birth cohort, compared to other society groupings. This finding can be explained if capitalist economic culture, where it is most advanced, assigns a relatively lower value to family.

Within our interviews, it became clear that there was very little time nowadays for 'real' friendships, but instrumental or 'useful' friendships seemed to still be in demand among busy post-communist business people. Comparative evidence from the World Values Survey also seems to indicate friendship as a favored value among the younger birth cohorts (Figure 9.6). Among OECD and developing country respondents, the value of friendship rises somewhat with newer birth cohorts, but this rise is steeper among the post-communists. The average value of friends is highest among OECD citizens and lowest among those from developing societies, although the oldest post-communist birth cohorts had an even lower friendship value than persons in developing societies. These results are harmonious with both the economic culture and post-materialism hypotheses. Within capitalist culture, thin and instrumentalized friendship networks are presumed to be useful for business purposes. This explains the rise in friendship values especially among post-communist and OECD respondents. In the meanwhile, the post-materialism hypothesis would suppose that those who grew up in wealthy societies become more pro-social, with wider and thinner social networks than those in poorer societies. These data confirm this; richer societies more highly value friendship.

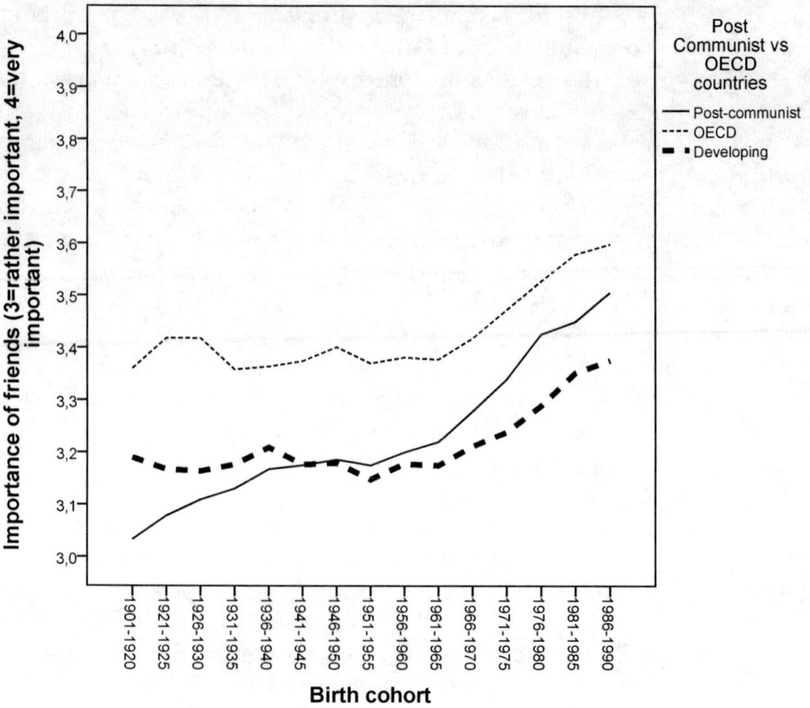

Figure 9.6 Importance of friends by birth cohort in post-communist, OECD, and developing societies, WVS 1990–2005.
Source: World Values Survey 1981–2008 Official Aggregate Files v. 20090901 and v. 20090914.

Our earlier results showed the importance of 'moral flexibility' for those successfully adapting to the new economy. I quantitatively measure this through whether or not respondents believe that good and evil are absolute, compared to whether they should be conditional. Comparative results on this item indicate that people in developing societies have the highest absolute standards for good and evil, and there is no significant difference for them across generations (Figure 9.7). OECD respondents have the lowest overall levels of moral absolutism, with only about 30 percent of the youngest cohorts adhering to the principle, compared to 50 percent of the youngest birth cohorts in developing countries. Post-communist respondents are exactly in between, with an overall level between the developing world and the OECD. In comparison with intergenerational stability in moral absolutism among respondents from developing countries, OECD and post-communist citizens become more 'morally flexible' with consecutive birth cohorts. This rate of decline is fairly strong in the OECD and moderate in post-communist countries. These results can be explained by the economic culture argument, since moral flexibility is a favored value in business culture. Therefore, the most economically developed societies have both the lowest levels of moral absolutism and the greatest rates of decline across generations.

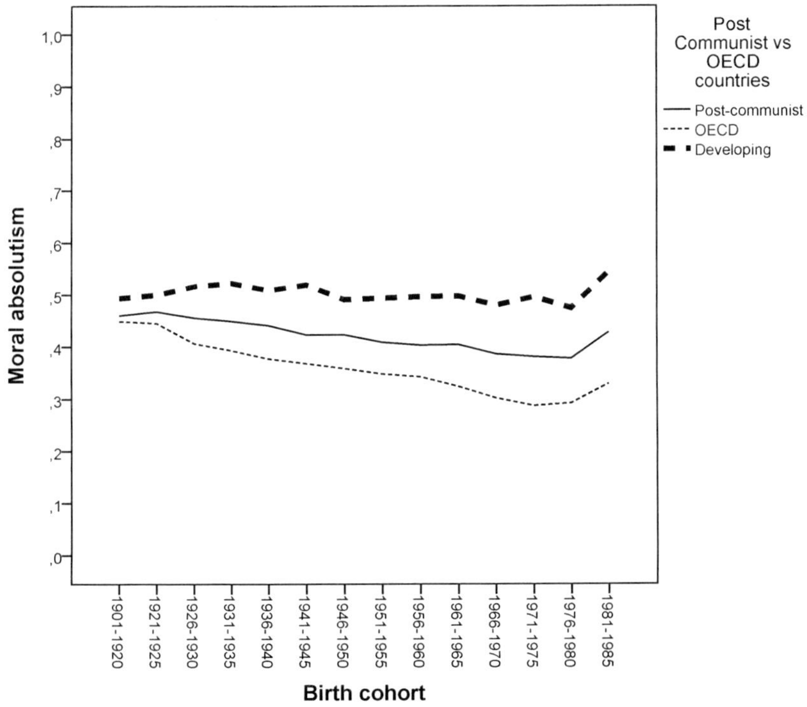

Figure 9.7 Moral absolutism by birth cohort in post-communist, OECD, and developing societies, WVS 1990–2005.
Source: World Values Survey 1981–2008 Official Aggregate Files v. 20090901 and v. 20090914.

A final group of results is related to the propensity for honesty. Here, we find that younger birth cohorts in all societies are more likely to believe that lying is justifiable, compared to older birth cohorts (Figure 9.8). People in developing societies are most honesty-oriented, followed by those in OECD societies, followed by the post-communists. The rates of intergenerational increase in the justifiability of lying are strong in all societies. This result can be explained using a combination of economic culture and pendulum effect arguments. Dishonesty can be beneficial in a capitalist institutional framework, which explains why those in developing societies find it less justifiable than those in the OECD. Yet, the post-communists' higher level of justifiability of dishonesty can be explained as an over-adjustment to a capitalist culture which they interpreted as wild, exploitative, and dishonest. Such evaluations were demonstrated in the qualitative interviews with post-communist business people.

The figures I have just presented in this chapter tell us that the post-communists are not a rare hyper-individualized and hyper-materialistic breed who are misfits to a world which becomes increasingly humane. Neither are they under-adapted homo-sovieticus dinosaurs who have much more to do with the traditional world than with capitalist modernity. Rather, in most

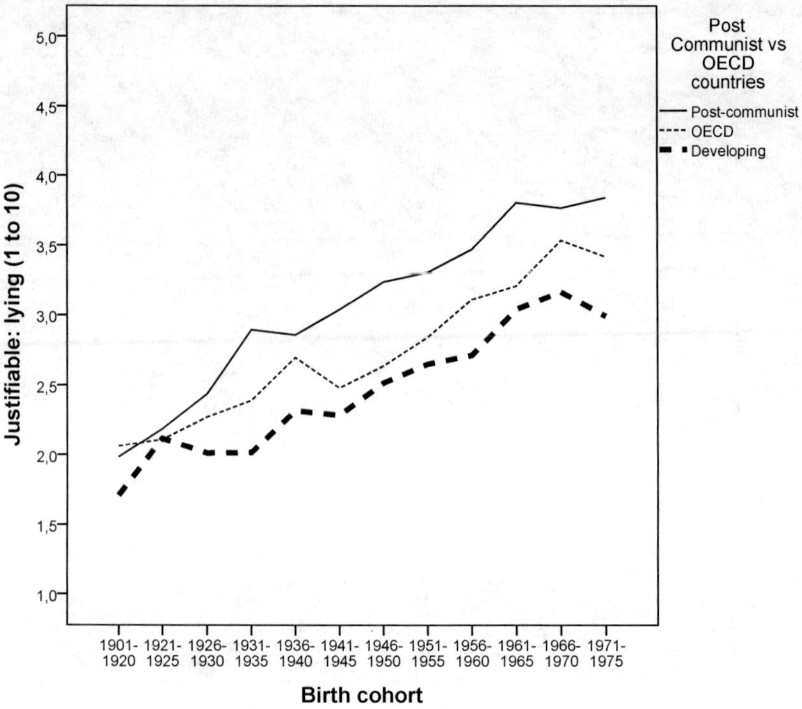

Figure 9.8 Justifiability of lying by birth cohort in post-communist, OECD, and developing societies, WVS 1990–2005.
Source: World Values Survey 1981–2008 Official Aggregate Files v. 20090901 and v. 20090914.

indicators, they align almost perfectly with individuals living in the OECD, and in the most 'individualized' direction prescribed by capitalist culture.

In the value of thrift, presumed as the opposite to consumption and investment culture, the post-communists are quickly declining toward the OECD level. Furthermore, post-communists are more focused on being rich than those in the OECD, but younger generations become more wealth-focused in both society-groupings at roughly the same rate. Also, and in line with some of our interview data supposing 'overadjustment,' post-communist citizens are more likely to believe in the justifiability of lying than are persons in the OECD, although younger cohorts increasingly justify dishonesty in all societies.

Yet in growing independence, risk-taking, friendship orientations, moral flexibility, diminished value of sacrificing for children, and the relative value of family, the post-communists and OECD nations are essentially the same and moving in the same direction.

10 Discussion
Ambivalent Individualization and Capitalist Culture

. . . Capitalism has survived itself.

—Leipzig informant's remark about the collapse of communism (L6)

Evidence from qualitative interviews comparing new-rich businessmen with their fathers supports a model by which the transmission of values from the capitalist economic culture to individuals appears to take place. People in post-communist societies were faced with a new economic system that implied both objective and subjective elements. Objectively, daily life shifted across two dimensions in fundamentally similar ways whether the individuals we are speaking of were living in China, Russia, or East Germany. The previous bounds and scope, both positive and negative, of the spheres of work and consumption were ripped open. Subjectively, this shift was interpreted through an ideological battleground forged by communist ideals of the past and a neo-liberal capitalism entering with force. These objective and subjective shifts result in a set of outcomes ultimately pushing the new value set in a direction we may label as individualization, one encompassing, in addition to positive aspects, enhanced latency of intimate social values.

On the one hand, individuals perceive the economic shifts outlined above and tend to respond to them in ways that are both creative and sensible. They consciously choose to adapt their behavior, and their values, in a way that they figure will allow them to succeed in the new economic environment. On the other hand, individuals are more than their conscious wills alone and are affected in unforeseen and unintended ways. For example, the clash between the habitus of values they bring from the past and those values that are functional 'tools of success' within the current economic arena results in cognitive dissonance. This dissonance tends to be resolved in the direction of least resistance: the latency of the intimate values that are not prioritized by capitalism.

Both conscious adaptation and cognitive dissonance are at least partially nested within a polarized ideological environment characterized by communism and capitalism in their ideal forms. This means that dissonance is magnified and that conscious choices are exaggerated to fit a capitalism seen through a communist lens—creative, competitive, and profitable yet also egoistic, hedonistic, materialistic, and immoral. That this result is also one of loosened valuation of sociality should not be underestimated. Finally, as Mannheim (1952) showed us, intergenerational changeover has a tendency to produce a comparative radicalization of values in the younger generation through several mechanisms. First, 'fresh contact' demonstrates how youth are socialized contemporaneous to social change, so that they experience the changing world simultaneous to their biological aging, and they thus carry less value baggage from the past. Second, post-communist individuals complained that their parents were poor role models during the transformation since they knew very little of the capitalist economy. As a result, the youth had to rely upon their equally young and radical peers for advice. Third, the socialization of children has metamorphosed, so that the new generations are increasingly stepping back from actively transmitting values to the youth, whether because of role confusion or a conscious choice to pass—or allow to be passed—'individualist' values to their children. Intergenerational changeover is an enduring producer of radicalized values, which has been no exception in this particular transformation. Yet the content and meaning behind 'radicalism' is formed as a conversation between the past and present cultural environments; it does not automatically embody individualism.

The mechanisms just described appear to be the dominant forces producing the main empirical outcome of this research: value tensions and gaps between generations, between new and old occupational groups, between the rich and the non-rich, and within individual persons, as demonstrated by both qualitative and quantitative data. These tensions indicate that the intrinsic valuation of close face-to-face ties loses out to terminal valuations of profit and self-realization, executed by various means, to include abstracted and instrumentalized relationships with others.

Empirically, I find that the value of work has expanded, so that the young working generation ambitiously views it as a means of self-realization and making money, in comparison with the older generation, which viewed it as a simple duty linked to the family and society. As a result, high work valuation—even approaching work as an 'end in itself'—pushes family and intimate social values into latency, as they compete for time and focus. In contrast, the older generation tends to see work and family as in harmony. The younger generation also has developed a new phasing of the life course, with a high work focus coming first, during the youth, and a focus on the existing family occurring only later, upon retirement, alongside other 'leisure' activities. As a result of this, parents tend to put less energy into the socialization of their children. Simultaneously, society loses respect for the outdated knowledge and capacities of older people, who represent the mistakes and failures of the past. Materialism is also a place of great tension between generations. The necessities of image cultivation and profit-orientations in work spur a consumerist orientation that is antithetical to traditional valuations of thrift. While such consumerist orientations are merely instrumental at the beginning as the material habitus develops, they both tend to colonize non-material spheres and spur conspicuous consumption for signifying success. Regarding wider social values, a trend seems to be the contraction of both patriotic and community orientations, a general de-politicization. This is coupled with the expansion of the value of 'independence' and the enhanced moral flexibility of post-communist populations. Morality is not seen as useful by successful young people involved in business. In addition, while the value of friendship may become more enhanced, qualitative data suggest this is a more instrumentalized, and less intimate friendship, one that is conducive to the 'networking' and weak-tie needs of the new economic culture.

The relay of individualized values from the economic culture to the individual through conscious adaptation does not occur as a uniform, unchallenged, or uncontextualized process, but rather it is shaped greatly by other factors. This individualization is catalyzed by intergenerational changeover, cognitive dissonance, ideological conflict, and state reinforcement of neoliberal values (especially in China during the 1990s). In the meantime, this individualization may be stymied by religiosity, the role of the welfare state in producing values emphasizing work-family harmony (in Germany), and by the female gender, as women appear—based on both this and outside research—more resistant to materialism, individualism, and competitiveness than men.

The analysis presented in this book tells us about value tensions which are apparent within those who were 'successful' during the post-communist transformation, and more widely as shown quantitatively, between social groupings within China, Russia, and Eastern Germany. It has also described the mechanisms whereby such value tensions tend to resolve themselves through the increasing latency of intimate sociality. Thereby, a principal finding strengthens—through describing the links between them—the conception of capitalism itself as a harbinger of individualization. Of course, socialist societies had dark repercussions for sociality as well. Keeping in mind the material scarcity and everyday wickedness (think of the Stalin purges, the East German Stasi, or the Chinese Cultural Revolution) during much of communist histories, the finding of, nonetheless, comparative de-socialization tensions between then and now is noteworthy.

Of course, there are plenty of grounds on which to critique this research. One involves the interpretation of birth cohort, rather than age, effects. One of this book's prime inferences is that intergenerational value gaps illustrate a tension that has relevance for social change in the long-term. Yet the father-son pairs interviewed here as well as the members of different generations responding to the World Values Survey are simultaneously representing people of different age groups. Thus, critics might argue that the value gaps reported here represent not social change crystallized within different generations but rather age dependent variations, or life-stage effects. While such argumentation can certainly not be wholly dismissed, as biological age and social change are always conflated (Mannheim 1952), this same fact is also the reason why it is impossible to explain most of these value gaps by age alone.

Further, the idea of universally valid life-stages across all cultures and epochs is clearly questionable. Chapter 9 of this book, for instance, demonstrates how life-stages and birth cohorts embody different values in different types of societies. An argument sometimes made against my findings is that members of the younger generation are more work oriented—and more conflicted—than those of the older generation because they are in the 'work phase' of their lives. Thereby, high work orientations are assumed to be universal and have nothing to do with post-communism or capitalism per se. What is it that causes us to label more than half of the life-span the 'work phase?' Moreover, considering that all but one of the younger generation informants of this study have children, why do we not assume them to be in the 'parenting phase' of their lives? Indeed my results suggest that exactly this phasation of 'work then family' is privileged within capitalist economic culture compared to within the planned economic model. All available data point in this direction: the crash of marriage and birth rates immediately upon transformation in post-communist societies, the fact that older informants recall having emphasized work-family harmony during their communist-era working years, that younger informants face major time pressures negotiating work together with family, and that older informants place far more emphasis on child-rearing than do the younger informants currently within their 'parenting phase' of life.

Methodologically, father-son pairing allows us to infer the difference between the two. Under normal circumstances, the father could be expected to impart his values into his son, and where unsuccessful, this difference in current values could be written up as due to age differences or social change. In addition, retrospective accounts of the fathers, although certainly imperfect due to nostalgia, bad memory, and influence of current value sets, give us a rough indicator as to what they were like during their younger years. By such accounts, the fathers speak with a vocabulary entirely different than their sons within every sphere of values: work, family, material values, and values related to more distant others. Many of the fathers' recollections are specific enough to be difficult to discount. For example, East German and Russian fathers vividly recall working on very few weekends compared to their sons today. Other informants recalled specific occasions where household duties were shared together with the wife for the purpose of maintaining family harmony; in contrast, their sons simply note that the wife should "understand" that work comes first. Nonetheless, even if we discount retrospective reports, the real-time differences in values between specific fathers and their sons, and between their generations as groups, are of a nature making them difficult to explain through a lifestage explanation alone. Why would people become more moral with age? Why would they come to believe that lying is less justifiable with age? Why would image cultivation and profit orientations decline with age? Why would parents care *less* about the socialization of their children than the grandparents? Why would people become more community-oriented and nationalistic with age? Of course, for each of these questions, we can come up with age-specific explanations, but these explanations become more and more arbitrary without reference to the central historical-contextual clue that unifies them all: the link to capitalist work and new routes to occupational success. My qualitative sample yields an important finding: a few of the older generation informants also had to adapt and 'reinvent' themselves during the transformation years, and they exhibit the same value adaptations as the working sons instead of the 'older generation' values. This indicates a transformation due to exposure to modern work rather than an aging effect.

Another point that reinforces the argument that emergent value tensions cannot be hastily dismissed is that many value gaps noted between generations harmonize quite obviously with specific social changes that have occurred. Young informants admit the allure of certain luxuries and advertisements for purposes of image cultivation, yet advertisements did not exist on the same scale during communist times, and luxuries themselves were scant to be found. Nonetheless we find this very expansion of consumerism within the younger generation coupled with a decline in traditional values of thrift. It is problematic to explain this value gap away through a life-stage effect alone since there was no readily comparable consumer culture, advertising industry, or readily available-for-purchase high-class luxuries to speak of during planned-economy times. Each of these has expanded notably over the past 15–20 years, and in the past, excessive displays of wealth were even condemned.

Finally, the qualitative nature of the data used here have allowed for some tracing of mechanisms of value change within individual minds. Individuals have both given specific accounts of how their own values have changed and provided the context for externally-observed value tensions within them. Sure enough, aging mechanisms are alluded to, since it is difficult for individuals to distinguish their 'own' psychological development from the influence of external events. Yet aside from allusions to the role of life-stage and biological aging, more telling for purposes here is that informants time and time again provided evidence of specific mechanisms, tied to socio-structural conditions, by which their values were affected. These mechanisms, already described above as cognitive adaptation to the economy, cognitive dissonance, ideological conflict, and intergenerational changeover, trace a drive toward value tensions from the macro-level of capitalist economic culture to the micro-level of the individual mind. These mechanisms thereby function as a roadmap that is analytically distinct from life-stage/age-effect argumentation through its strong links to specific socio-cultural changes.

My interviews were conducted with a diverse body of successful people in occupations favored by the new economy. We interviewed various types of entrepreneurs, managers, and businessmen. One might object that these different occupations should embody different sets of values, as the 'tools of success' for them may be very different. For instance, those who profited through acquiring privatized assets through questionable legal means, those who started a small business with very few political ties, and those who took a position as an upper-level manager in an international firm may have developed in very different ways in order to become successful. I do not doubt differences in habitus between these paths, but in fact, when recalling these men's stories of how they have changed over the years, and when comparing them to their own fathers, and to older generations as a group, it is the similarities that are startling. For most of them, a central orientation on profit-calculation, self-realization, and rigorous work is the dominant feature. Of course, I have found variations, but these were not based on differences in occupation. Modern capitalist work functions as a school in the dissemination, both structurally and agentically, of values (see Inkeles and Smith 1974).

Understandably the language used in this book may lead to the false impression that a claim for 'really-existing' social change has been made. Especially the use of ideal-typical language and the dichotomies it entails—capitalism versus communism, individualist versus social values—easily conjures movements across these dimensions. Naturally some readers might assume that my main claim here is that such a movement has occurred. Instead, my main argument is about the tendency toward a particular movement rather than movement itself, of the likelihood of this particular change in the long run due to the mechanisms I outlined.

The father-son pairs interviewed in each of three different countries cannot prove a universal change, nor could they even if they had been randomly sampled. Nor can each small country sample demonstrate a change within each society. The young businessmen interviewed are not representative of other segments of society. A purely urban qualitative sample does not translate immediately into repercussions for non-urban populations, especially in China, where three-fourths of the population are poor rural-dwellers or migrants. Yet none of these things was claimed. Rather this qualitative sample was chosen for a different reason: not to prove a specific shift but rather to mine for ideas on how such change is occurring, should it indeed be unfolding across a broader spectrum. The theoretical frame predicted that *if* a de-intimization of values would occur as a result of the transformation to capitalism, then *surely* it would occur in the theoretically most-affected places, among the most affected generation within those of the most-affected gender working in the most-affected occupations, and that this effect would be further magnified by contrasting this most-affected group with their less-effected and comparable fathers. Thereby, in this way, the results tell us two things. First, the fact that social values are indeed comparatively deteriorated in exactly the places the theory directed us to look strengthens the value of this particular theoretical setup. Any other finding would have called for a major revision. Second, and more to the point, this particular mix between theory and method provide a highly sensitive instrument for focusing on the capitalism-sociality link, so that the mechanisms and 'how' of this link may be illuminated.

The quantitative data analysis shown in Chapter 9 demonstrates how post-communist values are arrayed compared to value sets in other parts of the world. These post-communists are in a similarly individualized category as people in the rest of the developed world. This suggests a common line of development with particular tendencies. One major tendency is the 'digging in,' and further entrenchment of capitalist culture. This produces value repercussions that are well-described within modernization theories. Yet I wanted to outline, in addition to value outcomes that are 'positive,' some that are potentially problematic, such as the latency of social values.

Individualization is profoundly ambivalent. The individualized informants in this study displayed enhanced levels of personal ambition, tolerance toward others, self-reflexivity, independence, and confidence. Yet these positive traits are not without cost. Their personal ambition makes them focus increasing amounts of time on their own development at the expense of their loved ones, their tolerance of strangers is due to their indifference toward them, their self-reflexivity tends toward narcissism, their independence limits a dependence upon intimate relationships with others, and confidence makes them less likely to listen to or seek advice. A utopian view alone is incomplete.

Thereby, most broadly, the entrenchment of modern capitalism may help paint for us a vector for human sociality, whereby this sociality becomes latent, buried, as a result of the internal conflicts emerging as it comes into friction with an increasingly rationalized world. We should ask ourselves the extent to which the value tensions of the capitalist personality—and presumably, over the long-term, value shifts—found within the most-affected individuals and between social groupings may, as scouts, show us the terrain into which other populations—such as the rural, traditional occupations, and the poor—are drawn as they 'modernize.'

More work needs to be done to link multi-faceted individualization outcomes to diverse influences of modernization. Of course, economic development alone does not drive the enhanced latency of the valuation of face-to-face communication. In particular, the profound influences of the urban setting and technological developments need to be disentangled from those tied more directly to economic culture. In terms of methods, since values reside in the mind, research without qualitative components that deeply investigate the meaning and valuation processes within individuals has a built-in blind spot. Quantitatively, although intergenerational value shifts are a strong inference for change, and wave-to-wave changes can be calculated at the aggregate level, these cannot prove change. We urgently need international panel data that deal with values questions.

This project aims to contextualize optimistic modernization accounts on the topic of economic development and social values, thereby empirically demonstrating the plausibility of the correlation of modern capitalist development and de-intimization. There are at least two reasons to pursue this. First, the empirical foundation of this book provides a fuller understanding of the topic at hand. Second, this particular work also normatively suggests the problems inherent in a utopian interpretation of reality.

I would not have written this book if I thought that the valuation of face-to-face intimate ties is unimportant. Such ties are important for informal social control, as the means by which social norms (whichever they may be) are most effectively transmitted and reinforced. Instrumental ties embody less normative cohesion because they are interchangeable, more numerous, and temporally intermittent. Second, as social animals, close, intimate ties are also important for our physical and mental health.More mundanely, they make us happy. For these reasons, we should be very aware of the consequences of cultural development for these ties. Their active valuation is not a universal, stable 'given.'

Once such a warning is in hand, how might this project handle the task of moral praxis or action? While warnings may spur action, a problem is that the directionality and mechanics of social action are never implicit in knowledge. The how of praxis is not linked in a clear-cut way to the description of the problem but is rather an issue of politics and moral philosophy; it will thus have to be taken up elsewhere.

Nonetheless, there is no need to drop the issue entirely as one devoid of hope. If we happen to decide that the negative components of individualization outweigh the positive, research points to buffers that may slow the process. Religious values, since they offer a form of ultimate values in competition with the ultimate values of material culture, may offer solace. In addition, states which resist purified forms of the market economy, through providing alternative policy and values, such as the welfare state or the reinstatement of 'Confucian values,' may also fight against this particular individualization. Finally, females appear more able to maintain their sociality than men. What to do with these three points is not prescribed. While conservatives might hope for a return to the past in these dimensions, this is neither feasible nor superior to progressive alternatives.

Despite the difficulty, even impossibility, of acting based on a secure framework of knowledge, it may be necessary. In this regard, perhaps the more pragmatic course of action—as opposed to revolutionary approaches—of the communitarian approach is a way forward. For example, Etzioni's (1988) concerted attack on the classical economics mainstays of rationality and individualism, arguing instead for the insertion of emotions, values, community, and morality into our way of understanding the economy could be seen as an attempt to subvert economic logic from within, as a Trojan Horse.

Appendix A
Methods

MOST DIFFERENT CASE DESIGN

As already described at the end of Chapter 4, China, Russia, and Eastern Germany differ across all key identified dimensions (See Table A.1) relevant for value change except the common presumed cause (entrenchment of capitalist economic culture) and effect (latency of social values).

Table A.1 Comparison of Country Cases

	China	*Russia*	*Eastern Germany*
previous state of family development	traditional	mixed	modern
state-level family policy	one-child policy	initially nothing, then encourage child-bearing	encourage child-bearing
recent socialist history	disruption, Cultural Revolution	slow decay and demoralization	beginning of demoralization
urbanization level	low	medium	high
industrialization	medium	high	high
techno-bureaucratic development at time of transformation	low	high	highest
Spirituality	low to medium, Confucian, Buddhist roots, growing Christianity	weak, bourgeoning orthodoxy	medium, remnants of Catholicism, Protestantism survived
1990's economic conditions	strong growth	total collapse	near-total collapse

(continued)

Table A.1 (continued)

	China	*Russia*	*Eastern Germany*
economic restructuring	phased, gradual	fast-paced neo-liberal shock	colonial, fast transfer of West-German institutions
external economic support	very little	little	very high (from West Germany)
initial state value response to transformation	"get rich first"!	do nothing	work-family balance (welfare state)
later state value response	reintroduced Confucian values in schools	focus on Russian family (encourages procreation)	slight shift away from work-family balance with welfare reforms

LOGIC OF THE MIXED METHODS APPROACH

Values reside, before they result in behavior, in the head, and valuation is an act of cognition. Therefore, without an earnest exploration into the richness of this cognition, there is little hope at getting near the core of values. This is why interviews play a key role in this design. Quantitative methods provide the ability generalize such findings across a wider population, yet have a more difficult time dealing with the meaning and nature of values. This is not to say that quantitative research is unnecessary for values research, but rather that it is insufficient. Therefore, the qualitative analysis is used to uncover the mechanisms behind the emergence of a new class of values and the conflicts they spur, while quantitative data allow us to generalize value gaps to the wider population. Qualitative and quantitative indications will be used in parallel, to triangulate social value gaps across occupational groups, the rich and the others, and between generations.

Qualitative Methods

The principal method of unearthing value tensions here is through intergenerational interviews. (See Table A.2 for a description of the informants). Contemporary intergenerational value variations are sought, and these are tapped as possible indicators of social change. The assumption is that social changes crystallize into intergenerational value gaps as the younger generations adapt to, for the first time, a society considerably different from that of their predecessors (Mannheim 1952). vThis research is primarily

Table A.2 Basic Characteristics of 32 Informants (18 Businessmen, 13 Fathers, 1 Mother)

Interview Number	*Age at time of interview*	*Gender*	*Sector*	*Duration of marriage*	*Ages of children*	*Vacation days per month*	*Vacation days per month in 1990*
S4	72	male	former newspaperman	45 years	38, 43, 45	18	4
S5	32	male	construction design (SOE)	5 years	3	9	n.a.
S6	~65	male	industry	38 years	32, n.a.	8	4
S7	49	male	IT		19	2–3	2–3
S8	72	male	former soldier, transportation worker	50 years	49, 48	30	4
S9	37	male	bearings production (industry)	10 years	11	2	4
S11	32	male	auto components manufacturing	not married yet	none	8	4
S13	40	male	pharmaceuticals (SOE)	10 years	9	8	4
S14	65	male	n.a.	n.a.	40, n.a.	8	4
S15	32	male	insurance	3 years	3	8	4
S17	43	male	service sector	18 years	18	10	rarely
M1	42	male	construction, design	15 years	n.a.	3	0
M2	80	male	retired	55 years	42, 52	30	8
M5	47	male	marketing, advertising	6–8 years	from 3 to 24	n.a.	3
M6	77	male	retired, former engineer	25 years	2	30	30
M7	n.a.	male	financial markets	9	2, 6	4–5	8
M8	60	male	science (private research firm)	35	36	8	n.a.
M9	37	male	design	separated	7	8 (winter), 4–5 otherwise	8

(continued)

Table A.2 (continued)

Interview Number	*Age at time of interview*	*Gender*	*Sector*	*Duration of marriage*	*Ages of children*	*Vacation days per month*	*Vacation days per month in 1990*
M10	61	male	technology sales	35 years	36, n.a.	2	8
M11	36	male	sale of consumer products	11 years	11	6–7	8
M12	65	female	retired, former worker at the department of education	widowed	46 ,36	30	8
L1	33	male	Lawyer, freelance in joint office	5 years	2, 3	4–5	2
L2	61	male	Steel Worker, manager	34 years	29, 33	10	5–6
L3	34	male	engineer, owner	2 years	18 months	8–9	8
L4	n.a.	male	n.a.	n.a.	n.a.	n.a.	n.a.
L5	40	male	Advisor, information technologies	9 days	10, 16	4–6	8
L6	77	male	penioner, previously chemical research	46 years	45,41,36	30	6
L7	34	male	print company owner	girlfriend	6 months	4	8
L8	62	male	print company owner	26 years	34	4–5	4–5
L9	32	male	IT business	no	1, 6	7	8
L11	42	male	window builder, owner	19 years	13, 16	4–5	7–8
L12	69	male	window builder, owner	almost 50 years	40, 42	8–10	8–12

Odd number interviews are with the younger generation, while the even number above them is their father, if interviewed. The letter before the number stands for (S)hanghai, (M)oscow, or (L)eipzig.

n.a. Information is not available.

interested in how values change, how the valuation process occurs, and how tensions in valuation emerge and are resolved. This is information best garnered from individuals themselves, since the valuation occurs within individual minds. Thus, semi-structured qualitative interviews are chosen for this purpose. Through this rich information, I may triangulate what a person's values are through asking about them in a variety of ways. Informants' discussions of the tensions between their values give clues as to how 'old' and 'new' values contend with one another within individual minds. Through thick description, it also becomes clear how particular values derive from a specific cultural source, such as from religion or the market economic structure. Also, the respondents may offer us clues as to why their particular values have or have not changed. Finally, by comparing different groups of informants, representing the 'most-affected' and 'less-affected' cases, we can discern a possible change vector, which indicates the potential direction of change for the overall society through revealing underlying tensions.

The central idea behind the qualitative interviews in this study is to compare theoretically most-affected cases with less-affected cases. With this in mind, two categories of informants are interviewed: the 'most-affected"' young businessmen, entrepreneurs, and managers, and their own 'less-affected' fathers.

Men are interviewed, rather than women, because they are designated within this study as the theoretically 'most-affected gender.' This is confirmed by other research that indicates women tend to be more compassionate, less competitive, and less materialistic (Beutel and Marini 1995; See also Appendix C). Therefore, interviews are conducted with men and their fathers as these interviews will likely reveal the greatest contrasts and thus allow for a more vivid analysis.

Because values are promoted and interpreted primarily through family structures, this study used intergenerational qualitative interviews in order to attempt to gauge changes in social values. Interviews were conducted with new-rich businessmen (who have children) and with their surviving fathers. It can be assumed that the values of fathers and sons would roughly resemble each other, since fathers would be expected to socialize their sons with their own values. Differences then between the values of these generations thus symbolize the extent to which the father's values are no longer adequate and thereby serve as a proxy for social change.

It is assumed that the businessman's father possesses the state of values closer to that which existed before the transition to the market economy. His values would have been much less affected by the economic changes than his son's because the father (now approximately 60 years old) has been socialized long ago and now has minimal involvement in the economy and therefore less adaptive value modification. In contrast, successful businessmen, entrepreneurs, and managers are deemed to have adapted most toward the new economic system and thus most-directly reflect the new system's values.

Qualitative informants were not selected using any sort of random sampling. Rather, young informants were identified according to how well they fit with the ideal profile. This ideal profile consists of the following dimensions:

- Economically successful: the economic success of the young respondent identifies him as having successfully adapted to the new economy.
- Aged 35–45: informants between 35 and 45 years old would have been between 20 and 30 years old at the time of the transformation. Thus, their youthful socialization was nearly complete, and one can observe how they changed their values during this volatile period.
- Married, with children: bachelors would have different value systems than married men, and since I am interested in finding how the work sphere competes with the family, interviewing men with families makes sense.
- Minimal contact with the pre-market wealth and power structures: such a businessman has worked his way up the ladder of social mobility only within the new market-economic structures. Therefore, such structures should have had the greatest value impact on this person.

Respondents were identified through informal networking activities and the help of several local organizations; multiple snowball sampling was used. Informants in Shanghai were acquired primarily through the assistance of the sociology department of Shanghai University and the Shanghai Young Entrepreneurs Association. Leipzig informants were assembled through the assistance of the sociology department of Leipzig University and the assistance of the local *IHK* (Chamber of Commerce). Moscow informants were identified through the assistance of the sociology department of the National Research University Higher School of Economics and through personal networking. The final profiles of the informants, of course, differ from the ideal profile because of the restrictions of the profile itself and rejections encountered through asking informants for their father's contact information in order to conduct the second interview to complete the pair. Relevant information about the informants can be found in Table A.2, where the "L" interview numbers represent Leipzig interviews and "S" and "M" represent, respectively Shanghai and Moscow. Furthermore, each odd-numbered interview represents someone from the businessman cohort, while the subsequent even number is their own father. For example, M1 is the son of Moscow informant M2. In total, the qualitative data being analyzed here consist of interviews with 32 informants, a total of 18 younger generation businessmen and 14 from the older generation. The younger businessmen range in age from 32 to 49, while the older were between 60 and 80 years old. Each of the informants was male, with the exception of

M12, the Moscow mother of M11, because there was no surviving father. With two exceptions (S11, L7), each of the younger cohorts was either married or divorced, and only one of these two (S11) has no child, whereas all other informants have children. In terms of occupation, each of the younger cohort members is a manager, an owner, or an entrepreneur. They vary considerably in terms of wealth. At the low end, M9 could be described as middle to upper-middle class, and I would judge the wealthiest to be M5, a Moscow marketing tycoon. It was quite difficult to assemble full pairs in Shanghai because of the lack of trust of an outside foreign researcher and, in some cases, the son's desire to shield his father from potential embarrassment and hassle. As a result, only three of the four older generation informants from Shanghai may be compared directly to their own children. In Leipzig and Moscow, the construction of informant pairs was more successful, with five complete pairs in each city. In all cases, informants both young and old gave their consent for the interview and were assured that their data would be anonymized.

Interviews were conducted by native-speaking sociology students from Shanghai University, the National Research University Higher School of Economics, and Leipzig University. In half of the cases, the interview was conducted alone between the student and interviewee, whereas in the other half, the primary researcher was also in the room. This variation was intentional in order to determine the effect of a foreigner (the primary researcher) involved in the process. In addition, within several Shanghai interviews, additional persons were unavoidably present during the interview, usually entailing the persons who assisted as intermediaries in contacting informants. Interviews with fathers and sons were always conducted separately.

Interviews lasted, on average, about 90 minutes. The following information was collected within the interviews. First, a profile sheet was filled out which detailed the informant's age, sex, occupational sector, job position, self-assessment of income, number of years married, wife's work, number and ages of children, and whether or not the father lives nearby (for follow-up interview). At the beginning of the interview, the informant was asked to detail the structure of his daily activities in order to see how he distributes his time. First, they would estimate the number of "free days" they have per month today and 15 years ago. Then, they were asked to detail their typical work and vacation days now and 15 years ago within time diaries.

After completion of time diaries, the interview was begun according to the guideline. Interviewers used a guideline as a general roadmap (See Tables A.9, A.10, A.11, and A.12 at the end of this appendix for interview guidelines in English, Chinese, Russian, and German), but they were free to deviate from those questions written down as long as they stayed within the general theme. Additionally, interviewers were encouraged to pursue relevant leads as they saw fit.

The first guideline topic was the 'ostensible prioritization of values: the informant was directly asked which things are most important to him, through questions such as "What are the most important things in your life?" or "Which are the moral principles which guide your behavior?" Thereafter, the interviewer asked about 'goal-based prioritization of values': informants were asked to name their biggest goals in life, how they imagine their lives in the future, who their role-models are, and which values they try to pass on to their children/grandchildren. Informants were thereafter asked, through direct and goal-based questions, to recall their values and moral principles 15 years ago.

In the next step, informants were asked if and why their values changed during the transformation years and also to reflect on how the new economic structure might have affected their values through, for example, heightened aspirations, increased cost-benefit analyses in the life sphere, through perceived material exploitation by and of others, and through the impacts of material culture, such as advertisements, TV shows, and movies.

Finally, informants were asked whether or not their own values were in conflict, what the causes of those conflicts might be, how they justify and attempt to resolve the conflicts, and how the conflicts make them feel.

The interviews, in total, over 300 pages of data, were coded in two main sweeps using ATLASTI software. First, they were coded *structurally*, in direct accordance with the interview guideline. Thereby informant responses may be categorized according to their parallel answers to the same questioning scheme. Second, the interviews were coded line by line *contextually*, according to specific values which became apparent despite where they were found in the interview. This contextual coding was dense, resulting in 441 raw codes across a wide variety of dimensions: timing of the particular value (whether recollections of 1990 or assessments of 2005–6), individual achievement values, materialist values, family values, work values, the value of honesty, education, politics and nationalism, perceptions of change, examples of personal value change, perceptions of value conflicts and interpersonal conflicts, et cetera. These codes were overlapping, meaning that multiple codes may be assigned to the same body of text. They were later collapsed into four main families for analysis: work values, family values, materialist values, and other values.

Social change is inferred through the interviews in three ways. First, value change is looked at within the interviews based on the informants' *personal retrospective detailing* of how their values might have changed during the transition period. Second, the father's cohort and the son's cohort are compared with one another *as groups*. Third, *direct father-son pair comparisons*, where available, are used to look at value change, inferring that the values of fathers and sons should be similar, except for the changes induced by the new environment. These three methods, incorporating both interview utterances and reference to the informants' time diaries, are used to triangulate value gaps in each city.

Quantitative Design

Within representative quantitative samples from China, Russia, and Eastern Germany, the value gaps discovered within the qualitative interviews are looked at across the wider population to see if they correspond to parallel tensions between young and old birth cohorts, between new occupations and occupations favored by the old economy, and between the wealthiest respondents and others. Over-time, or between-wave, changes are not reported in this book, because samples in particular World Values Survey (WVS) societies (especially China) are sometimes quite skewed between waves. As a result, differences in means between waves often reflect these different samples rather than differentiation over time. To avoid this problem, I use birth cohort comparisons, as well as occupation and income-group comparisons, using pooled waves, in order to infer change.

The quantitative portion of this study's method is conducted using data from the WVS, an ambitious cross-sectional multi-national collection of attitudes at the individual level collected from a large variety of nations, including the post-socialist societies under research here. It is virtually the only one capable of contributing to an intimate social values argument that has collected data from most post-communist countries, to include China.

A description of the datasets used for China, Russia, and Eastern Germany can be found in the Table A.3. The sample is taken from four consecutive waves of the cross-sectional World Values Survey, collected in 1990, 1995–1997, 1999–2001, and 2006–2007 within China, Russia, and Eastern Germany. Sample sizes for each country and each wave range between 999 and 2500 persons.

A birth cohort variable was created in order to determine how values are arrayed in younger generations compared to older generations. The oldest birth cohort was constructed of those born between 1901 and 1920; this 20-year range allowed pooling an adequate number of respondents into the category. All other birth cohorts were constructed in five year increments, for example 1921–1925, 1926–1930, and so on, through to 1986–1990.

Additionally, a variable was built to differentiate those within 'new' occupational fields from others. The new occupations included respondents working in occupations favored by the new economy, such as owners, managers, office supervisors, office workers, and professionals. These occupations are the most rapidly growing and prestigious within the new economy compared to the manual workers, foremen, skilled workers, farmers, and others represented by the other occupations. These 'new occupations' parallel the occupations of the young businessmen and managers qualitatively interviewed within this study.

A relative income variable was also constructed from the existing income variable within the data. Within each country, I collapsed a number of the upper categories of the 10-point income scale roughly equal to the upper 15 percent of persons into one 'wealthy' indicator.

Table A.3 Description of WVS Data Used to Compare China, Russia, and Eastern Germany

	China	*Russia*	*Eastern Germany*
number of respondents	5515	8534	4420
female	48,9%	57,1%	55,2%
Modern occupations	21,4%	42,2%	49,5%
"Wealthiest"	17,3%	13,2%	15,4%
1901–1920 birth cohort	0,6%	3,1%	4,8%
1921–1925 birth cohort	0,8%	3,7%	4,3%
1926–1930 birth cohort	2,0%	6,3%	5,7%
1931–1935 birth cohort	2,3%	5,5%	7,0%
1936–1940 birth cohort	5,7%	8,9%	10,7%
1941–1945 birth cohort	7,7%	4,9%	8,5%
1946–1950 birth cohort	9,4%	9,0%	7,9%
1951–1955 birth cohort	11,9%	10,6%	10,1%
1956–1960 birth cohort	11,8%	12,0%	9,5%
1961–1965 birth cohort	14,6%	9,8%	11,0%
1966–1970 birth cohort	13,8%	8,8%	8,5%
1971–1975 birth cohort	9,6%	6,6%	5,3%
1976–1980 birth cohort	5,2%	4,9%	4,0%
1981–1985 birth cohort	2,8%	2,9%	1,8%
1986–1990 birth cohort	1,6%	2,7%	0,9%
Wave 2 (1989–1993)	18,1%	23,0%	30,2%
Wave 3 (1994–1999)	27,2%	23,9%	22,8%
Wave 4 (1999–2004)	18,1%	29,3%	22,6%
Wave 5 (2005–2007)	36,5%	23,8%	24,3%

Source: World Values Survey 1981–2008 Official Aggregate Files v.20090901 and v.20090914

Operationalization of key concepts, at first glance, might look complicated because of the number of variables involved within the World Values Survey. Yet a number of factors allowed for the quick reduction of the possible number of variables to be used, such as the poor variation of certain indicators and missing data within certain countries. Quantitative descriptions of the variables used may be found in Tables A.4, A.5, and A.6. The value categories of interest are the same as those tapped within the analysis of the qualitative interviews: individualism, ambition work, materialism and consumerism, family and friends, and politics and morality. The reason for choosing these particular variables, and their interpretations, is clarified within the relevant chapters.

Table A.4 Description of Key WVS Variables, China, Pooled Waves 2 through 5

	N	*Mean*	*Std. Deviation*	*Min–Max possible*
Child independence	5515	0,670	0,469	0–1
Work	5340	3,448	0,697	1–4
Non–material job ambitions	3500	0,401	0,331	0–1
Risk–taking	2430	4,460	3,075	1–10
Thrift	5515	0,600	0,489	0–1
Good pay	3500	0,710	0,456	0–1
Being rich	1924	3,197	1,403	1–6
Exploitative wealth	3819	3,251	2,340	1–10
Easy Money	2767	2,290	1,068	1–5
Job security	3500	0,610	0,488	0–1
Sacrifice for children	3395	0,604	0,489	0–1
Respect parents	3429	0,826	0,380	0–1
Relative importance of family	5106	1,658	0,560	.25–4
Importance of friends	5367	3,075	0,685	1–4
Politics	4908	2,744	0,870	1–4
Importance of god	2715	2,880	2,698	1–10
Importance of Religion	4737	1,608	0,827	1–4
Moral Absolutism	3143	0,378	0,485	0–1
Justifiability of Lying	979	4,020	2,799	1–10

Source: World Values Survey 1981–2008 Official Aggregate Files v.20090901 and v.20090914

Table A.5 Description of Key WVS Variables, Russia, Pooled Waves 2 through 5

	N	*Mean*	*Std. Deviation*	*Min–Max possible*
Child independence	8528	0,320	0,467	0–1
Work	8359	3,292	0,872	1–4
Non–material job ambitions	6501	0,337	0,321	0–1
Risk–taking	6113	5,250	2,869	1–10
Thrift	8528	0,550	0,498	0–1
Good pay	6501	0,880	0,329	0–1
Being rich	1958	3,150	1,437	1–6
Exploitative wealth	5449	4,877	2,979	1–10
Easy Money	2396	2,360	1,047	1–5
Job security	6501	0,590	0,492	0–1
Sacrifice for children	6082	0,566	0,496	0–1
Respect parents	6270	0,837	0,369	0–1
Relative importance of family	8078	1,681	0,588	.25–4
Importance of friends	8437	3,106	0,733	1–4
Politics	8322	2,202	0,899	1–4
Importance of god	8014	5,210	3,225	1–10
Importance of Religion	8160	2,319	0,973	1–4
Moral Absolutism	5944	0,386	0,487	0–1
Justifiability of Lying	4297	3,060	2,351	1–10

Source: World Values Survey 1981–2008 Official Aggregate Files v.20090901 and v.20090914

Table A.6 Description of Key WVS Variables, Eastern Germany, Pooled Waves 2 through 5

	N	*Mean*	*Std. Deviation*	*Min–Max possible*
Child independence	4413	0,640	0,479	0–1
Work	4289	3,444	0,801	1–4
Non–material job ambitions	3272	0,482	0,323	0–1
Risk–taking	2314	6,690	2,498	1–10
Thrift	4413	0,570	0,496	0–1
Good pay	3324	0,720	0,449	0–1
Being rich	1071	2,623	1,268	1–6
Exploitative wealth	3303	4,225	2,656	1–10
Easy Money	2013	2,910	1,304	1–5
Job security	3328	0,760	0,430	0–1
Sacrifice for children	3287	0,650	0,477	0–1
Respect parents	3105	0,721	0,448	0–1
Relative importance of family	4220	1,514	0,524	.25–4
Importance of friends	4382	3,325	0,651	1–4
Politics	4364	2,413	0,876	1–4
Importance of god	4366	3,370	3,141	1–10
Importance of Religion	4318	1,801	0,985	1–4
Moral Absolutism	3229	0,248	0,432	0–1
Justifiability of Lying	2287	2,930	2,153	1–10

Source: World Values Survey 1981–2008 Official Aggregate Files v.20090901 and v.20090914

The variables above were each analyzed graphically by nation and birth cohort, and T-tests were performed to test for significant differences between birth cohorts, persons of different occupational fields, and persons of different levels of wealth.

Post-communist vs. OECD versus Developing Country Analysis

The classification of countries into country groupings is straightforward. From all available WVS countries, if a society is formerly communist, it is put into that grouping, even if it is also an OECD member. Remaining OECD members are grouped together, and all developing countries are classified as such (Table A.7). The few societies that do not fit into the classification, such as Singapore, were removed, as was described in Chapter 9. The characteristics of the dataset used to compare post-communist respondents as a whole to others in the world are displayed in Table A.8. Waves 2 through 5 of the main WVS data set are used.

Table A.7 OECD, Post-communist, and Developing Societies Included in Chapter 9 Analysis

Post-communist	*OECD*	*Developing*
"Albania"	"Australia"	"Algeria"
"Azerbaijan"	"Canada"	"Argentina"
"Armenia"	"Chile"	"Bangladesh"
"Bulgaria"	"Finland"	"Brazil"
"Belarus"	"France"	"Colombia"
"China"	"Israel"	"Cyprus"
"Croatia"	"Italy"	"Dominican Republic"
"Czech Republic"	"Japan"	"El Salvador"
"Estonia"	"South Korea"	"Ethiopia"
"Georgia"	"Mexico"	"Ghana"
"Hungary"	"Netherlands"	"Guatemala"
"Kyrgyzstan"	"New Zealand"	"India"
"Latvia"	"Norway"	"Indonesia"
"Lithuania"	"Spain"	"Iran"
"Moldova"	"Sweden"	"Iraq"
"Poland"	"Switzerland"	"Jordan"
"Romania"	"Turkey"	"Malaysia"
"Russian Federation"	"Great Britain"	"Mali"
"Slovakia"	"United States"	"Morocco"
"Viet Nam"	"Germany West"	"Nigeria"
"Slovenia"		"Pakistan"
"Ukraine"		"Peru"
"Macedonia"		"Philippines"
"Germany East"		"Puerto Rico"
"Serbia"		"Rwanda"
"Montenegro"		"Saudi Arabia"
"SrpSka—Serbian Republic of Bosnia"		"South Africa"
"Bosnia Federation"		"Zimbabwe"
		"Thailand"

(continued)

Table A.7 (continued)

Post-communist	*OECD*	*Developing*
		"Trinidad and Tobago"
		"Uganda"
		"Egypt"
		"Tanzania"
		"Burkina Faso"
		"Uruguay"
		"Venezuela"
		"Zambia"

Table A.8 Description of WVS Data Used to Compare OECD, Post-communist, and Developing Societies

	Post-communist	*OECD*	*Developing*
number of informants	69853	67071	109427
female	53,3%	52,2%	50,3%
Modern Occupations	34,8%	46,7%	31,8%
"Wealthiest"	18,7%	26,3%	18,5%
1901–1920 birth cohort	1,8%	2,4%	0,5%
1921–1925 birth cohort	2,7%	2,6%	0,7%
1926–1930 birth cohort	4,5%	3,9%	1,6%
1931–1935 birth cohort	5,5%	4,8%	2,4%
1936–1940 birth cohort	7,5%	6,0%	3,9%
1941–1945 birth cohort	6,4%	7,1%	4,2%
1946–1950 birth cohort	8,7%	8,4%	6,0%
1951–1955 birth cohort	10,2%	9,1%	7,6%
1956–1960 birth cohort	10,8%	10,5%	9,6%
1961–1965 birth cohort	10,6%	11,1%	11,1%
1966–1970 birth cohort	9,9%	11,3%	13,1%
1971–1975 birth cohort	8,9%	9,6%	13,4%
1976–1980 birth cohort	7,9%	7,7%	12,8%
1981–1985 birth cohort	3,2%	3,9%	8,9%
1986–1990 birth cohort	1,4%	1,5%	4,2%
Wave 2 (1989–1993)	10,9%	13,8%	8,2%
Wave 3 (1994–1999)	47,2%	29,9%	22,8%
Wave 4 (1999–2004)	18,7%	22,7%	31,7%
Wave 5 (2005–2007)	23,2%	33,6%	37,2%

Source: World Values Survey 1981–2008 Official Aggregate Files v.20090901 and v.20090914

Table A.9 English Interview Guide

	Topic	*Time Allotment*	*Example Questions*
VALUES NOW	Ostensible Prioritization of Values	3	1a) What are the most important things in your life? 1b) Which values are important to you? 2) Are there any moral principles that guide you? If so, what are they?
	Goal-Based Prioritization of Values	7	3a) What are your biggest goals in life? 3b) How do you imagine your life in the future? 4) Who is your biggest role model and what do you admire about them? 5) Which values do you try to instill in your grandchildren?
VALUES BEFORE	Previous (15 years ago) ostensible prioritization of values	3	6a) What were the most important things in your life? 6b) Which values were important to you? 7) Are there any moral principles that guide you? If so, what are they?
	previous (15 years ago) goal-based prioritization of values	7	8a) What were your biggest goals in life? 8b) How did you imagine your life in the future? 9) Who was your biggest role model and what do you admire about them? 10) Which values did you try to instill in your grandchildren?

CAUSES OF VALUE CHANGE	Causes of Value Change—Individual answer	2	11) Why did your values change between 1990 and today?
	Causes of Value Change—hypotheses	13	12) Do you think more about money and material things than you did before? 13) Do you think more about costs and benefits nowadays, for example about the costs of getting married, having children, or going on vacation, than you did before? 14a) Compared to before, do you think people more often use you for money or material gain? 14b) Compared to before, is it more tempting to think about using others for material or monetary gain? 15a) How do you feel when you see an advertisement that encourages you to spend more money or buy certain products in order to be successful? 15b) Do company advertisements influence you to buy more or to work harder now compared to before? 16a) How do you feel when you see movies or television shows that show a rich man as the model of success? 16b) Do movies and television influence you to buy more or to work harder now compared with before?
VALUE CONFLICTS	Value Conflicts	10	17a) Do you think any of your values are in conflict with others? 17b) For example, are your work values in conflict with your family values? 18) How do you justify one value with another if they are in conflict? 19) Are these conflicts a source of anxiety or do they make you feel bad? 20) How do you think these conflicts can be resolved?
		45 minutes	

Table A.10 Chinese Interview Guide

1)	在您的人生中，最重要的东西是什么？
2)	是否有某些道德准则指导着您？如果有，它们包括哪些？
3)	在您的人生中，最大的目标是什么？
4)	谁是您最重要的榜样？您欣赏他们的哪些方面？
5)	您会把哪些准则/价值观念灌输给您的子女/孙子女？
6)	在您的人生中，最重要的东西是什么？
7)	是否有某些道德准则指导着您？如果有，它们包括哪些？
8)	在您的人生中，最大的目标是什么？
9)	谁是您最重要的榜样？您欣赏他们的哪些方面？
10)	您会把哪些准则/价值观念灌输给您的子女/孙子女？
11)	90年代至今，为什么这一阶段您的准则/价值观念会发生改变？
12)	对比过去，现在您是否对钱和物质方面的东西考虑的更多些？
13)	对比过去，现在您是否对开支和收益考虑的更多些？比如说关于结婚，抚育小孩，或者是度假等项目开支的考虑？
14a)	和过去相比，您是否认为他人更多地利用了您的关系获得物质利益？
14b)	和过去相比，您是否会更多地倾向于考虑利用别人的关系来获得物质利益？
15)	当您看到那些为体现成功，而鼓动您花费更多的钱，或者是购买某种商品的广告时，您会怎样看待？
16)	当您看到那些把富人作为成功象征的电影或电视节目时，您会怎样看待？
17)	在您看来，您的一些准则/价值观念与其他准则/价值观念之间发生过冲突么？例如，您的工作准则/价值观念与家庭准则/价值观念之间存在冲突么？
18)	您是怎样在相互冲突的准则/价值观念之间作出判断的？
19)	这些冲突是否给您带来焦虑，或者它们使您感到不安？
20)	您认为怎样才能处理好这些冲突？

Table A.11 Russian Interview Guide

1a)	Что для вас самое главное в жизни?
1b)	Какие ценности для вас важны?
2)	Какие моральные принципы влияют на ваше поведение?
3a)	К каким высоким целям вы стремитесь в жизни?
3b)	Как вы представляете себе свою жизнь в будущем?
4)	С кого вы берете пример и какие черты вам в нем/ней нравится?
5)	Какие ценности вы стремитесь передать вашим детям/внукам?

(continued)

Table A.11 (continued)

6a)	Что для вас было самое главное в жизни, 15 лет тому назад?
6b)	Какие ценности были для вас важны, 15 лет тому назад?
7)	Какие моральные принципы влияли на ваше поведение, 15 лет тому назад?
8a)	К каким высоким целям вы стремились в жизни, 15 лет тому назад?
8b)	Как вы представляли себе свою жизнь в будущем, 15 лет тому назад?
9)	С кого вы брали пример и какие черты вам в нем/ней нравились, 15 лет тому назад?
10)	Какие ценности вы стремились передать вашим детям/внукам, 15 лет тому назад?
11)	Насколько понятия ценности изменились для вас с 1990ого года по сегодняшений день?
12)	vПочему понятия ценности изменились для вас с 1990ого года по сегодняшений день?
13)	Думаете вы сегодня о деньгах и материалном положении больше чем раньше?
14)	Думаете вы сегодня вольше чем раньше о расходах будничной жизни, если вы хотите съездить в отпуск, жениться/выйти замуж, или завести детей?
15a)	Насколько больше вы сегодня, по сравнению с прошлым, склоны использовать других людей ради своего материального благосостояния?
15b)	Насколько вы думаете, по сравнению с прошлым, используют вас другие для своего материального благополучия?
16a)	Какого мнения о рекламе, которые вас вынуждают тратить больше денег или покупать определенные вещи, чтобы считаться успешным?
16b)	Каким образом, по по вашему мнению, влияют на вас реклама вынуждая вас вольше тратить или больше работать, по сравненнию спрошлым?
17a)	Что вы думаете о фильмах, телевидении, и музыке, которые представляют вогатого человека ака образ упеха?
17b)	Насколко фильмы, музыка, телевидение влияют на вас вынуждая вольше тратить или больше работать, чем раньше?
18)	Каким образом, по вашему мнению, некоторые из ваших ценностей вступают в конфликт с другими ценностями? На пример, в какой мере ваши ценности на работе вступают в конфликт с вашими ценностями связанными с семьей?
19)	Каким образом вы объясняете ваши ценности, если они вступают в конфликт друг с другом?
20)	Какие чувства вы испытываете в связи с этими конфликтами?
21)	Как эти конфликты могут быть решены?

Table A.12 German Interview Guide

	Thema	*Zeitvorgabe*	*Beispielfragen*
Werte jetzt	Generelle Wertegewichtung	3	1a) Was ist Ihnen das Wichtigste im Leben? 1b) Welche Werte sind Ihnen wichtig? 2) Gibt es irgendwelche moralischen Prinzipien, die sie leiten? Wenn ja, welche?
	Zielorientierte Wertegewichtung	7	3a) Was sind die höchsten Ziele in Ihrem Leben? 3b) Wie stellen Sie sich Ihr zukünftiges Leben vor? 4) Wer ist Ihr grösstes Vorbild und was bewundern Sie an ihm/ihr? 5) Welche Werte versuchen Sie Ihren Enkeln zu vermitteln?
Werte früher	Generelle Wertegewichtung vor 15 Jahren	3	6a) Was war Ihnen das Wichtigste im Leben? 6b) Welche Werte waren Ihnen wichtig? 7) Gab es irgendwelche moralischen Prinzipien, die sie leiteten? Wenn ja, welche?
	Zielorientierte Wertegewichtung vor 15 Jahren	7	8a) Was waren die höchsten Ziele in Ihrem Leben? 8b) Wie haben Sie sich Ihr zukünftiges Leben vorgestellt? 9) Wer war Ihr grösstes Vorbild und was haben Sie an ihm/ihr bewundert? 10) Welche Werte versuchten Sie Ihren Enkeln zu vermitteln?

Ursachen des Wertewechsels	Ursachen des Wertewechsels—Individuelle Antwort	2	11) Warum haben sich Ihre Werte zwischen 1990 und jetzt geändert?
	Ursache des Wertewechsels—Hypothesen	13	12) Im Vergleich zu früher (vor ca. 15 Jahren), wie oft denken Sie heute an Geld und materielle Dinge?
			13) Im Vergleich zu früher, wie oft denken Sie heute an Kosten und Nutzen, z.B. bei der Entscheidung, zu heiraten, Kinder zu bekommen oder zu verreisen?
			14a) Im Vergleich zu früher, wie oft werden Sie von anderen benutzt, die sich an Ihnen materiell bereichern oder durch Sie Geld verdienen wollen?
			14b) Im Vergleich zu früher, wie verlockend ist es, darüber nachzudenken, andere zu Ihrem eigenen Vorteil zu gebrauchen?
			15a) Was denken Sie über Werbung, die Sie dazu anregen soll, mehr Geld auszugeben oder bestimmte Dinge zu kaufen, die Sie erfolgreich machen?
			15b) Inwieweit werden Sie von Werbung dahingehend beeinflusst, mehr zu kaufen oder, im Vergleich zu früher, härter zu arbeiten?
			16a) Was empfinden Sie, wenn Sie in Filmen oder Fernsehshows einen reichen Mann als Erfolgsmodell dargestellt sehen?
			16b) Inwieweit werden Sie durch Film und Fernsehen beeinflusst, mehr zu kaufen oder, im Vergleich zu früher, härter zu arbeiten?
	Wertekonflikte	10	17a) Inwiefern stehen manche Ihrer Werte in Konflikt mit anderen ihrer Wertvorstellungen?
			17b) Können Sie zum Beispiel Arbeit und Familie gut miteinander vereinbaren?
			18) Wie rechtfertigen Sie die jeweiligen Werte, wenn sie in Konflikt miteinander geraten?
			19) Wie fühlen Sie sich, wenn derartige Konflikte auftreten? Werden Sie unsicher oder fühlen Sie sich deshalb schlecht?
			20) Wie denken Sie könnten diese Konflikte gelöst werden?
		45 Minuten	

Appendix B
T-test Results

Table B.1 Two–tailed T–test Mean Comparisons of Key Variables Measuring Individualism, Ambition, and Work, WVS 1990, 1995, 2000, 2005 Waves

Value	*Comparison groups*	*N*	*Mean*	*Std. Deviation*	*Comparison*	*Highest significant p–value*
Child independence	China (C)	5515	0,670	0,469	R<E<C	0,002
	Russia (R)	8828	0,320	0,467		
	Eastern Germany (E)	4413	0,640	0,479		
	1901–1920 cohort	513	0,300	0,460	1920<1990	0,001
	1986–1990 cohort	355	0,640	0,481		
	New occupations	5885	0,540	0,499	New>Other	0,001
	Other occupations	10066	0,500	0,500		
	Richest 15%	2491	0,570	0,494	Rich>Other	0,001
	Other incomes	14136	0,490	0,500		
Work	China (C)	5340	3,448	0,697	R<C,E	0,001
	Russia (R)	8359	3,292	0,872		
	Eastern Germany (E)	4289	3,444	0,801		
	1901–1920 cohort	494	2,887	1,143	1920<1990	0,001
	1986–1990 cohort	342	3,228	0,796		
	New occupations	5793	3,441	0,770	New>Other	0,001
	Other occupations	9778	3,370	0,810		
	Richest 15%	2465	3,487	0,695	Rich>Other	0,001
	Other incomes	13796	3,360	0,826		
Non–material job ambitions	China (C)	3500	0,401	0,331	R<C<E	0,001
	Russia (R)	6501	0,337	0,321		
	Eastern Germany (E)	3272	0,482	0,323		
	1901–1920 cohort	500	0,347	0,327	1920<1980	0,001
	1976–1980 cohort	496	0,462	0,330		
	New occupations	4284	0,445	0,327	New>Other	0,001
	Other occupations	7036	0,364	0,329		
	Richest 15%	1999	0,424	0,330	Rich>Other	0,001
	Other incomes	10303	0,385	0,329		

(continued)

Table B.1 (continued)

Value	*Comparison groups*	N	*Mean*	*Std. Deviation*	*Comparison*	*Highest significant p–value*
Risk–taking	China (C)	2430	4,460	3,075	C<R<E	0,001
	Russia (R)	6113	5,250	2,869		
	Eastern Germany (E)	2314	6,690	2,498		
	1901–1920 cohort	388	4,620	2,893	1920<1990	0,001
	1976–1980 cohort	350	6,070	2,744		
	New occupations	3629	5,440	2,815	New>Other	0,001
	Other occupations	5657	5,190	3,050		
	Richest 15%	1538	5,820	2,850	Rich>Other	0,001
	Other incomes	8676	5,280	2,957		

n.s. not statistically significant.

Source: World Values Survey 1981–2008 Official Aggregate Files v.20090901 and v.20090914

Table B.2 Two–tailed T–test Mean Comparisons of Key Variables Measuring Materialism and Consumerism, WVS 1990, 1995, 2000, 2005 Waves

Value	*Comparison groups*	N	*Mean*	*Std. Deviation*	*Comparison*	*Highest significant p–value*
Thrift	China (C)	5515	0,600	0,489	R<E<C	0,041
	Russia (R)	8528	0,550	0,498		
	Eastern Germany (E)	4413	0,570	0,496		
	1901–1920 cohort	513	0,680	0,467	1920>1990	0,001
	1986–1990 cohort	355	0,430	0,495		
	New occupations	5885	0,510	0,500	New<Other	0,001
	Other occupations	10066	0,610	0,489		
	Richest 15%	2491	0,520	0,500	Rich<Other	0,001
	Other incomes	14136	0,580	0,493		
Good pay	China (C)	3500	0,710	0,456	C,E<R	0,001
	Russia (R)	6501	0,880	0,329		
	Eastern Germany (E)	3324	0,720	0,449		
	1901–1920 cohort	504	0,690	0,464	1920<1985	0,005
	1981–1985 cohort	70	0,830	0,380		
	New occupations	4300	0,770	0,419	New<Other	0,001
	Other occupations	7055	0,810	0,393		
	Richest 15%	2000	0,780	0,416	Rich<Other	0,044
	Other incomes	10346	0,800	0,401		

(continued)

Table B.2 (continued)

Value	*Comparison groups*	*N*	*Mean*	*Std. Deviation*	*Comparison*	*Highest significant p–value*
Being rich	China (C)	1924	3,197	1,403	E<C, R	0,001
	Russia (R)	1958	3,150	1,437		
	Eastern Germany (E)	1071	2,623	1,268		
	1931–1935 cohort	80	2,338	1,124	1935<1990	0,001
	1986–1990 cohort	127	3,252	1,345		
	New occupations	826	2,696	1,271	New<Other	0,001
	Other occupations	2169	3,104	1,409		
	Richest 15%	222	3,000	1,342	n.s.	n.s.
	Other incomes	2299	2,968	1,365		
Exploitative wealth	China (C)	3819	3,251	2,340	C<E<R	0,001
	Russia (R)	5449	4,877	2,979		
	Eastern Germany (E)	3303	4,225	2,656		
	1901–1920 cohort	340	3,791	2,776	1920<1990	0,001
	1986–1990 cohort	333	5,288	2,923		
	New occupations	4156	4,283	2,758	New>Other	0,001
	Other occupations	6841	5,190	4,012		
	Richest 15%	1487	3,940	2,584	Rich<Other	0,001
	Other incomes	10036	4,192	2,819		
Easy Money	China (C)	2767	2,290	1,068	C<R<E	0,025
	Russia (R)	2396	2,360	1,047		
	Eastern Germany (E)	2013	2,910	1,304		
	1921–1925 cohort	155	2,480	1,175	1925<1980	n.s.
	1976–1980 cohort	530	2,740	1,141		
	New occupations	2201	2,480	1,176	n.s.	n.s.
	Other occupations	4026	2,420	1,133		
	Richest 15%	1116	2,360	1,066	Rich<Other	0,001
	Other incomes	5238	2,510	1,189		
Job security	China (C)	3500	0,610	0,488	R<C<E	0,041
	Russia (R)	6501	0,590	0,492		
	Eastern Germany (E)	3328	0,760	0,430		
	1901–1920 cohort	504	0,530	0,499	1920<1980	0,001
	1976–1980 cohort	497	0,630	0,482		
	New occupations	4303	0,600	0,489	New<Other	0,001
	Other occupations	7056	0,660	0,473		
	Richest 15%	2000	0,640	0,480	n.s.	n.s.
	Other incomes	10350	0,640	0,480		

n.s. not statistically significant.

Source: World Values Survey 1981–2008 Official Aggregate Files v.20090901 and v.20090914

Table B.3 Two–tailed T–test Mean Comparisons of Key Variables Measuring Family and Friendship Values, WVS 1990, 1995, 2000, 2005 Waves

Value	*Comparison groups*	*N*	*Mean*	*Std. Deviation*	*Comparison*	*Highest significant p–value*
Sacrifice for children	China (C)	3395	0,604	0,489	R<C<E	0,001
	Russia (R)	6082	0,566	0,496		
	Eastern Germany (E)	3287	0,650	0,477		
	1901–1920 cohort	483	0,770	0,421	1920>1980	0,001
	1976–1980 cohort	480	0,452	0,498		
	New occupations	4149	0,561	0,496	New<Other	0,001
	Other occupations	6729	0,626	0,484		
	Richest 15%	1940	0,580	0,494	n.s.	n.s.
	Other incomes	9924	0,603	0,489		
Respect parents	China (C)	3429	0,826	0,380	E<C, R	0,001
	Russia (R)	6270	0,837	0,369		
	Eastern Germany (E)	3105	0,721	0,448		
	1901–1920 cohort	483	0,888	0,315	1920>1980	0,001
	1976–1980 cohort	483	0,741	0,438		
	New occupations	4128	0,779	0,415	New<Other	0,001
	Other occupations	6802	0,835	0,372		
	Richest 15%	1925	0,815	0,389	n.s.	n.s.
	Other incomes	9961	0,805	0,396		
Relative importance of family	China (C)	5106	1,658	0,560	E<C<R	0,028
	Russia (R)	8078	1,681	0,588		
	Eastern Germany (E)	4220	1,514	0,524		
	1901–1920 cohort	467	1,805	0,675	1920>1990	0,001
	1986–1990 cohort	337	1,546	0,524		
	New occupations	5662	1,606	0,540	New<Other	0,001
	Other occupations	9391	1,658	0,579		
	Richest 15%	2420	1,584	0,520	Rich<Other	0,001
	Other incomes	13363	1,647	0,577		
Importance of friends	China (C)	5367	3,075	0,685	C<R<E	0,013
	Russia (R)	8437	3,106	0,733		
	Eastern Germany (E)	4382	3,325	0,651		
	1901–1920 cohort	497	2,976	0,830	1920<1990	0,001
	1986–1990 cohort	354	3,517	0,539		
	New occupations	5855	3,216	0,674	New>Other	0,001
	Other occupations	9864	3,093	0,716		
	Richest 15%	2469	3,213	0,680	Rich>Other	0,001
	Other incomes	13945	3,130	0,711		

n.s. not statistically significant.
Source: World Values Survey 1981–2008 Official Aggregate Files v.20090901 and v.20090914

Table B.4 Two–tailed T–test Mean Comparisons of Key Variables Measuring Morality, Religion, and Political Values, WVS 1990, 1995, 2000, 2005 Waves

Value	*Comparison groups*	*N*	*Mean*	*Std. Deviation*	*Comparison*	*Highest significant p–value*
Politics	China (C)	4908	2,744	0,870	R<E<C	0,001
	Russia (R)	8322	2,202	0,899		
	Eastern Germany (E)	4364	2,413	0,876		
	1901–1920 cohort	494	2,279	1,004	1920>1990	0,004
	1986–1990 cohort	345	2,099	0,826		
	New occupations	5774	2,493	0,899	New>Other	0,001
	Other occupations	9411	2,386	0,920		
	Richest 15%	2422	2,568	0,886	Rich>Other	0,001
	Other incomes	13531	2,388	0,916		
Importance of god	China (C)	2715	2,880	2,690	C<E<R	0,001
	Russia (R)	8014	5,210	3,225		
	Eastern Germany (E)	4366	3,370	3,141		
	1901–1920 cohort	485	5,850	3,664	1920>1990	0,001
	1986–1990 cohort	316	4,630	3,070		
	New occupations	5252	4,240	3,228	n.s.	n.s.
	Other occupations	7551	4,250	3,310		
	Richest 15%	1743	4,150	3,145	n.s.	n.s.
	Other incomes	11809	4,270	3,293		
Importance of Religion	China (C)	4737	1,608	0,827	C<E<R	0,001
	Russia (R)	8160	2,319	0,973		
	Eastern Germany (E)	4318	1,801	0,985		
	1901–1920 cohort	497	2,598	1,109	1920>1990	0,001
	1986–1990 cohort	329	2,009	0,899		
	New occupations	5641	2,012	0,974	New>Other	0,005
	Other occupations	9202	1,965	0,990		
	Richest 15%	2357	1,896	0,926	Rich<Other	0,001
	Other incomes	13253	2,009	0,996		
Moral Absolutism	China (C)	3143	0,378	0,485	E<C,R	0,001
	Russia (R)	5944	0,386	0,487		
	Eastern Germany (E)	3229	0,248	0,432		
	1926–1930 cohort	742	0,426	0,495	1930>1980	0,001
	1976–1980 cohort	476	0,233	0,423		
	New occupations	4148	0,350	0,477	n.s.	n.s.
	Other occupations	6347	0,361	0,480		
	Richest 15%	1898	0,292	0,455	Rich<Other	0,001
	Other incomes	9562	0,361	0,480		

(continued)

Table B.4 (continued)

Value	*Comparison groups*	*N*	*Mean*	*Std. Deviation*	*Comparison*	*Highest significant p–value*
Justifiability of Lying	China (C)	979	4,020	2,799	E<R<C	0,021
	Russia (R)	4297	3,060	2,351		
	Eastern Germany (E)	2287	2,930	2,153		
	1901–1920 cohort	361	1,970	1,602	1920<1980	0,001
	1981–1980 cohort	261	4,160	2,484		
	New occupations	2763	3,130	2,335	n.s.	n.s.
	Other occupations	3458	3,170	2,410		
	Richest 15%	1000	3,580	2,469	Rich>Other	0,001
	Other incomes	5925	3,090	2,356		

n.s. not statistically significant.
Source: World Values Survey 1981–2008 Official Aggregate Files v.20090901 and v.20090914

Table B.5 Two-tailed T-test Mean Comparisons of Key Variables across Post-communist, OECD, and Developing Societies

Value	*Comparison groups*	*N*	*Mean*	*Std. Deviation*	*Comparison*	*Highest significant p–value*
Child independence	Post–communists	68902	0,470	0,499	PC<OECD	0,001
	vs. OECD	67071	0,520	0,500		
	vs. Developing	109427	0,420	0,493	PC>Dev	0,001
	1901–1920 cohort	3385	0,280	0,451	1920<1980	0,001
	1986–1990 cohort	6812	0,540	0,499		
Risk–taking	Post–communists	41315	5,280	2,929	PC<OECD	0,001
	vs. OECD	26697	5,380	2,784		
	vs. Developing	25393	4,950	3,219	PC>Dev	0,001
	1901–1920 cohort	2157	4,690	2,885	1920<1980	0,001
	1976–1980 cohort	5271	5,660	2,949		
Thrift	Post–communists	68902	0,480	0,499	PC>OECD	0,001
	vs. OECD	67071	0,340	0,475		
	vs. Developing	109427	0,320	0,467	PC>Dev	0,001
	1901–1920 cohort	3385	0,450	0,497	1920>1990	0,001
	1986–1990 cohort	6812	0,330	0,471		
Being rich	Post–communists	15555	3,010	1,381	PC>OECD	0,001
	vs. OECD	20297	2,469	1,261		
	vs. Developing	33242	3,401	1,622	PC<Dev	0,001
	1901–1920 cohort	241	2,523	1,357	1920<1990	
	1986–1990 cohort	5903	3,519	1,578		

(continued)

Table B.5 (continued)

Value	*Comparison groups*	N	*Mean*	*Std. Deviation*	*Comparison*	*Highest significant p–value*
Parental sacrifice	Post–communists	50802	0,665	0,472	PC<OECD	0,001
	vs. OECD	44210	0,681	0,466		
	vs. Developing	63078	0,830	0,376	PC<Dev	0,001
	1901–1920 cohort	2908	0,800	0,400	1920>1985	0,001
	1981–1985 cohort	5177	0,756	0,430		
Friends	Post–communists	69123	3,231	0,706	PC<OECD	0,001
	vs. OECD	64357	3,416	0,696		
	vs. Developing	104537	3,228	0,790	PC, Dev n.s.	n.s.
	1901–1920 cohort	3207	3,208	0,818	1920<1990	0,001
	1986–1990 cohort	6556	3,428	0,704		
Moral absolutism	Post–communists	48066	0,413	0,492	PC>OECD	0,001
	vs. OECD	37725	0,346	0,476		
	vs. Developing	46939	0,497	0,500	PC<Dev	0,001
	1901–1920 cohort	2529	0,461	0,499	1920, 1985 n.s.	n.s.
	1981–1985 cohort	3387	0,464	0,499		
Lying	Post–communists	9883	3,200	2,461	PC>OECD	0,001
	vs. OECD	8041	2,850	2,470		
	vs. Developing	8914	2,680	2,557	PC>Dev	0,001
	1901–1920 cohort	3385	0,280	0,451	1920<1990	0,001
	1986–1990 cohort	6812	0,540	0,499		
Relative family value	Post–communists	66975	1,635	0,546	PC>OECD	0,001
	vs. OECD	62831	1,532	0,492		
	vs. Developing	102850	1,607	0,523	PC>Dev	0,001
	1901–1920 cohort	2987	1,745	0,638	1920>1990	0,001
	1971–1975 cohort	6423	1,526	0,501		

n.s. not statistically significant.
Source: World Values Survey 1981–2008 Official Aggregate Files v.20090901 and v.20090914

Appendix C

Results on Social Values and Gender

The quantitative sample used in this book contains both men and women. In comparison, the qualitative sample involved exclusively men, with the exception of one Moscow mother, because of the assumption that men are more individualized than women. While the quantitative analyses above meshed quite well with the qualitative results, it is worth asking to which extent these quantitative results were affected by adding women to the analysis, especially considering men were chosen qualitatively because of their 'most-affected' position in terms of their values being more likely pulled toward those demanded by the economy.

In order to approach this question, T-tests were performed on all the variables used in this book, pooled across waves using China, Russian, and the East-German samples. Table C.1 displays these results. These findings are remarkably consistent with those of Beutel and Marini (1995), who found men to be more competitive, materialistic, and less compassionate than women. In comparison, results here indicate that women to be less individualistic, less work oriented, less ambitious toward work, more risk-adverse, more thrift-oriented, less focused on 'good pay' and becoming rich, more oriented toward job security, more highly valuing sacrificing oneself for one's children and unconditional respect for parents, less politically oriented, more god-oriented and religious, and less likely to believe that lying is justifiable. On three indicators, there was no difference between men and women: the belief that wealth accumulation is exploitative, the value of 'easy money,' and moral absolutism.

Thereby, men are indeed much more affected by the individualization processes mentioned here, while women seem to embody some sort of resistance. Notably, this makes this study's overall quantitative change findings more conservative than would an exclusive focus on male businessmen, who indeed embody these individualization tensions the most. Nonetheless, women in the sample experience the same growth of individualized values among the younger cohorts.

Table C.1 Two-tailed T-test Mean Comparisons of Key Variables by Gender in China, Russia, Eastern Germany, 1990–2005

Variable		*N*	*Mean*	*Std. deviation*	*Comparison*	*Significance*
Child independence	Male	8453	0,540	0,502	M>F	0,001
	Female	10014	0,470	0,501		
Work	Male	8275	3,446	0,763	M>F	0,001
	Female	9711	3,313	0,844		
Non-material job ambitions	Male	6115	0,410	0,338	M>F	0,001
	Female	7228	0,364	0,335		
Risk-taking	Male	5519	4,690	3,837	M>F	0,001
	Female	6522	4,330	3,886		
Thrift	Male	8453	0,560	0,501	M<F	0,006
	Female	10014	0,580	0,496		
Good pay	Male	6115	0,800	0,402	M>F	0,003
	Female	7228	0,780	0,420		
Being rich	Male	2282	3,175	1,426	M>F	0,001
	Female	2671	2,951	1,383		
Exploitative wealth	Male	5982	4,189	2,812	n.s.	n.s.
	Female	6587	4,232	2,788		
Easy Money	Male	3875	1,440	2,621	n.s.	n.s.
	Female	4774	1,420	2,564		
Job security	Male	6115	0,620	0,486	M<F	0,044
	Female	7228	0,640	0,484		
Sacrifice for children	Male	5868	0,578	0,494	M<F	0,001
	Female	6894	0,616	0,487		
Respect parents	Male	5875	0,791	0,407	M<F	0,001
	Female	6927	0,819	0,385		
Relative importance of family	Male	8037	1,573	0,562	M<F	0,001
	Female	9365	1,686	0,570		
Importance of friends	Male	8335	3,163	0,702	M>F	0,019
	Female	9849	3,138	0,711		
Politics	Male	8167	2,519	0,923	M>F	0,001
	Female	9425	2,308	0,895		
Importance of god	Male	6817	3,520	3,051	M<F	0,001
	Female	8405	4,780	3,383		
Importance of Religion	Male	7929	1,823	0,923	M<F	0,001
	Female	9284	2,139	1,022		
Moral Absolutism	Male	5734	0,341	0,474	n.s.	n.s.
	Female	6580	0,355	0,478		
Justifiability of Lying	Male	3474	3,300	2,511	M>F	0,001
	Female	4209	2,900	2,329		

n.s. not statistically significant.

Source: World Values Survey 1981-2008 Official Aggregate Files v.20090901 and v.20090914

Feng, Shuliang. 2001. "Crime and Crime Control in a Changing China." In *Crime and Social Control in a Changing China*, edited by Jianhong Liu, Steven F. Messner, and Lening Zhang, 123–130. London: Greenwood Press.

Festinger, Leon. 1957. *A Theory of Cognitive Dissonance*. Stanford: Stanford University Press.

Finley, Moses I. 1973. *The Ancient Economy*. London: Chatto & Windus.

Flockton, Chris, Eva Kolinsky, and Rosalind Pritchard. 2000. "The New Germany in the East: An Introduction." In *The New Germany in the East: Policy Agendas and Social Developments since Unification*, edited by Chris Flockton, Eva Kolinsky, and Rosalind Pritchard. London: Frank Cass.

Folbre, Nancy. 2001. *The Invisible Heart: Economics and Family Values*. New York: The New Press.

Fourcade, M. 2011. Price and Prejudice: On Economics and the Enchantment (and Disenchantment) of Nature." In *The Worth of Goods: Valuation and Pricing in the Economy*, edited by Jens Beckert and Patrik Aspers, 41–62. Oxford: Oxford University Press.

Fourcade, M. and Kieran Healy. 2007. "Moral Views of Market Society." *Annual Review of Sociology* 33, 285–311.

Freeland, Chrystia. 2000. *Sale of the Century*. New York: Crown Publishers.

Froese, Fabian J. 2007. "The Future of Asia: Work Values and Career Goals of the Young Elite in Shanghai, Tokyo, and Seoul." Conference Paper. American Sociological Association, 11 to 14 August, 2007, New York.

Frone, Michael R., Marcia Russell, and M. Lynne Cooper. 1992. "Prevalence of Workfamily Conflict: Are Work and Family Boundaries Asymmetrically Permeable?" *Journal of Organizational Behavior* 13: 723–729.

Gandhi, Mahatma. 1946. *Hind Swaraj: Or, Indian Home Rule*. Ahmedabad: Navajivan Publishing House.

Giddens, A. 1991. *Modernity and Self-Identity: Self and Society in the Late Modern Age*. Cambridge: Polity Press.

Goedicke, Anne. 2006. "A "Ready-Made State": The Mode of Institutional Transition in East Germany After 1989." In *After the Fall of the Wall: Life Courses in the Transformation of East Germany*, edited by Karl Ulrich Mayer, Martin Diewald, and Anne Goedicke, 44–64. Stanford: Stanford University Press.

Gold, Thomas B. 1985. "After Comradeship: Personal Relations in China Since the Cultural Revolution." *China Quarterly* 104: 657–675.

Grancelli, Bruno. 2002. "Networks, Social Capital, and Leadership: Methodological Remarks on Approaches to the Study of Postcommunist Transformation." In *Postcommunist Transformation and the Social Sciences: Cross-Disciplinary Approaches*, edited by Frank Bönker, Klaus Müller, and Andreas Pickel. New York: Rowman & Littlefield.

Granovetter, Mark. 1985. «Economic Action and Social Structure: The Problem of Embeddedness." *The American Journal of Sociology* 91(3): 481–510.

Granovetter, Mark. 2005. "The Impact of Social Structure on Economic Outcomes." *The Journal of Economic Perspectives* 19(1): 33–50

Grant, Geoffrey. 1989. "The Family and Social Control: Traditional and Modern." In *Social Control in the People's Republic of China*, edited by Ronald J. Troyer, John P. Clark, and Dean G. Rojek, 17–25. New York: Praeger.

Greenhaus, J.H., and N.J. Beutell. 1985. "Sources of Conflict between Work and Family Roles." *The Academy of Management Review* 10: 76–88.

Grix, Jonathan. 2003. "Recasting Civil Society in East Germany." In *Women in Eastern Germany Since Unification*, edited by Eva Kolinsky and Maria Nickel Hildegard. London: Frank Cass.

Habermas, Jürgen. 1989. *The Theory of Communicative Action, Volume 2: Lifeworld and System: A Critique of Functionalist Reason*. Boston: Beacon Press.

Hall, Peter A. and David Soskice (eds). 2001. *Varieties of Capitalism: The Institutional Foundations of Comparative Advantage.* Oxford: Oxford University Press.

Hansen, Mette H., and R. Svarverud. 2010. *IChina: The Rise of the Individual in Modern Chinese Society.* Copenhagen: NIAS.

Hareven, T.K. 1990. "A Complex Relationship: Family Strategies and the Processes of Economic and Social Change." In *Beyond the Marketplace: Rethinking Economy and Society*, edited by R. Friedland and A.F. Robertson, 215–244. New York: Aldine de Gruyter.

Haub, Claudia. April 22nd, 2011." Russian Birth Rate Continues to Rise." *Population reference Bureau.* Accessed on May 6th, 2012. http://prbblog.org/index.php/2011/04/22/russian-birth-rate-continues-to-rise/.

Hessel, A., M. Geyer, J. Würz, and E. Brähler. 1997. "Psychische Befindlichkeiten in Ost: und Westdeutschland im seibten Jahr nach der Wende." *Aus Politik und Zeitgeschichte* 13: 15–24.

Hirschi, Travis. 2002. *Causes of Delinquency.* London: Transaction Publishers.

Hitlin, Steven, and Jane Allyn Piliavin. 2004. "Values: Reviving a Dormant Concept." *Annual Review of Sociology* 30: 359–393.

Horkheimer, Max, and Theodor W. Adorno. 2002. *Dialectic of Enlightenment: Philosophical Fragments.* Stanford: Stanford University Press.

Huinink, Johannes, and Michaela Kreyenfeld. 2006. "Family Formation in Times of Abrupt Social and Economic Change." In *After the Fall of the Wall: Life Courses in the Transformation of East Germany*, edited by Martin Diewald, Anne Goedicke, and Karl Ulrich Mayer, 170–190. Stanford: Stanford University Press.

Huinink, Johannes, and Michael Wagner. 1995. "Partnerschaft, Ehe und Familie in der DDR." In *Kollektiv und Eigensinn: Lebensverlaüfe in der DDR und danach*, edited by Johannes Huinink, Karl Ulrich Mayer, Martin Diewald, Heike Solga, Annemette Sorensen, and Heike Trappe. Berlin: Akademie Verlag.

Humphrey, Caroline. 2002. "The Villas of the 'New Russians.'" In *The Unmaking of Soviet Life: Everyday Economies after Socialism*, Caroline Humphrey. Ithaca, NY: Cornell University Press.

Humphreys, S.C. 1969. "History, Economics, and Anthropology: The Work of Karl Polanyi." *History and Theory* 8: 165–212.

Inglehart, Ronald. 1990. *Cultural Shift in Advanced Industrial Society.* Princeton: Princeton University Press.

Inglehart, Ronald. 1997. *Modernization and Postmodernization. Cultural, Economic, and Political Change in 43 Societies.* Princeton: Princeton University Press.

Inglehart, Ronald. 2000. "Globalization and Postmodern Values." *The Washington Quarterly* 23: 215–228.

Inglehart, Ronald, and Wayne E. Baker. 2000. "Modernization, Cultural Change, and the Persistence of Traditional Values." *American Sociological Review* 65: 19–51.

Inglehart, Ronald, and Christian Welzel. 2005. *Modernization, Cultural Change and Democracy.* Cambridge: Cambridge University Press.

Ingram, David, and Julia Simon-Ingram. 1992. *Critical Theory: The Essential Readings.* St. Paul: Paragon House.

Inkeles, Alex. 1983. *Exploring Individual Modernity.* New York: Columbia University Press.

Inkeles, Alex, and David Smith. 1974. *Becoming Modern: Individual Change in Six Developing Countries.* Cambridge, MA: Harvard University Press.

International Bank of St. Petersburg. 2002. "Annual Report: Key Macroeconomic Trends in 2002." St. Petersburg, Russia.

T

thrift, 115–116, 121–123, 175–177
time, value of, 56–57
tools of success. *See* best-practices
Tönnies, Ferdinand, 29
transitology, 40–44; technocratic nature of, 40–42

V

values, 12–44, 183–190; definition of, 15–19; state policies of, 49; in tension, 45–76

W

Weber, Max, 14, 23, 26–27, 29–32, 72, 96–97, 119
welfare state, 50, 74
work, focus, 54, 71–72, 94–112; as career, 107–108; as enslavement, 104, 111; as family, 140, 155; as salvation, 103, 109–110

Z

Zelizer, Viviana, 38–40, 67